Daily Guideposts, ™ 1996

Publishers Since 1798

THOMAS NELSON PUBLISHERS

Nashville • Atlanta • London • Vancouver

Published in Nashville, Tennessee, by Thomas Nelson, Inc., and distributed in Canada by Word Communications, Ltd., Richmond, British Columbia, and in the United Kingdom by Word (UK) Ltd., Milton Keynes, England.

ACKNOWLEDGMENTS

All Scripture quotations, unless otherwise noted, are from *The King James Version of the Bible.*
Scripture quotations marked (RSV) are from the *Revised Standard Version of the Bible.* Copyright © 1946, 1952, 1971 by the Division of Christian Education of the National Council of Churches of Christ in the U.S.A. and are used by permission.
Scripture quotations marked (NIV) are from the *Holy Bible, New International Version.* Copyright © 1973, 1978, 1984 International Bible Society. Used by permission of Zondervan Bible Publishers.
Scripture quotations marked (NRSV) are from the *New Revised Standard Version Bible.* Copyright © 1989 by the Division of Christian Education of the National Council of Churches of Christ in th U.S.A. Published by Thomas Nelson, Inc., Nashville, TN 37214.
Scripture quotations marked (TLB) are from *The Living Bible.* Copyright © 1971. Used b permission of Tyndale House Publishers, Inc., Wheaton, IL 60189. All rights reserved.
Scripture quotations marked (NAS) are from the *New American Standard Bible.* Copyright © 1960, 1962 1963, 1968, 1971, 1972, 1973, 1975, 1977 by The Lockman Foundation. Used by permission.
Scripture quotations marked (NKJV) are from *The New King James Version of the Bible.* Copyright © 1979, 1980, 1982 by Thomas Nelson, Inc., Nashville, TN 37214.
Scripture quotations marked (GNB) are from *The Good News Bible, the Bible in Today's English Version.* Copyright © American Bible Society, 1966, 1971, 1976.
Scripture quotations marked (PHILLIPS) are from *The New Testament in Modern English.* Copyright © 1958 by J.B. Phillips. Used by permission of the Macmillan Company.
"My Gift Today . . ." series was written by Elizabeth Sherrill.
"The Surprises of Easter" series was written by Keith Miller.
"Journey Toward the Light" series was written by Pam Kidd.
"My New Year's Wish" by Mary J. Lewis was quoted by permission from *Sourcebook of Poetry* Copyright © 1968, 1992 by Al Bryant. Published by Kregal Publications, Grand Rapids, MI.
"Stay Thy Heart on Me" by Amy Carmichael is from *Amy Carmichael of Dohnavur,* by Frank I Houghton. Copyright © 1953, The Dohnavur Fellowship. Published by The Christian Literatur Crusade, Fort Washington, PA. Used by permission.
"Fireflies" by Jane Hess Merchant. First printed in *Halfway Up the Sky,* Jane Hess Merchant permission granted by Elizabeth Merchant.
"Pass on the Torch" by Allen Eastman Cross reprinted with the permission of The Pilgrim Press.

Designed by Holly Johnson
Artwork by Monica Ice
Indexed by Patricia Woodruff
Typeset by Metro PhotoType
Printed in the United States of America

ISBN 0-7852-7624-6

1 – 96

TABLE OF CONTENTS

TABLE OF CONTENTS

INTRODUCTION

A reader from San Augustine, Texas, wrote to us saying, "As a result of having read *Daily Guideposts* for several years, I feel that you people are my friends. I have to get the annual devotional book; otherwise I'd lose my friends. Thank you for sharing your lives with others, giving guidance and encouragement." The inspiration that so many have found in this book springs from readers like this.

Daily Guideposts turns twenty this year — a reason to celebrate! Each new volume reaches out by word of mouth, through a gift or just by chance to new readers who join the growing *Daily Guideposts* family. Through all these twenty years, the spirit of the book has grown strong through the support of all of you who make a small but precious place for *Daily Guideposts* in your lives. Whether in the morning or in the evening, alone or with loved ones, those moments with *Daily Guideposts* glow warmly through every hour of the day.

Fifty-one writers here share with you the special moments of their lives, moments of laughter and moments of revelation. They offer us what they learned and how they learned it, to help us through every day of 1996. They draw on the strength of *Daily Guideposts* readers and gain inspiration from your letters. An unseen gathering of readers is at the shoulder of every contributor.

Some of our writers have been thinking this year about finding lights in the darkness. We hope that *Daily Guideposts, 1996* will share some of the lights they have found and reach out a helping hand to those who, for whatever reason, find themselves temporarily lost in the darkness. One longtime Daily Guideposter in Seattle, Washington, told us, "*Daily Guideposts* is of such great comfort and peace to me that I don't know how I ever got along without it. It has given strength, encouragement and a much deeper faith than I ever could have had without it." It took a loyal reader to put our goal into words.

Each year *Daily Guideposts* is a gathering of people, their stories and their spiritual growth. Some are familiar: Fred Bauer, who has been with the book since the beginning; Mary Lou Carney, who also edits our children's magazine *Guideposts for Kids*; Arthur Gordon, Marjorie Holmes, Marilyn Morgan Helleberg and many others.

Then each year brings newcomers, often moved to write by what they have read in previous years' *Daily Guideposts*: Edward Grinnan of the *Guideposts* magazine staff makes his first appearance, as does Katherine Paterson, a minister's wife and mother of four, who is also the author of the award-winning books for young people *Bridge to Terabithia* and *Jacob Have I Loved*.

As you journey through the year 1996, finding light, laughter, love and, above all, God's presence in these pages, you, the very special reader, are in our thoughts and in our prayers. May God bless you.

— *The Editors*

And God said, Let there be lights in the firmament of the heaven to divide the day from the night ... to give light upon the earth: and it was so.

—GENESIS 1:14–15

JANUARY

S	M	T	W	T	F	S
	1	2	3	4	5	6
7	8	9	10	11	12	13
14	15	16	17	18	19	20
21	22	23	24	25	26	27
28	29	30	31			

1 | M O N | *For he is our peace ... and has broken down the dividing wall of hostility.* —Ephesians 2:14 (RSV)

On the window ledge of our kitchen there sits a small chunk of concrete. There is nothing impressive or beautiful about it except its meaning, for this is a piece of what was once the Berlin Wall. Our German exchange student Jordis chipped it herself and brought it to our family as a gift. Sometimes I reach up and touch it with a sense of wonder, as though that small object were part of a miracle. And in a way it was. How many of us believed that the Wall would come down in our lifetime?

Not a day goes by that I don't look at this fragment from history and think of the hope it symbolizes. On this, the first day of 1996, it takes on special significance. I don't know exactly what lies ahead in the new year, but for certain change is in the air. The last of our children will be graduating from high school. I will need to hone my work skills. My husband Terry is looking at shifts within his career. We even wonder if we'll remain in Alaska. And what about "us"— how will we weather being alone again after all these years?

So it is that I need hope — the reassurance that God encompasses any wall I might face and that wonderful, impossible things can happen. Today I look at this bit of "the Wall that wasn't coming down" and find I am ready to run with confidence into the future.

Let's do it!

Father, because You are God of the impossible, what is impossible to me becomes possible with You. Thank You for such a magnificent hope. —Carol Knapp

2 | T U E | *I will bless the Lord at all times: his praise shall continually be in my mouth.* —Psalm 34:1

Every year during the first week of January, I take time with my Bible to search out the one Scripture passage that I can make my spiritual focus for the year ahead. Last January, as I began my search, God seemed very far away. Budget cuts in California had put on hold many of the engineering consulting projects my husband John counted on to supplement his retirement check. Our daughter Katrelya had moved back home as she struggled to get her word processing service started. We were constantly jostling one another and getting in each other's way. In addition, walking for exercise in the wrong kind of sneakers had produced painful bruises on my feet. Emotionally, I felt resentful and stretched to a snapping point.

Taking comfort from a late night cup of tea, I opened my Bible at the Psalms. A verse I had read many times suddenly jumped out at me: "Thou art holy, O thou that inhabitest the praises of Israel" (Psalm 22:3). *What a strange idea!* I thought. *What does it mean? How does God live in His people's praises? Does that mean that praising God brings Him into my life? And the more I praise Him the more assurance I have that He is with me?*

Excited, I turned to other praise portions of the Psalms. The emphasis on praise was certainly there. "I will bless the Lord at all times: his praise shall continually be in my mouth" (Psalm 34:1). "I will hope continually, and will yet praise thee more and more" (Psalm 71:14).

I had found my spiritual focus. My New Year's resolution would be that instead of grumbling about all the *what isn'ts* in my life, I would praise God for *what is!* Family and home: Yes, I am glad that our daughter is home and we are here to help her. Simple pleasures: John and I hand-in-hand on an early morning walk to the village (in comfortable sneakers) for sweet rolls and coffee that even a cut budget can manage. And the greatest blessing of all: the reality of God's presence, dwelling with me as I praise Him.

Throughout this coming year, dear Lord, I will focus on Your blessings and give You the gift of my grateful heart. —Fay Angus

3 | W E D | *To win the contest you must deny yourselves many things that would keep you from doing your best....*
—I Corinthians 9:25 (TLB)

For many years, when the University of Wisconsin Badgers football team wasn't doing so well, we still had our spectacular marching band. Everybody loved their wild and crazy "fifth quarter" presentation after each game. But in the fall of 1993 something wonderful happened. The Badgers had a 10-1-1 season and made it to the Rose Bowl for the first time in thirty-one years!

Armed with his recent "Most Valuable Percussionist" award, my son Michael and his fellow Badger band members were off to Pasadena. Oh, how I wanted to go to that game! I searched my savings and checking accounts, desperately trying to figure out a way to afford the airfare and hotel costs. I entered a newspaper contest where the prize was a trip to the game. I warned my out-of-state relatives who were planning to come to my home for New Year's weekend that I might be going to the game in person.

Well, none of it happened. I stayed home, the relatives came (all thirteen of them!), and we watched Michael on TV as the camera focused in on him playing his duos and high-stepping his way through the most exciting day of his life. And we cheered, laughed, whooped and hollered as we watched the Badgers beat the UCLA Bruins in an upset.

I learned something that day. We humans don't always know what's best for us, but God sure does. I was much better off with my big family in my own home than I would have been in Pasadena fighting the crowd by myself. And I wouldn't have seen my son as clearly on his proudest day had I been there.

Today, Lord, remind me that Your plan for me is always, without a doubt, the best plan — no matter what.   — Patricia Lorenz

4 | T H U *And as ye would that men should do to you, do ye also to them likewise.*   — Luke 6:31

The other day, someone who knew that I had interviewed many people in my writing career asked me which one had impressed me most. "Which one said something that has stayed with you ever since?"

Well, that wasn't an easy question, but I found my mind going back to something Dr. Karl Menninger said when I was visiting him at the Menninger Foundation in Topeka, Kansas. I can recall his office very vividly: the Navajo rugs on the floor; the Native American artifacts everywhere; Dr. Karl wearing a yellow shirt with turquoise cufflinks, peering at me through horn-rimmed glasses with eyes that were both penetrating and kind.

We were talking about the importance of hope in human affairs. "If you lose all hope," the doctor said, "you stop trying and you stop caring. That won't do. I think each of us is put here to help dilute the misery in the world. You may not be able to make a big contribution, but you can make a little one, and you've got to try."

Help dilute the misery in the world. It's a tremendous challenge and an unwavering yardstick to measure yourself by. Before you fall

asleep tonight, ask yourself which of your actions during the day
came close to fitting that definition. Let small ones count as much
as large ones. If you can think of a few, sleep soundly. If not, don't
despair. The sun will rise tomorrow. You'll have plenty of opportunities then.

Dear Jesus, Healer of hurts, be our Guide.   —Arthur Gordon

5 | F R I | *Strait is the gate, and narrow is the way, which leadeth unto*
life....   —Matthew 7:14

Never have I felt so close to Jesus as I have these past few months. I
see His face when I awake; He's with me in the kitchen and as I tidy
up the house. He's beside me all day at my desk: those tender, deeply
caring eyes; that kind little smile on His lips. It's a portrait that had
been lying unwrapped in the basement ever since I moved back to
Virginia after losing my husband George. My son finally rescued it,
exclaiming, "Mother, have you seen this? Just look at what it says!"

> I never said it would be easy.
> I only said it would be worth it.

The words were inscribed on either side of His face. I had never
seen it and didn't remember — so many people had been so kind with
their gifts. Thrilled, I hugged it to my heart. The portrait was so
amazing I wanted to learn more about it.

A little investigation put me on the trail of Marty Peterson, a missionary in Japan. Marty told me that he was very young and insecure
when he first arrived in that country. Suffering from culture shock
and desperately needing encouragement, one day he spied a small
picture of Jesus gazing at him from a store window. "I bought it and
wrote on it the words He seemed to be saying: 'I never said it would
be easy. I only said it would be worth it.' " It helped him so much, he
sent a copy to his parents to help them.

Later, Marty met the artist Scott Snow, who agreed to paint a
larger picture that would capture and enhance that wonderful look.
"Eyes that see right into your soul!" And a calligrapher inscribed the
famous phrase that makes this work so powerful.

With Jesus' face before me, my prayer life is better. I have something tangible to reassure me that He hears. And like so many of

us, I sometimes wonder, *How can I go on?* Then I see that gentle reminder: "I never said it would be easy. I only said it would be worth it."

And Jesus was right. It is!

Dear Lord, keep us close to You every day.   — Marjorie Holmes

---

POINT OF LIGHT

MY NEW YEAR'S WISH

What shall I wish thee this new year —
Health, wealth, prosperity, good cheer,
All sunshine, not a cloud or tear?
Nay, only this:

That God may lead thee His own way,
That He may choose thy path each day,
That thou mayest feel Him near
Always, for this is bliss.
                              — Mary J. Lewis

---

6 | S A T | *My mouth praises thee with joyful lips, when I... meditate on thee....*   — Psalm 63:5 – 6 (RSV)

I was gently mincing the onion on the chopping board for gua-camole — gently because I didn't want to disturb Julee, my wife. I try never to bother her during her daily quiet time.

I had made a paste of one garlic clove and two teaspoons of salt, and set it aside in a small dish. Now I added the onion to a big bowl of ripe, peeled avocados and various spices. I'm not the chef in the family, but I can follow recipe instructions.

Julee's profession can be stressful and draining, as it had been this afternoon, and she went into the bedroom for her quiet time as an antidote to the daily tumult. What puzzled me, though, was how these relatively few minutes of spiritual solitude amidst all the hours of chaos in the day seemed to make such a dramatic difference for her. Julee explained that it was a simple matter of "getting back into rhythm with God." Still, I wondered.

The guacamole was done. I dredged a finger through it for a quick taste. Something was wrong. I added a shake of hot sauce. Then a frantic dash of cilantro. Just then Julee emerged from her room, stretching.

"I ruined it," I announced. Julee smiled and pointed to the garlic and salt paste, which I'd forgotten to add. "That's not going to do it!" I snapped. My wife took the dollop of paste, whipped it through the guacamole and held out a finger full. The guacamole was transformed.

"Powerful stuff," she said. "A little goes a long way."

I dutifully thanked Julee for revealing the secret of guacamole. And of her quiet time with God.

God, a little of Your peace goes a long way. Teach me to stay in rhythm with You throughout the day.   —Edward Grinnan

7 | S U N | *"Cure the sick.... You received without payment; give without payment."*   —Matthew 10:8 (NRSV)

A friend from my church was to be admitted to the hospital where I work. I learned about this when she shared the news during the worship service and asked for prayer. A biopsy had confirmed her worst fears, and she was scheduled for a mastectomy the following week.

The women in her Bible study group got busy that week in a very special quilting bee. When Gen came up to her room after surgery, she found her hospital bed covered with a beautiful quilt. Each square proclaimed an embroidered Scripture promise and the loving get-well wishes of the quilter. Gen carried that quilt with her everywhere she had to go in the hospital. No X ray was made, no test was performed without the comfort of her comforter.

A visit to Gen's room reminded me again how important it is not only to treat the body in sickness, but also to provide comfort and help for the mind and spirit. Although I wasn't Gen's doctor, I saw ways that I could help her. I taught her all the techniques I know for making doctors and insurance companies listen to what a patient has to say.

Gen is still on her journey toward wholeness; she's preparing for a bone marrow transplant. But I know that her quilt will go with her, as

will her newfound communication skills. And perhaps these gifts that
were given freely will prove to be the most important in the fight for
her life.

Lord, show me new ways to bring comfort and healing in Your
name.   —Diane Komp

8 | M
    O Now therefore let it please thee to bless the house of thy
    N servant, that it may be before thee for ever: for thou blessest,
O Lord, and it shall be blessed for ever.   —I Chronicles 17:27

For five years I rented the third floor of my house to a young couple
with a growing family—and growing problems. I enjoyed the babies,
and often baby-sat. But over the years the parents' arguments and
fights increased in number and intensity. Then the husband moved
out, leaving his wife with three small children. Eventually they, too,
moved out, and I spent June through August having the apartment
refurbished and trying to find a tenant.

With a new kitchen, redone walls and ceilings, and new linoleum,
the apartment looked light and pleasant. But though a number of folk
came to see it, and even said they'd rent it, the apartment remained
empty until another young couple with a baby actually came through
and moved in. But they, too, fought and argued. In two months, they
had broken up and moved out.

"The walls of the apartment must be soaked with ugly words,
angry cries, tears and the sounds of violence," I said to my friend
Tessie at church. "How do I counteract that?"

"Why not have a house blessing service?" she said.

That was my answer. Some time before Christmas, Pastor
Clemente came over and we prayed through the apartment, asking
God to remove any negative influence and make it a place of serenity.

The next person who came to see the apartment was a young professional woman. That very evening we agreed on the details, and she
moved in at the beginning of January. She's quiet and considerate—
and, I discovered afterward, a practicing Christian. "This apartment
has been a real blessing," she said to me recently.

"A blessing—and blessed," I replied, and then I told her why.

Lord, may Your blessing be on all our houses, so that our homes may
radiate Your love and peace.   —Mary Ruth Howes

9 | T U E | *Make love your aim, and earnestly desire the spiritual gifts....* —I Corinthians 14:1 (RSV)

Last year, in an after-Christmas visit with my friend Charlene, I noticed she had a new lamp. Its base was a plaster likeness of a dog with a bandanna tied around its neck. This new piece was definitely not Charlene's refined taste, and I questioned her about it.

"Oh, it was a Christmas gift. One of my favorites." I could hardly believe it and said as much. Charlene laughed. "The gift wasn't the lamp. The gift was my grown son searching out something unique for me."

I'm reminded of that conversation today as I put away one of my own Christmas presents: a large paperweight with a real tarantula inside. Instead of this hairy creature, I'm seeing my friend Carol searching for something unique to add to my paperweight collection. I'm reveling in her spirit of giving, even more than I am in the gift itself. I'm remembering Charlene's words: "The gift wasn't the lamp."

She's right, of course. The real gifts of Christmas were the loving thoughts of my family and friends as they chose something special to give me. That, too, was my gift to them. The packages, whatever they contained, were just a happy extra.

Thank You, Father, for Your gift of love to me. May we each learn to share that love all year long. —Mary Lou Carney

10 | W E D | *O Lord, be not far from me.* —Psalm 35:22

My husband David and I have just worked out at our neighborhood YMCA, and I am waiting for him near the men's dressing room. I have no less than a *jillion* things to do before the day is over, and the thought of the long day ahead fills my insides with a familiar panic. I pace up and down the hall, and when I look up, I find myself staring at a sign posted on the wall. *You are here*, it says. A red arrow points to a certain location marked with an X on the building's blueprint.

I am still standing there looking at the sign when David comes. "This is crazy," I say to him, "but I feel so reassured knowing exactly where I am in this busy day." David laughs, puts his arm around my shoulder and off we go.

Later, I am working at my computer when the buzzer on the dryer sounds. On my way to remove David's shirts, I smell the chicken dish

cooking in the kitchen and change my direction to check on it.
Passing the dining room, I notice that I haven't yet set the table for
tonight's guests. A moment of cold fear falls over me. *Can I really handle all of this?* Then I remember the sign. "You are here," I remind myself as I open the oven door. The casserole is fine.

After I have the shirts on hangers, I return to my desk and jot down
all the things I need to accomplish before the day ends, numbering
them by priority. "You are here," I say out loud as I draw a red arrow
to number one on the blueprint of my day.

Realizing that today actually can be managed, one task at a time, I
stop and smile. "I am here," I say to God, "and You are here. Let's
turn this into a good, productive day together." And we do!

Dear Father, my days are so full and I find myself overwhelmed.
Give me the peace that comes from knowing that where I am, You
are, and together we can handle whatever comes.   —Pam Kidd

11 | T *Hearken unto this...stand still, and consider the*
    | H *wondrous works of God.*   —Job 37:14
    | U

My mother had few material things in her life, but cared for what she
did have lovingly. With ten children in the house, sometimes some of
her little treasures got broken. I can see her still, patiently trying to
glue them back together.

"Why don't you just throw it in the trash, Mama?" I would ask.

"But you'll hardly be able to tell it's been broken when I finish with
it," she would reply.

As for myself, I wanted nothing broken or ruined. When something bad happened to anything of mine, it went straight into the
trash can. I demanded this kind of perfection for many years.

Then, seven years ago, I had a serious stroke and was left with several side effects, among them the inability to write or type. Doctors
told me that I probably would never be able to do either again, and I
was crushed. But I have since proven them wrong, and now can do
both. Not perfectly, of course, as I once did, but I thank God every
day for each imperfect page I am able to turn out, and I consider
them miracles.

Today, I find much value and beauty in things that are imperfect.
For example, the very elderly neighbor who is right now approaching my door walks slowly and painfully with a metal walker. But her

mind is so keen and her conversation so brilliant and interesting, a visit from her is always a joy. Incidentally, her walker is exactly like the one that was delivered to me a few days ago.

Oh, God, help me to ever see the value that often lies in imperfection.
— Dorothy Nicholas

12 | F R I | *Joy cometh in the morning.* — Psalm 30:5

I had the very great privilege of being in the birthing room when my granddaughter Saralisa was born. What an honor it was to be with my daughter Karen through all of her pain and hard work, to experience the moment when that tiny pink body fell into Dr. Wier's hands, to wait through the next few breathless moments and finally hear the first little cry that told us all was well! I'll hold the memory of that moment in my heart forever.

As the waiting hours passed that January night, I thought about how often great joy follows on the heels of great pain, and that in some mysterious way, the joy is made sweeter by the pain that precedes it.

Just that morning, a project over which I'd labored long and hard had come back rejected, and it felt like a stab wound. But as I held my new little granddaughter in my arms and kissed her soft cheek, I knew beyond all doubt that *only love matters*. And I said a prayer in my heart, entrusting little Saralisa to the love that is God. Then I released my future work ventures to the same love.

I'm very pleased to tell you that Saralisa, now two years old, is happy, beautiful and thriving. And I'm working on a new project that comes from a place of deep love within me.

If you're suffering today, maybe you'll take heart knowing that pain is often the mother of true joy.

Thank You, Lord, for the great joy that so often grows out of pain.
— Marilyn Morgan Helleberg

13 | S A T | *...That I may daily perform my vows.* — Psalm 61:8

I walked into traffic school that snowy Saturday morning seething with resentment over the ticket I'd received for speeding. I'd protested it in court—I'd been a good driver for forty-five years. Yet here I was, surrounded by other traffic offenders, attending school by order of the judge.

The teacher, a retired police officer, began the class by showing us a film that outlined twenty common driving errors, illustrated by scenes of accidents. My resentment faded when I realized that my driving skills had indeed become rusty, and I had forgotten many safety rules. At the end of the day, I made a fervent vow to drive more carefully. Every driver in America, I decided, should be required to attend traffic school at regular intervals to review the rules of good driving.

But then I got to thinking: *Wouldn't it be a good idea to review the rules periodically in other areas of my life—like marriage?* So when our wedding anniversary approached, I typed up the wedding vows we had made. I included them in the card I gave Larry, along with a note: "Let's review these vows together." The resulting discussion led to a deeper understanding of our relationship, and a commitment to keep our vows fresh.

Reassessment. Recommitment. To safe driving and vows of marriage. And what about the vows I took when I accepted Jesus into my life? Yes, I think it's time to reaffirm those, too.

Heavenly Father, help me to review—and renew—the vows I have made in my life.   —Madge Harrah

14 | S U N   *Let us think of one another and how we can encourage one another to love and do good deeds.*
—Hebrews 10:24–25 (Phillips)

Yesterday, I drove by a building that had just been razed. Once its impressive façade had dominated the horizon, but that piece of sky was now vacant and the structure lay in ruins. A demolition company had felled its twelve stories with explosives so that a new building could take its place. The whole process of tearing down, I read, took about eight seconds.

The question that I pondered was the time it took to put the building up. From conception and design to completion and occupancy, probably several years. Years to construct, eight seconds to destroy.

Buildings and people have at least one thing in common. They can both be built up or ripped down. Not long ago I overheard a manager tell an employee, "I can always count on you. Thanks for working late and completing the order." Compare that with another boss' complaint to an overworked secretary: "You never get anything done on time. Can't you work any faster?" Both incorporated two highly charged words: *always* and *never*. Used positively, those words build up. Used negatively, they tear down.

When it comes to people, you and I can choose which it will be. We can be in either the construction business or the demolition business. We can help loved ones, friends and associates with uplifting praise and compliments, or we can hurt them with faultfinding and criticism that tears down self-confidence and self-esteem. Either can be accomplished in eight seconds ... maybe less.

> *Stop me, God, when I would be acidic,*
> *Help me be a builder-upper, not a critic.*

— Fred Bauer

15 | M O N | *Our Father which art in heaven ... deliver us from evil....*
— Matthew 6:9, 13

In 1985, my husband Alex and I were in South Africa on business. Our host, Werner, and Alex were collaborating with a "colored" (mixed race) scientist on a project, yet this brilliant man could not ride in the same train car with them or swim at the same beach! Whites, coloreds and blacks were rigidly separated.

There was one bright spot, however. One evening we worshiped at an interdenominational fellowship in Stellenbosch and saw an unimaginable sight: coloreds, blacks and whites joining hands to sing and pray.

After we left the country, violence escalated. I hoped for the best, yet I prayed with little faith. Through the turmoil, Christians in South Africa continued to proclaim love between races, meeting despite the danger and praying vigilantly. Finally, in April 1994, peaceful elections were held. The headline of a Durban newspaper exulted: *God Steps In to Save South Africa!*

Martin Luther King, Jr., urged prayer against the evils of racial injustice and insisted on conquering hate with love. He proclaimed, "With Him we are able to rise from the fatigue of despair to the buoyancy of hope ... from the midnight of desperation to the daybreak of joy."

Today, I read accounts of a riot in an American urban center, of a bloody takeover by a dictator, of refugees fleeing a war-torn country. But I no longer feel defeated praying for situations enmeshed in evil. In each situation, God's people are working, loving, praying. I can join with them and persevere in prayer, asking expectantly for peace.

Oh, Father, may Your kingdom come, may Your will be done.

— Mary Brown

MY GIFT TODAY . . .

At mid-month throughout the year, Elizabeth Sherrill will share with us one gift she looks for every day at home that becomes a shining light pointing to God's love and care. We invite you to find similar gifts around your home and record them on the diary pages, "Gifts of Light," at the end of each month. Elizabeth tells us more about these daily gifts in today's devotional.

—The Editors

16 | T U E   THE BOOKMARK

Every good gift and every perfect gift is from above, and cometh down from the Father of lights....   —James 1:17

January. Cheerless and cold. The Christmas decorations are put away, and my mood can be as dark as the days outside. I've battled these low spells all my life, and not just in January. I know — in theory — what the cure is. Gratitude.

The problem is, how do you conjure up gratitude while the dark clouds hover? Over and over I remind myself of the stupendous gifts of God: life; health; the love of friends and family; this beautiful world. But this only compounds depression with guilt. How can I feel low with so very much to be grateful for?

So much to be grateful for.... It was on a January afternoon about five years ago that a thank-you note from a friend suggested I was approaching gratitude from the wrong end. The Christmas gift I'd sent was such a tiny thing! A bookmark! Just a small strip of paper, so inconsequential I'd hesitated to send it at all. To read my friend's letter, though, I might have sent gold. The bookmark had arrived on the anniversary of a miscarriage I hadn't even known about. Somehow the flowers around the border had spoken to her of new beginnings and made a dark day bright.

Maybe, I thought, *that was my mistake on my own dark days: trying to see through the clouds all the way to heaven. What if I were to start out by being grateful, not for all the great gifts, but for just one small one.*

From that day on I've followed a little ritual: finding that day's gift. Not some lofty abstraction, but something tangible: the bedroom rug beneath my feet on a winter morning; a grandchild's artwork on the refrigerator door.... There are only two rules: I must find the gift right here at home, and each day it must be something different.

How many hundreds of days in five years, and not once have I had to repeat. The mysterious chemistry of gratitude sets to work on those dark clouds. The light of God shines through the tiniest crack.

Father of lights, Giver of all good gifts, shine Your light into our darkness, today and all year long.   — Elizabeth Sherrill

17 | W E D | *O Lord, my rock and my Redeemer.*
          —Psalm 19:14 (NAS)

Ideally, I like to begin my day in my office at home with Bible reading and prayer. But yesterday, when my working day came to an end, my Bible had not been opened. It was buried beneath the details of one project after another that needed to be handled immediately. I could see this might become a recurring problem, and I wondered what might be the best way to correct my priorities.

That evening on a TV nature show, I found my answer. The screen came to life just in time for me to see the tail of a desert mouse disappearing into its sandy burrow for the night. Once inside, the mouse closed the hole behind it by deftly pulling a small stone across the opening. "You've just witnessed a nightly, routine performance," the narrator explained. "The pebble neatly camouflages the entrance to keep out any predators.

"But the stone serves another purpose," the narrator continued. "As the hot desert air cools off during the night, a single drop of dew condenses on the surface of the stone. In the morning, just as the sun begins to rise, the thirsty mouse emerges from its dark burrow to drink that one life-giving drop of precious water. It's enough fluid to carry the tiny creature through another day of dry, searing heat."

Such mouse ingenuity gave me an idea. Before going to bed, I went downstairs to my office and thumbed through my Bible until I located the passage listed for today's date in my daily reading guide. Then I positioned the open Bible in a conspicuous place on my desk.

This morning, when I came to my desk, there it was waiting for me, precious truth condensed in a single verse, Psalm 37:4 (NAS): "Delight yourself in the Lord, and He will give you the desires of your heart." The verse became a refreshing dewdrop of living water that helped me keep my perspective through another long day of juggling priorities.

Father, please help me daily to position Your Word front and center.
— Alma Barkman

---

18 | T H U | *For I am in distress, make haste to answer me.*
—Psalm 69:17 (RSV)

I felt a lot like that sad little character from the "Lil Abner" cartoon strip, that poor guy with the ever-present rain cloud looming over his head. Tomorrow's forecast had major storm fronts gathering for me: chemistry test third period, trigonometry for fifth and an oral report on John Steinbeck's *The Grapes of Wrath* scheduled for eighth. I began to think of the Joad family's travails as a vacation lark compared to what I had to face on Friday.

My bedroom floor was awash with texts and scattered notes, and I looked around frantically for some kind of organizational life raft to cling to. My annoyance sonar was finely tuned to the slightest distractions and, naturally, distractions were everywhere. I heard a car's door slam and flew to the window to glower.

Instead, I saw my childhood pal Paulie, now seventeen, and his mom arriving home. I had forgotten that Thursday was my old friend's chemotherapy day, and I watched as Paul, slighter and seemingly more vulnerable now than he had been at ten, shuffled his way tiredly up his front steps. Pausing to catch his breath, he noticed me, smiled wanly and called with effort, "Nice day, huh, Jen? How's it goin'?"

At that moment, with a sure and direct hand, God cleared the clouds above me and gave me pause to see with a clearer perspective. I shot Paulie a "thumbs up" and managed to choke out, "Got it made, Paulie! I got it made!"

Lord, thank You for making my burdens light with Your love.
— Jenny Mutzbauer

---

19 | F R I — *Homes are built on the foundation of wisdom and understanding.* — Proverbs 24:3 (GNB)

In a few months, I will graduate from college and nervously enter the "real world." This anxiety only increased when I went home last weekend to find that my youngest sister had moved into my bedroom.

As I stood staring at Stephanie's personal belongings mixed in with my own, I was struck by a feeling of loneliness. *Does being in school mean that I am no longer a part of my home? What will happen to me when I graduate?*

I puttered around the house with this question still in my mind when my mother came home from work. Upon seeing the look on my face, she asked, "Are you all right, Jen? You look so preoccupied."

"Oh, I was just thinking about graduation," I answered vaguely, not wanting to reveal my true concern.

When my sisters came home from school a little while later, Stephanie greeted me briefly and went straight to my room. She soon walked out of it, carrying her belongings in her arms. "Your room is back the way you left it, Jen!" she smiled, and went upstairs to her old bedroom.

"Jennifer, please come set the table!" my mother called from the kitchen, just like always.

And as I set the table for all of us, I knew that I had been wrong to lose faith in family, because no matter where I go, I will never really be leaving home.

Assure us, Father, that we can always come home.
— Jennifer Thomas

20 | S A T

All the earth shall worship thee, and shall sing unto thee....   —Psalm 66:4

It was a Saturday morning at church, and, as usual, a horde of homeless people and residents of local single-room occupancy hotels was lined up at the soup kitchen. I saw my friend Carol Chickering sitting behind her desk, counseling those who requested help, giving them referrals to social services in the area.

"Are you going to the service later?" I asked her. A longtime parishioner had died, and the memorial was being held in the sanctuary that morning.

"I'll be there," she said.

As the service began, I couldn't find Carol among the small crowd assembled in the chancel. Then from the choir loft behind, I heard her gorgeous, bell-like soprano voice. "I know that my Redeemer liveth," she sang. Her phrasing was limpid, her tone like spun gold, reassuring us of the hope that overcomes sorrow, of the joy found after mourning.

Afterward, I went back to the choir loft to tell her how much her music meant to me, but she was already gone. Only on my way out of the parish house did I spot her: back at her usual Saturday position, behind her desk, counseling the needy, giving hope to the poor.

Someone once said that "worship service" is a redundant phrase. Worship *is* service, and service, at its best, is worship. I had just seen the two as one.

Lord, I will worship You with my thoughts, words and deeds.
                                                        — Rick Hamlin

21 | S U N

"Were not our hearts burning...while He was explaining the Scriptures to us?"   —Luke 24:32 (NAS)

I often think about a student of mine from my teaching days. Her name was Susie, and she was one of the students in my preaching class whom I challenged to prepare and deliver a sermon in a different-than-usual form.

When Susie's turn came, she walked to the front of the room, paused for a moment to make sure she had everyone's attention, then said, "My name is Gomer. You know all about my husband. But I think it's about time you heard my side of the story." Then she kept our attention riveted as she retold the story of her marriage to Hosea. She changed nothing in the Bible story but the perspective. Suddenly, that familiar story came alive. She sent everyone scrambling to the Old Testament to reread the prophet's message.

Ever since that day in class, as I read the wonderful stories in the Scriptures, I sometimes pause in my reflection and reread the passage from the perspective of one of the people in the account. I've reread the account of the Prodigal Son from everyone's viewpoint: the mother, the elder brother, the pig merchant. It makes the story come alive in a new and different way.

Today, try picking out a Bible passage you've read so many times over the years that you've quit learning from it. But this time look at everything that is said and done through someone else's point of view, and let the Word come alive for you.

Dear God, today, help us to find fresh meaning in Thy Word and in our lives.   —Kenneth Chafin

22 | M O N   *I am with thee … in all places whither thou goest….*
                                                        —Genesis 28:15

I've written about my friend Agnes before. She is now in her ninety-ninth year and growing frailer and frailer. I still drop in on her once a week, and our conversations are as lively as ever. There's nothing frail about her ability to interest and amuse.

Lately, we've been delving more and more into memories. Yesterday, we talked about a custom in her family that she'd almost forgotten. "If I had something difficult to do and was worried about it," Agnes said, "my parents would ask me, 'Who is with you, Agnes?' and I'd reply, 'God is.' If I were heading back to college, my father would ask me the same question. Sometimes even if I was just going down to the grocery for a dozen eggs, my mother would say, 'Who's with you, Agnes?' and I'd reply, 'Oh, Mom, you know Who it is.' 'Then say it,' she'd say, and I'd say, 'God is!' "

Later in my visit with Agnes that day, we talked about death. Not unusual for us. She often mentions it matter-of-factly. "I have my bags packed," she has told me more than once.

"I hope I'm around when you pick up those bags," I told her.

"Why's that?"

"Because I'm going to ask you a question."
She looked blankly at me for a moment and then her eyes filled with luminous comprehension.
"Touché, my friend, touché," she smiled sweetly.

There's no need for me to reach out and touch You, Lord. I know that You are there.   —Van Varner

23 | T U E   *And then there are the sailors sailing the seven seas, plying the trade routes of the world. They, too, observe the power of God in action.*   —Psalm 107:23–24 (TLB)

Several times a day I rehearse a little nautical prayer that gives me great peace. It's painted on a delicate porcelain cup that my wife Sharon keeps on a bathroom cabinet shelf, surrounded by pretty seashells. The cup is guarded by two miniature figurines, a sailor and a fisherman. Whenever I shave or comb my hair, I repeat the prayer aloud: "From rocks and sands and every ill, May God preserve the sailor still."

Rocks: Those terrifying dangers that leap out of the fog and call for drastic action. Several of my friends from college days have hit those rocks. Failed marriages, career mistakes, bankruptcy. The wise kings David and Solomon hit those rocks in middle age. Am I wiser than they? So I pray for God's help in the fog of life.

Sands: Those subtle, hidden sandbars that can strand a ship unexpectedly. Laziness, apathy, compromise—these are the sands that threaten me. The closer I get to my heavenly port, the easier it seems to be bogged down in the sands of making a living. I pray for guidance around these invisible enemies.

And every ill: Scurvy, seasickness, loneliness were the ills that stalked the ancient mariners. I, too, wrestle with loneliness—the kind that thrives in a crowded world. And I get sick from the waves of rapid change that leave me dizzy.

So I keep saying my little prayer from my heart and turning my world over to the Captain of the Ship of Life. He alone knows the way through the rocks and storms.

"From rocks and sands and every ill, May God preserve the sailor still." Amen.   —Daniel Schantz

24 │ W E D │ *I have been a stranger in a strange land.*
                                                    —Exodus 2:22

When my stepfather came to live with me a few years ago, he was
quite depressed. Although he realized he couldn't go on living alone,
he missed the home he had known for so many years. Whenever his
friends called to see how he was, he would always say the same thing:
"I never got a chance to go back home. I just went into the hospital
and then I came here."

I thought my dad's sadness would go away, but when it didn't, I
spoke to our family doctor about it. "Be patient," the doctor told me.
"He needs more time. When we get older, it takes longer to feel comfortable in new places." I never said anything to Dad; I just kept on
trying to make him feel welcome. But sometimes when I saw the
loneliness in his eyes, I thought my heart was going to break.

A few weeks ago, my dad and I went to a christening and a recep-
tion. We were away a full day, and when we came home my dad stood
quietly at the back door while I fumbled for my keys. "You know," he
said, "I had a very good time—but it's good to be home!" He was
looking around at all the trees and smiling, as if he owned the place.
And there wasn't a bit of loneliness in his eyes. Our doctor was right.
My dad just needed more time to make himself at home.

Gentle Jesus, give us the patience and understanding we need to be
good caregivers.   —Phyllis Hobe

25 │ T H U │ *...A time to laugh....*   —Ecclesiastes 3:4

I was baby-sitting three of my grandchildren, and it was time to bathe
two-year-old Thomas. I got him and all his toys into the tub, and
began to wash him, sitting at an angle on the edge so I could continue
talking with Jamie and Katie, his sisters. Then before I could catch
myself, I lost my balance, slipped backward and fell into the tub—
fully clothed!

My granddaughters laughed hysterically. Thomas, observing them
for a few seconds, threw his head back and joined in the laughter. As
I sat in the warm water with my arms and legs extended, I felt this
tremendous laugh making its way out. I leaned against the pink tiles

and let it come. The four of us were joined together by our laughter, which lasted for perhaps three minutes and was exhausting and satisfying and unforgettable.

Of course, I wouldn't have laughed in my young motherhood days. I would have resented anything that made me look less than perfect, and would have been in a nasty mood for the rest of the evening, probably not speaking. And we would never have mentioned the incident again.

I'm glad I have finally learned — through experience, age and God's grace — that there's a time to laugh, even at myself and my humanness.

Father, help me to see the lighter side of things.
— Marion Bond West

26 | F R I   *God is light, and in Him there is no darkness at all.*
— I John 1:5 (NAS)

Hustle-Bustle, our turquoise parakeet, was part of the family. Welcomed at our table, he'd sample bread crumbs or nibble from a bowl. Nestled on a shoulder or perched in his cage, he'd repeat the compliments he'd memorized. "Pretty Hustle-Bustle," he'd croon. "Pretty boy."

Hustle-Bustle was almost human in another way. He disliked darkness. If we turned out the light in one room, he'd head for the light in the next room. We used to laugh about it, but there came a time when I could not only sympathize with him but also follow his example.

I was going through a dark time of depression when it seemed someone had turned out the lights in my life. Watching Hustle-Bustle showed me a way to get through my dark times — that is, to follow whatever light I did have. I found that if I looked, those lights were there. Some days it was just the lyrics of a song or a friend's kind word. Other times it was just remembering that for the wise men, one star in a blackened sky offered enough light to mark a path. By seeking the light, I found my way back into it.

Lord, when I am lost in darkness, please enable me to put out my foot in faith and follow the light.   — Joan Rae Mills

27 | SAT | *Whatever your hand finds to do, verily, do it with all your might....* — Ecclesiastes 9:10 (NAS)

One hectic Saturday morning, I ran a few errands for my mother and dropped by to make a delivery and return her change. "Thanks for everything," she said as I started to leave. "And especially for that last little gift."

"What are you talking about?" I asked. "I didn't give you anything."

"This," Mother said as she cupped her hands over mine and gave them a gentle squeeze. "You probably did it without even knowing it, but it was just like heaven reaching down to touch me."

I thought about that little incident on the way home. While it comforted me in some ways, it also disturbed me. *Was our world really so fast-paced and impersonal that a little squeeze of the hand could mean that much?*

Later, during the noon rush hour at a fast-food drive-through window, the cashier looked especially harried. "I said a large order of fries!" a man barked into the intercom.

"Give me a break," she muttered under her breath.

As I counted out the $2.34 for my order, my thoughts drifted back to Mother. On impulse, I softly sandwiched the cashier's hand in mine as I pressed the money into her palm. For an ever so brief moment, her brown eyes, framed in red tortoiseshell glasses, met mine. "Thanks. I really needed that," she said, smiling.

What began as a spur-of-the-moment gesture is now a tradition for me whenever I sense a need for it. It's nothing dramatic, but that subtle squeeze rarely fails to bring a smile.

Mother was right. In these life-in-the-fast-lane times, just about everyone can use an extra pair of hands.

Lord, we really are Your hands extended. Show me someone who needs Your touch today. — Roberta Messner

28 | SUN | *Grace be with all them that love our Lord Jesus Christ....* — Ephesians 6:24

The thing I found myself least prepared for when my husband Norman died was the crushing loneliness. We had shared more than sixty-three years together and had become inseparable. During the days, family, friends and associates filled the hours. But when I went home at night to our big old farmhouse, the loneliness descended. The place seemed like an empty barn.

One Sunday evening I was sitting in our family room watching the sun set and feeling the loneliness creep in. Every creak of the house made it seem more isolated because each noise reminded me that Norman was not there to make any noise. Just then the telephone rang.

"Grandma," exclaimed my granddaughter Becca from New York City, "are you all right?"

"Of course, Becca," I replied. "Why do you ask?"

"Well, I was reading a book and fell asleep on my couch and had a dream. Grandpa came to me and said clearly, 'Tell Grandma to turn on the alarm. Do it now, Becca.' And then I woke up and just had to call you."

"Isn't that strange," I said. "I haven't switched on the security system yet, and your grandfather always liked to have it on whenever we were in the house for the night."

Becca and I chatted a bit more, and then we hung up and I turned on the system. And I wondered, *Did Norman somehow look down from heaven and put a thought in Becca's head to call me?* I leave the theological debates and discussions to others, but I do know this: The Lord used that experience to remind me that Norman is very much alive and with Him, and that their love will always be with me.

Lord, thank You for the mysteries that remind us that You are in control and that we are deeply loved.   —Ruth Stafford Peale

29 | M O N   *Make the best use of your time....*
                    —Ephesians 5:16 (Phillips)

Recently, I served on a pastoral nominating committee at our church. Our major task was to call a new senior pastor, but early in the process, we got bogged down in writing out a questionnaire to the congregation, asking for feedback about the kind of person we needed. One night we worked until nearly eleven, struggling with the wording of a section on "personal characteristics." It seemed we couldn't agree, and we were getting nowhere.

Finally, one exasperated member asked, "Will this questionnaire bring in the kingdom?" It made us all stop and wonder what our real priorities were, and it helped us slice through the bog of our differing opinions so we could move on toward our more important goal. As we continued to meet, this question became a handy tool that kept us moving forward. Eventually, we reached our goal and called a wonderful new pastor to our church.

Our committee dissolved after that, but the "kingdom question" continues to help me move through the less important tasks in my life so that I can get on with the more important ones. *Will this bring in the kingdom?* I ask myself, because when I measure the value of the task in God's eyes, I sort through my priorities more quickly.

Father, sometimes I get bogged down in places where I shouldn't. Help me to recognize those places, move through them more quickly, and get on with Your work at hand.   — Carol Kuykendall

30 | T U E   *O sing unto the Lord a new song....*   — Psalm 96:1

One late winter evening, after the children and my wife were asleep, I turned the floodlights on in the backyard. It was snowing, and already a few inches had accumulated. I grabbed my coat, turned off the floodlights, quietly opened the back door and walked to the middle of the lawn. I stooped to the ground, gathered a handful of snow and licked it. Then I stooped again and rolled a snowball into my hands, pulled my arm back and let fly my missile at a tree.

In the silence, I looked to my left, then to my right, checking the empty street. Then I fell backward into the snow. I waved my arms up and down, spread my legs open and closed, then quickly stood up. A snow angel.

I began to feel the cold, but then I had a final idea. Once again I gathered snow into a ball and began to roll it in front of me. Within a few minutes my ball was more than half my size. Then I rolled a second ball, not as large as the first. After I rolled the third ball, it was the labor of the next few minutes that revealed the sure shape of my snowman. Putting my cap on the snowman's head, I returned to the house. From the back window, with the lights on again, I could see him, frozen in midnight, a man with a green cap.

The next morning I woke up to the sound of my three children hooting and laughing in the backyard. I opened the blinds and saw the children at work building their own snowmen, three children snowmen standing beside the one I had built the night before. It was a singular moment linked to my moment the night before. One that spelled God's blessings.

Thank You, God, for the joy of snowy days and nights, and for the chance to be a child again.   — Christopher de Vinck

31 | W E D   *"Choose for yourselves today whom you will serve...."*
                    —Joshua 24:15 (NAS)

"I want to share with you a saying that has really helped me," my friend Charles told me recently, after a seminar on time management. "'Every time you say yes to one thing, you say no to another.'"

Since then Charles' short maxim has helped me tremendously. Yesterday, for instance, I received an invitation to speak to a civic club in our city. I was honored by the invitation and wanted to say, "Yes, I'd love to." But the invitation was for Friday, my day off. Normally, I would have accepted the invitation. This time, though, I asked myself, *By saying yes, to what am I saying no?*

The answer was that I would be saying no to my wife and no to my hobbies and leisure. I would also be saying no to my church and its members, who expect me to take a day off each week so that I'll be rested and vital for their ministry. When I saw all the things to which I was saying no by saying yes, I politely declined the invitation.

Charles' saying has helped me put all my decisions to a spiritual test: How can I spend my time most wisely in God's service?

Father, I want to please You in all my life. Give me the wisdom to know when to say yes *and when to say* no. *Amen.*   — Scott Walker

GIFTS OF LIGHT

1 _____

2 _____

3 _____

4 _____

5 _____

6 _____

7 _____

8 _____

9 _____

10 _____

11 _____

12 _____

13 _____

14 _____

15 _____

16 _____

17 _____

18 _____

19 _____

20 _____

21 _____

22 _____

23 _____

24 _____

25 _____

26 _____

27 _____

28 _____

29 _____

30 _____

31 _____

For thou wilt light my candle: the Lord my God will enlighten my darkness.

—PSALM 18:28

FEBRUARY

S	M	T	W	T	F	S
				1	2	3
4	5	6	7	8	9	10
11	12	13	14	15	16	17
18	19	20	21	22	23	24
25	26	27	28	29		

1 | T H U | *To every thing there is a season, and a time to every purpose under the heaven.* — Ecclesiastes 3:1

Today's mail brought a letter from my lifelong, hometown friend Rachel, who had a brush with death a few months ago, resulting in heart bypass surgery. She was exuberant. "Marilyn, the most wonderful thing I've learned about prayer is that God does answer, in His own time. After spending forty-five years on my knees praying for Dan to be with me in church, it has finally happened! I guess it took my near-death experience for God to get through to him!"

Rachel's husband is tall, strong, confident; a medical doctor who seemed to rely only on science for his truths. As far as I know, he hadn't set foot in church except for weddings and funerals since he was a child.

Daniel in church! A miracle! But the thing that really struck me was my friend's faithfulness in prayer. *Forty-five years* without giving up. That, too, was a miracle — a miracle of unwavering trust in God. And during all that time, Rachel stayed loving and faithful and non-blaming. She didn't turn Daniel off. She just continued to pray, quietly believing in miracles.

I've been about ready to give up on a prayer I've held in my heart for four years, but Rachel's letter has renewed my hope and fortified my faith in God's perfect timing. Have you been getting discouraged about some long-term prayer? Maybe a miracle is worth a bit more time on our knees!

My prayer is in Your hands, Lord. I trust Your plan ... and Your timing!
— Marilyn Morgan Helleberg

2 | F R I | *Why are you cast down, O my soul ...? Hope in God; for I shall again praise him ....* — Psalm 42:11 (RSV)

"I feel very blue today," I said to my husband as we raced out of the house.

"It's the rain," he replied matter-of-factly.

But it wasn't. I had no real reason to be down, but nothing seemed to matter. I felt as if the light had been switched off in my life. My mother always said, "Keep your bad moods to yourself," and she was usually right about those things. So I put on a smile when I got to the office and went to check my schedule with a colleague.

She was not at her desk, but her computer was switched on. I focused on the words of green light moving endlessly across the dark screen. Usually, these gadgets to protect the screen are jokes, shapes or flying toasters, but not this time. "In a dark time," the line read, "the eye begins to see." Then it disappeared off the screen and began again at the other side. The words, she later told me, were a line from a poem she'd known since high school, "In a Dark Time" by Theodore Roethke.

"In a dark time, the eye begins to see," I said to my depressed heart. And I began, then and there, to count my blessings, to see in the darkness. I thought of faith, how prayer had comforted me when I lost my job; of my husband and three children; and friends, old and new. Those few scrolling words evoked them all.

The light came on again in my world that morning, and I remembered other words, learned in my childhood, from a very old prayer, giving "most humble and hearty thanks for all thy goodness and loving-kindness to us, and to all men. We bless thee," it goes on, "for our creation, preservation and all the blessings of this life."

No more than two minutes had passed. The owner of the office reappeared saying, "Well, don't you look cheerful today."

I praise You, O God, for these gifts of light in my life:
_____ ; _____ ; _____ .

— Brigitte Weeks

3 | S A T | *Thou shalt love thy neighbor as thyself....*
                                        —Leviticus 19:18

After years of living in apartments and rented houses, we purchased our first home when my husband was transferred to Washington, D.C. We couldn't afford the house, but we couldn't resist the view. It was on the crest of a hill flowing down to luxurious green meadows and beautiful woods. All the neighbors praised that view. It didn't occur to us that it could ever be taken away.

But after a few years, rumors began: "They're going to build a development of townhouses there." Meetings were held, petitions signed. But the juggernaut of progress came rolling over the landscape, devouring *our* meadows, *our* forest, *our* view! Our disappointment made us self-righteous. And the seeming injustice was compounded by the dust, the traffic, the noise. How dare they!

But we were also curious. And in the evenings when it was silent, we explored the unfinished streets — and were pleasantly surprised. The houses were different but lovely, the whole layout inviting.

Lights began to bloom in the new village, like little flags of friendship in the night. And the new people were so nice. Soon we were pausing to chat as we walked our dogs or met in the supermarket. Our children ran back and forth to play. Our churches called on them. And exciting things happened. Interesting couples discovered each other; strong friendships developed.

The drawbacks we had dreaded failed to appear. And, gradually, we forgot all about the view that we had guarded so jealously. For now, on the once empty sloping meadows had risen something far more beautiful: homes with warm, loving families in them. Lives that were full and rewarding as they blended and entwined with our own. They had given us back far more than they had taken away.

Dear Father, help me to remember that You created this earth for us to share. And that we can make it more beautiful for each other by the lives we lead while we are here.   — Marjorie Holmes

4 | S U N   *The entrance of thy words giveth light....*
                                        —Psalm 119:130

When I was thirteen years old, I began attending a Christian school. One day, in jest, I said to a friend, "You're a fool!"

"Don't say that!" said Eddie, one of my classmates. "If you do, you're in danger of hellfire."

"What?" I exclaimed.

"That's what it says in the Bible," he assured me.

What else is in the Bible? I wondered. I hadn't read it much. The Bible was a thick black book I'd had in my room as a child, a book too sacred to rest my juice glass on.

I went to see Mr. Boronow, one of my teachers. "How can I know everything that's in the Bible?" I asked him. "How can I know all the warnings — all the things I need to do?"

Mr. B — that's what we called him — looked at me with kind but serious eyes. "Robin, you don't need to know everything that's in the Bible. You just need to give your life to Jesus. Then, bit by bit, as He lives in you, He'll open up His Word to you and you'll understand all you need to live for His pleasure."

Right there in Mr. B's office, I asked the Lord Jesus to forgive me and come live in my heart.

Mr. B was right. I still don't know everything that's in the Bible. But bit by bit, over the years, I have not only learned from the Bible how to live for Jesus, but I have also found that His pleasure is my highest goal.

Lord Jesus, teach me again today how to please You.
                                                — Robin White Goode

5 | M O N   *"Why have you despised the word of the Lord, to do what is evil in his sight?..."*   — II Samuel 12:9 (NRSV)

During my medical school days, I decided that if innocent children suffer, there can't be a God. And if there isn't a God, then the Bible is useless. From there I went on to decide for myself what was right and wrong, and to trust my own judgment about my life and career.

One day, many years later, one of my medical students asked me a question. He wanted to be like me, he said, so he asked what my greatest goal in life was. "To find a cure for cancer?" he wondered.

A suffocating darkness filled my heart when I heard his assumption. If I answered him honestly, I would have to say that my goal was to *treat* cancer, rather than to *cure* it. If cancer was cured, what did that leave for me to do with my life? At some subconscious level, I *wanted* cancer to continue to exist! As I heard myself talking in my heart, I was afraid. With notions like that, how could I trust my own judgment?

I stammered out some answer to the student and then excused myself. But in the years that followed, I began to let God back into my life. Today, that student is a fine doctor with the gift of healing. I have to thank him for his question, which showed me the terrible price I was paying for ignoring the Word of God, and which was another step that started me on the path to my own healing and new life.

O Lord, You bring Your Word to us through many messengers. Help me always to be open to You.   — Diane Komp

6 | T U E   *The mountains shall bring peace to the people....*
                                                — Psalm 72:3

As I sit in my college adviser's office, I find myself pouring out all of my worries to her: "I have to finish school this semester, and I have eighteen really tough hours to go. How am I going to make it? But I have to make it because my sister Keri starts college next year, and I need to be out and working to help put her through school. And speaking of working, will I be good enough to get the job I really want? What if I fail? What if—"

"Hold it, Brock," my adviser stops me in mid-sentence. "I want to see you succeed so much that I'm going to give you an assignment."

One more thing to do! Is this woman crazy? I thought I was making it pretty clear that I am at the end of my rope. I look at my adviser, dumbfounded. She is reviewing my schedule, pointing to a break in classes that I have every Thursday when I finish at 1:00 P.M. "I'm going to sign you up for a weekly class during this period," she says, handing me something she's written down.

Outside her office, I stop and read her assignment: "Two hours on a hiking trail in the Great Smoky Mountains each Thursday from 2-4 P.M. Weekly report expected!" The woman, I'm convinced, is truly mad, but I know she's serious, so the next Thursday off I go!

The day is clear and cool. I follow the arrows that point to the 2.4-mile hiking trail. The only sounds are the wind in the trees, a squirrel cutting a nut with its teeth, a distant mockingbird's song. The air smells clean. The mountains of east Tennessee fill me with peace.

I find my thoughts are sorting themselves out. Somehow, I know everything is going to be all right down there at the university and beyond. From up on the mountain, none of the problems below seems so difficult. This assignment is a true stress-reliever. Then and there, I decide that this "class in the woods" will be a lifelong elective for me.

When I am weak, God, let me seek Your creation for strength.
—Brock Kidd

7 | W E D | *Has not God chosen those who are poor in the world to be rich in faith...?* —James 2:5 (RSV)

My little dog Sally Brown teaches me many things, and as usual I learn in spite of myself. The other day on my lunch hour I was impatiently walking her around the block (dragging might be a better word). I didn't have much time, and I let her know it. But cocker spaniels have relentless noses.

Around the corner came a man—I'm tempted to say old man, but there was really no telling—dressed in a soiled and ragged overcoat, grubby strands of dark hair half-tucked up under a frayed watch cap, his eyes sagging and sad. I, a seasoned New Yorker, glanced away.

But Sally made a kind of scurrying beeline to him, her stubby remnant of a tail vibrating in excitement. It was an utter mystery to me why she picked out this sorry soul to greet with the joy of a long-lost friend. My hand tightened on the leash. I wanted to pull her back, but self-consciousness got the better of me and I slackened my grip.

Sally sat demurely, obligingly allowing herself to be adored and stroked by the grimy hands. She gazed up at her admirer appreciatively. His features softened, a spark ignited in his eyes, and he smiled. "You *beeeaauutiful* girl, you!" he exclaimed quietly. "Thanks for saying hello."

He never looked at me. Quickly, he straightened up and was off. I stood and watched the man disappear down the street, wondering how he would have responded if it had been I who had stopped to say hello.

God, sometimes Your smallest creatures have the largest hearts. Help me do unto others with a larger heart.   —Edward Grinnan

8 | T H U   *Let the word of Christ dwell in you richly....*
                              —Colossians 3:16 (NRSV)

I was standing in line, waiting for the clerk in the produce department to weigh all the fruits and vegetables I had gathered up for my family of six. The woman at the head of the line had even more than I, and since she kept chatting with the clerk, most of us in the line were shifting grumpily from one foot to the other.

As the clerk and the customer made small talk, the line grew, snaking through the displays. I sighed impatiently, catching the eye of an elderly man who was standing just behind me. He returned my wry smile with a warm smile of his own. *What a nice man.* A bit of my annoyance drained away.

Then I noticed that he had only one item to be weighed, a small bag of mushrooms. I imagined a wife at home who had hurriedly dispatched him to pick up the one forgotten ingredient, and here he was trapped in a line of housewives with dozens of items. As the woman at the head of the line began moving her cart at last, I nodded at him. "You've only got one thing, and I have so many. Why don't you just go ahead of me?"

"No," he said, smiling his lovely smile again, "thanks just the same. You know, I've made a study and I've discovered that I have to spend sixteen percent of my life waiting. So I decided that I should learn how to wait graciously."

I've never forgotten that man. I have no idea how he came up with his sixteen percent figure, but fifteen years later he still comes to mind when I am forced to wait by people or circumstances. I am still trying to learn to wait graciously...to slow myself down...to think, as he did, of the other people in a tiresome line. That horrible "please hold" time, why not use it for prayer? And when my minister husband is late for lunch once again, I can remember to thank God that I have a good husband coming home, whose tardiness usually means he is out caring for people in need.

Lord, You are infinitely patient with me. Teach me how to open my times of waiting to Your grace. — Katherine Paterson

9 F R I *"Call to me and I will answer you...."*
— Jeremiah 33:3 (NIV)

A few years ago, I began volunteering one night a week on a San Francisco hotline for parents, children and teens under stress. Though I was happy to be that listening ear, I confided to my supervisor late one night, "We get so many crank calls. I'll answer saying, 'Talk Line,' and someone hangs up. Or I hear breathing on the other end, and even when I say, 'Hello, hello,' nobody replies."

"Those calls are very important," she replied. "It could be an adult who used this line as a teen and just needs to know that this hotline still exists now that he or she is a parent. Or it could be a child who saw our number and wants to check that we're really here. One thirteen-year-old told me she called six times before she got up the courage to speak. So even if we don't hear anything on their end, they hear that we're still available to talk, even if we don't have a long conversation every night."

I looked at the scarred wooden desk and the old black rotary phone. The next time I got one of those "crank calls," I would say softly, "I'll be here to listen whenever you're ready to talk." Just as God is always there for me.

Dear God, whether all my prayers are short or long, they are a way of keeping me connected to Your love. — Linda Neukrug

10 | S A T *Be kindly affectioned one to another....*
                                                    —Romans 12:10

My stepfather, who is in his eighties, grew up in more formal times. He has very good manners, and in today's casual world they're noticeable. He stands up when a woman enters a room; he holds the door for people; he offers his hand when he's introduced to someone; he doesn't interrupt when others are speaking; he says "Excuse me" if he needs to pass you; he writes thank-you notes and even tips his hat.

When my dad first came to live with me, my friends and neighbors were always telling him, "Oh, don't bother to get up, Ray," or "You don't have to do that, Ray." They meant well. He walks with a quad cane and has arthritis, so it takes him a little time to stand up and move around. Nevertheless, he stuck to his good manners. "I'm comfortable this way," he confided to me.

I was brought up with good manners, too, but I had let them slip away. I thought they were old-fashioned gestures that didn't mean anything. Now I realize I was wrong.

I've noticed that my dad's good manners are rubbing off on all of us who know him. We're saying "Thank you" more often. We offer our hands to newcomers. We don't interrupt each other when we're speaking. I even received a thank-you note from a neighbor's son. In fact, he was the one who came up with an explanation for our increasing politeness. "I like the way Ray treats people," Jeff told me. "He makes me feel special."

I've decided to keep my good manners. Yes, they are gestures, but they're very important ones. They're a way of telling someone, "I acknowledge your value as a human being—God's creation."

Lord Jesus, teach us how to honor each other.   —Phyllis Hobe

11 | S U N *"I will be a Father to you, and you will be my sons and daughters, says the Lord Almighty."*
                                                    —II Corinthians 6:18 (NIV)

I was astonished to tears at the lifelike oil portrait my artist friend Eva Llanos did for the three- to five-year-olds' Sunday school classroom. It was a copy of the famous one by Frances Hook, where Jesus is holding a child's face in both of His strong, carpenter's hands. The outstanding feature of this picture is the unconditional love burning in Jesus' eyes as He gazes into the face of this child.

I hung it over our altar where we gather for storytime and worship. But it wasn't just the children who were mesmerized. The adults, too, came to see. Early one Sunday, a woman I didn't know came in and stood for a long time not saying anything, just looking over the altar into the picture. Finally, I heard her whisper, "I wish my father would have looked at me like that."

I didn't answer. She wasn't talking to me. But a moment later her face lit up like the child's in the picture, and I knew God had slipped the truth into her heart: Her Father does look at her like that. And at you and me.

Lord Jesus, thank You for showing us the face of the Father in the face of Jesus. Help us, through faith, to accept His love.

— Shari Smyth

POINT OF LIGHT

EVERLASTING LIGHT

Almighty God, whose light is of Eternity and knoweth no setting, shine forth and be our safeguard through the night; and though the earth be wrapped in darkness and the heavens be veiled from our sight, let Thy brightness be about our beds, and Thy peace within our souls, and Thy Fatherly blessing upon our sleep this night. Amen.

— Author Unknown

---

12 | M O N *"Be merciful and kind to everyone."*
— Zechariah 7:9 (TLB)

Nancy Hanks Lincoln, Abraham Lincoln's mother, couldn't read. Nevertheless, she gathered her children around her nightly and from the light of the open fire recited prayers and Bible stories she had memorized. Times were severe. Food and physical warmth were scarce. The family was crowded into a tiny, makeshift log cabin, sometimes forced to stay inside for weeks until the heavy snow drifts melted.

Nancy Lincoln died at the age of thirty-four from an illness called "milk sickness." She had been faithfully caring for her sick relatives when she caught the disease. As she lay on her deathbed, she called her children around and gently gave them these final instructions. "Be good and kind to Father and to one another and to the world." Young Abraham helped his father make her simple pine coffin. It was spring before a minister came to the area to preach a brief message over her grave.

"Be good and kind ... to one another and to the world." It is a challenge I accept for myself, and one that I extend to you this day.

Father, help me to fill this world with kindness — today and every day.
— Marion Bond West

13 | T U E | *Blessed are all they that put their trust in [the Lord].*
—Psalm 2:12

Once in New York City I visited the shop of a violin maker. A craftsman who had learned the trade from his father, the man patiently explained the art of violin-making to me, demonstrating the use of his wood-shaping tools.

"I suppose the wood used in your instruments is the most important element," I suggested, pointing to some pieces of maple and spruce that he had imported from the highlands of Germany.

"It is imperative that you use high quality, seasoned wood to achieve resonance," he agreed. "But there is something more important to the finished product: the musician who plays it. In the hands of a master, even a flawed instrument can produce beautiful music."

I've thought of his words many times since. What is true of violins is also true of people. Not long ago, I met a young man who because of an auto accident had lost the use of his legs. He had been an outstanding athlete, but now is reduced to watching sports. I say "reduced," but that is a misnomer. He is as full of life and as involved in life as anyone I've ever met; active as a church officer, baseball coach and community leader.

"I can do all things through Christ which strengtheneth me," he testifies joyfully (Philippians 4:13). His body may not be perfect, but his spirit more than compensates for it. And because he has put himself in the hands of the Master, his life produces beautiful music.

God can do the same for you and me, no matter what our shortcomings, no matter what our flaws.

Teach us, God, to...
> *Live life without complaint,*
> *To hug what is, not what ain't.*

—Fred Bauer

14 | W E D *There is no fear in love; but perfect love casteth out fear....*
—I John 4:18

Today is Valentine's Day, a day when affection can be expressed in endless ways. On this day, I learned an old and unexpected lesson.

I remember Valentine's Day 1943 — not for what I did, but for what I neglected to do. Ruby and I had been married five months, and I made the rounds to the florist, the card shop and the candy store. How proud I was when I gave these gifts to her. In my clumsy way, I was proving that our courtship didn't end with the wedding ceremony.

Two weeks later, as we entered our church, the landlady turned and said, "Happy belated birthday, Ruby!" Ruby dropped her eyes and thanked her.

I gasped. Of course! Six days after Valentine's Day is Ruby's birthday. I had forgotten *her* day! I was embarrassed and ashamed. What could I do? How could I make up? I ended up ignoring my oversight and didn't say a word for fear of Ruby's response. I remained haunted over that birthday error of years ago.

Last Valentine's Day, I finally apologized to Ruby for my long-ago oversight. Ruby couldn't remember it, but she said, "I was probably hurt. Not because you forgot my birthday, but because you didn't come to me, and trust me and let me comfort you. If you had done this, you would have grown ten feet in my estimation."

I blinked. Ruby had given me a gift of love I would never forget. All I could do was utter, "Amen."

Blessed Father, help me to see the possibility of love in others and to understand that their forgiveness comes from You.

— Oscar Greene

15 | T H U | *MY GIFT TODAY...*
THE PILL BOTTLE

Thou hast delivered ... mine eyes from tears, and my feet from falling.   —Psalm 116:8

"Go through your medicine chest," the safety manual advised, "and throw out any prescription more than two years old." Guiltily, I opened the linen closet where a shelf held medications dating back decades.

I got a wastebasket and began tossing out syrups for forgotten ailments and tubes of salve with illegible labels. A small bottle bore the sticker of a pharmacy long closed. I read the directions: "Codeine. One tablet every four hours when needed for pain." I looked at the date: 1981.

Our doctor had written out that prescription before my husband and I left for China. "Just in case," he'd said. "One of you could have a toothache, sprain an ankle."

I unscrewed the cap. The bottle was full. We hadn't had toothaches on the trip, or sprains, or any of the thousand things that "could" have happened.

Standing there in the hallway, I recalled the grace one of our children once offered at the dinner table. Covered with the bumps and scrapes of any active youngster, six-year-old Donn said fervently, "Thank You, God, for all the places that don't hurt."

All the bumps we don't get, the illnesses and accidents that don't happen. As I tossed it in the wastebasket, I thought, *An unused bottle of pain pills is a gift indeed.*

Thank You, Father, for all the "coulds" that never happen.
                                              —Elizabeth Sherrill

16 | F R I | *Let each of you look out not only for his own interests, but also for the interests of others.*
                                          —Philippians 2:4 (NKJV)

"The windchill at O'Hare International Airport is officially twenty-five degrees below zero," the radio announcer said cheerfully. I pulled into long-term parking, feeling anything but cheerful. I hated these cold weather flights: the treacherous freeway driving to get to the airport; waiting for the bus to take me to the terminal; the inevitable ice delays. But I had committed to a project that required several flights during the winter months. Dragging my suitcase, I hurried toward the bus shelter.

It was full. I stood outside, shivering. Other people arrived, but the bus didn't. I was cold! Then, suddenly, I felt a decrease in the wind. A businessman had stepped in closer to me. Soon, a woman and her teenaged son followed suit. One by one we passengers gave up our lonely vigils and huddled close together, gathering warmth from each other. Someone laughed, and we all smiled through chapped lips, sensing that in that small act of cooperation we had ceased to be strangers.

And when, finally, the bus did arrive, no one seemed in a hurry to push forward and be the first inside.

Dear Lord, in a world of strangers and coldness, let us be aware of small chances that come our way to warm each other.

— Mary Lou Carney

17 | S A T *Oh, restore me to health and make me live!*
— Isaiah 38:16 (RSV)

Rob Pierce, a fifteen-year-old boy in our church, was in the hospital after having accidentally snapped himself in the eye with a bungee cord. His family and friends were all concerned about possible vision impairment — but that had paled beside his personality dip. Rob changed from a spunky teen to someone who barely mumbled when we spoke to him.

Steps were taken to reduce his medication, known to contribute to depression, and he underwent surgery to release pressure in his eye. Still, he continued to retreat; he wanted the curtains drawn and refused to open his one good eye. His parents didn't wish to add to his suffering by pushing him to respond to them. But one day, visiting with some members of the youth group, I appealed to him, "Rob, you *can* crawl out of this hole. Let us help you. Let's get some light in here. Open your good eye and look at your wacky balloons. And no more mumbling. Talk to us. We want you back."

We prayed together then, thanking Jesus that He understood Rob's confusion and fear and asking Him to give Rob the courage to get up. And a wonderful thing happened. Rob propped up on his elbow and opened a droopy eyelid. We had him back. Later on, he recovered most of the sight in his injured eye.

There have been times when I have holed up inside myself because I haven't wanted to face something, even something as common as a rainy day. But I hadn't considered how unsettling such dark mood swings must be for those closest to me until I saw the effect Rob had on his family and friends. I only hope I'll remember the joy on the faces of Rob's parents when he perked up again. Keeping that kind of spark in the eyes of those I love is one powerful antidepressant.

Lord, my down days often keep others from enjoying an up day. For their sakes, and mine, give me the courage to "pull up the shades" and look on life with hope. — Carol Knapp

18 | S U N *In my Father's house are many mansions.... And if I go and prepare a place for you, I will come again, and receive you unto myself; that where I am, there ye may be also.*
— John 14:2–3

We had guests one night for dinner, and somehow we got into a discussion about heaven. One woman said, "I don't mean to sound blasphemous, but the thought of a heaven with gold streets and marble walls turns me off a little. I'd like there to be green grass, beautiful trees, lovely flowers, sparkling streams and the sound of birds singing."

"There will be — somewhere around," someone else said. "God would never take all those wonderful things from us."

Then I spoke up, "Well, I'm hoping to find a heavenly library there. I know I'll still want books."

"What would you like to have in heaven, Fred?" someone asked my husband.

"Two good legs," he answered, "so that I won't have to go around limping all the time. And the constant sight of God's face beaming at me." Fred had had polio when just a one-year-old baby, and one leg was so affected he had to limp his way through life.

Then a woman said, "We're individuals here on earth, and we don't all yearn for the same things. I think we'll still be individuals in heaven, and that God will give to each of us those special things we long for. Heaven is going to be all things to all people, and God is preparing it that way for us now."

I spoke up again. "I think one of the nicest things about it will be not having to pack anything up and move when it's time to go. I'd hate to think about getting in another U-Haul truck, even for a move to heaven."

Everyone laughed, but the conversation had touched all of us. The evening ended with the group holding hands and saying individual prayers. Each prayer carried thanks to God for our future heavenly home awaiting us.

Dear Lord, let us keep our minds on You and be ever ready to meet You in those mansions on high.   — Dorothy Nicholas

19 | M O N   *And he led them on safely, so that they feared not....*
                    —Psalm 78:53

The summer of 1950 was a strange one for me — and for our nation. Just as I arrived in Washington, D.C., to do some research for a degree in history, the Korean War began. I took lodging in a rooming house close enough to the National Archives for me to walk there. Every day my journey took me past the White House, then undergoing major reconstruction. Everything in its interior had been removed; only its walls were left standing.

Often when I'd leave the archives at day's end, I'd find myself falling into stride with an old gentleman on his regular evening stroll. He was an odd bird, courtly in Southern mien and dressed most picturesquely in swallowtail coat and string tie. His wife had died, he told me; he didn't have to tell me he was lonely.

One evening I described to him a disturbing experience I'd had the previous night while walking home late by the White House. "The moon was shining through its walls," I said. "What with this new war on, and the president's house a shell, empty, I had an awful feeling that the country had no leader."

"Stop inventing trouble, son," the old man said. "The White House is indeed a symbol, but a symbol only. Next time you go by there, I'd advise you to look across the street to Blair House where President Truman is in residence. He's alive, and he's in charge. Just pray to keep him that way."

Ever since then, especially with the assaults that they — and we — have endured, I have prayed for the safekeeping of our presidents. It's something to keep in mind, I think, especially in the passionate heat of an election year.

(By the way, though I didn't know it at first, the old man was The Honorable Clyde Roark Hoey, Senator from North Carolina.)

Lord, protect those whom we have chosen as our leaders. Keep them strong and well in body, mind and spirit.   — Van Varner

20 | T U E   *As iron sharpens iron, so one man sharpens another.*
— Proverbs 27:17 (NIV)

Some time ago, I received a call from Jim, a businessman here in Mendenhall, Mississippi. I'm sorry to say my first reaction was, *This must be some kind of emergency for a white man to be calling a black man.* Even though Jim wanted to talk about the problems facing us in Simpson County, and how blacks and whites needed to work together to solve them, I was suspicious. Based on past experience, I was sure that after a few months, I wouldn't hear from him again.

But as we talked longer, something prompted me to say, "Jim, let's get together sometime, not just to discuss issues, but to get to know each other."

To my surprise, Jim said, "Okay, I'd like that." We agreed to meet for lunch once a month.

During one of our times together, we discussed Jim's feelings about the ugly history of racism in our area. To my astonishment, Jim said, "Dolphus, I saw it. I disagreed with it then, and I disagree with it now." After that we began to talk about our families and to share our hopes and dreams.

Then, in February 1990, my home was flooded with twelve inches of water. I was busy pulling up carpet and shoveling out mud when Jim arrived. Without hesitation, he pulled off his suit coat and began helping me clean up.

At that moment, I identified with the Scripture, "As iron sharpens iron, so one man sharpens another." We were two men, each learning about the other — as friends.

Do you have a Jim in your life who is helping you destroy years of cultural and racial differences? If so, praise God!

Lord, today help me to accept those You bring into my life who are different from me.   — Dolphus Weary

21 | W E D *[Christ Jesus] humbled himself, and became obedient unto death, even the death of the cross. Wherefore God also hath highly exalted him....* — Philippians 2:8–9

In church last Sunday, we were given small slips of paper at our morning services. "Write on them," we were told, "those things in your lives that you would like to put under the mercy of the Lord. Pain from a memory or a current hurt. Sins confessed. The need to forgive someone who has offended you. A habit that needs breaking. The commitment to help a homeless family...."

All over the congregation there were tears as we wrote. Then we came to the front of the church and one by one we placed these small pieces of our lives onto smoldering coals in an urn, to be burnt and turned into ash. These are the ashes that today, Ash Wednesday, will be used to mark our foreheads with the sign of the cross — a reminder of our own mortality and the sacrificial death of our Lord and Savior, Jesus Christ.

As my forehead is marked, I think of those intermingled ashes — my pain, with other people's pain, mixed together and given to the Lord. They not only speak to me of our common humanity, but they also point to the ultimate answer to suffering: Christ's forgiveness, His healing and His resurrection power!

As we remember Your pain and the suffering of Your passion, beloved Lord Jesus, we ask for Your forgiveness and healing grace. Come into our hearts — in glory! — Fay Angus

22 | T H U *Better poor and humble than proud and rich.* — Proverbs 16:19 (TLB)

During a three-day visit to Philadelphia, I toured Congress Hall, Independence Hall and Carpenter's Hall — restored buildings that tell the secrets of where and how the Declaration of Independence was written and where the first presidency was carried out.

I felt a sense of awe as I gazed at the elaborate silver inkstand used to sign the Declaration of Independence more than two hundred years ago, and then ran my hand down the banister on the same stairway George Washington used in Independence Hall during his two terms as president from 1789 to 1797. From 1790 to 1800, the nation's capitol was in Philadelphia, while Washington, D.C., was being built.

What amazed me most about my trip through American history was Washington's humility. Our guide told us that the people of Philadelphia built an elaborate palace for Washington outside the city. Yet he refused to live in it, feeling his place was among the people. He also refused to serve more than two terms as president, even though he would have been easily reelected to a third term. Rather than follow the example of England's monarchs who ruled for their lifetime, Washington felt that no U.S. president should be in power more than eight years. In a precedent-setting act of humility, after just two terms, he stepped down and, in effect, handed the presidency to John Adams.

Today, on George Washington's birthday, what act of humility can we practice that could set a precedent for our families? Perhaps planning a vacation centered on the interests of other members of the family instead of our own. Or quietly doing things for them without any announcement. If we humble ourselves by being servants to those we love, perhaps we'll be revered in God's eyes the way Washington was revered by his countrymen.

Today, Lord, help me to humbly serve others, creating precedents that will last for generations. —Patricia Lorenz

23 | F R I *One must help....* —Acts 20:35 (RSV)

I was driving my brand-new car on Interstate 80 early in the morning, trying to beat the traffic jams and to arrive at work early to finish a project. Suddenly, in the distance, I saw to the side of the highway a collection of people. The closer I zoomed toward them, the more I realized they had car trouble. I raced past them, but then as I looked in the rearview mirror, they were still waving. I pulled over and then backed up to the stranded people.

"Do you know car?" the man asked in broken English as he stood in front of the open hood.

The wife smiled. She was missing many teeth. One of the four children, an older boy, stepped up and said with a shy manner, "We are going to visit my uncle. He's getting married this morning."

"Can you fix?" the father asked.

I know absolutely nothing about cars. I looked up and down the empty highway hoping to see a police car, a tow truck, anyone who might be able to help. Then I looked at the family. "Where is the wedding?" I asked.

"Ten miles over the mountain," the wife said with another smile.

I arrived at work four hours late that morning. "What happened?" my supervisor asked.

"Well, I went to a wedding."

Three weeks later, I received a postcard from the Bahamas signed by the groom. It read, in part, "Thank you for my brother. His car is good again. My wife, she is going to name our first son Christopher."

In all likelihood, you will come across someone today in need of help. If you can, help. If you cannot, offer a silent prayer for them. You may not always get a thank-you postcard — unless it's one signed by God. It's called a blessing.

Lord, help me to help those who are in need of help.

— Christopher de Vinck

24 | S A T   *Be kind to one another....*   —Ephesians 4:32 (NAS)

It was 6:30, and I was back at the restaurant for the second morning in a row, for a wake-up cup of coffee before the conference activities started on the campus of Georgetown College in Kentucky. The breakfast buffet looked tempting, but I resisted it and ordered what I had ordered the day before. "All I want is a cup of coffee and one biscuit with a little gravy on it."

"I can't serve you just one biscuit," the waitress snapped. "You have to buy a whole order of two biscuits."

When I explained that I was just ordering what I had gotten the day before, she put her hands on her hips and with a head gesture toward the kitchen said, "Those girls aren't supposed to do that. All they do is make me look like an old grump." I told her to forget the biscuit and bring me a cup of coffee.

While I was sipping my coffee and trying to recover my focus, a different waitress came to my table. She wanted to explain what had happened. "Your waitress yesterday did bring you just one biscuit, but she charged you for a whole order as she is required to do." Then, with a twinkle in her eye, she asked, "Would you like for me to bring you your other biscuit from yesterday?"

She brightened my whole day, and I was better at everything I did as a result. Driving home to Louisville after the conference was over, I thanked God for her simple ministry to me and promised myself to look for some situations each day when I could bring someone his or her "other biscuit."

Lord, let me brighten someone's day with a fresh solution to some small problem.   — Kenneth Chafin

25 | S U N | *He that shall endure unto the end, the same shall be saved.* — Mark 13:13

All churches have something to say to a visitor, I think, if you will just stand still and listen....

The other day I found myself in the First African Baptist Church in my hometown, Savannah, Georgia. It stands facing Franklin Square, gaunt and angular, but with a certain power that is hard to explain unless you know something about its history.

It was built by slaves just at the beginning of the war between the states. Their owners allowed them to work on it at night by the light of bonfires after their other tasks were done. Many were illiterate, but some were also skilled carpenters and masons. Their wives brought bricks in their aprons to the men as they worked. Records of the construction are almost nonexistent, except for a single phrase in an old ledger: "The man who laid the first brick was the man who laid the last."

How could people held in bondage and denied education build a brick edifice capable of seating more than a thousand worshipers today? The answer is someone must have led them, one of their own number, someone who laid the first brick with faith and hope and determination and then four years later laid the last. No one knows for certain who that leader was, but the church is his monument and his glory.

More often than I like to acknowledge, I have become discouraged in the middle of a project. Sometimes I have given up altogether. But now I think I have a phrase to remember when that temptation comes, when the going gets tough, when it's much easier for me to stop than go on. *The man who laid the first brick laid the last.*

Grant me that kind of faith and courage, O Lord.
                                    — Arthur Gordon

26 | M
     O
     N   *If only I knew where to find him....*   —Job 23:3 (NIV)

We have call waiting, call recording, call interrupting; a portable
phone; a modem; not to mention a newfangled bulletin board and a
stack of little yellow Post-Its for writing notes. You would think that
with all these communications devices, our family would communicate. But no!

Just the other day, I pressed the wrong button on the telephone and
wiped out the message that my son Tim was coming home from the
city for dinner. The portable phone went stone dead from being left
all night under a pile of magazines, so I never got to remind eighth-
grader Geoffrey that I'd be late coming home. The dry-erase pen for
the new bulletin board ran out of ink. Forget the modem—no one
knows how to work it. And my Post-It note reminding my husband to
buy groceries for dinner fell off the door and disappeared.

Somehow, despite the technological snafus, the day ended in a moment of flawless information exchange among all significant parties.
Seated around a table laden with take-home Chinese that evening,
we grasped hands, bowed our heads and, faster than a speeding
microchip, found each other and our Lord.

Prayer, after all, is the perfect telecommunications system.
Instantaneous. Unfailing. A wire straight from our hearts to heaven.

Whenever I call, Lord, You are waiting. Hear my prayer.
                                              —Linda Ching Sledge

27 | T
     U
     E   *I will praise thee; for I am fearfully and wonderfully
          made....*   —Psalm 139:14*

All my life I've felt self-conscious about my teeth. You see, they're
crooked. When I was a child, my parents could not afford to have
them straightened, and after Larry and I got married, we couldn't
afford it either. Now whenever I look in a mirror, I see graying hair,
trifocal glasses, wrinkles ... and crooked teeth.

Recently, two of our son's young daughters came to visit us for the
weekend. On Saturday morning six-year-old Cheyanne looked up
from her bowl of breakfast cereal and said to me, "Grandma, you're
so nice and you're so pretty. When I grow up, I want to be like you
and look like you."

Caught up in my old insecurity, I replied, "Oh, no, Cheyanne, I'm not pretty, not with these crooked teeth. But I'm glad you love me anyway."

I guess she must have brooded about this all day, for at bedtime she turned to me suddenly and said in a fierce voice, "Grandma, you *are* pretty! And so are your teeth!"

My granddaughter's forthrightness jolted me. But it was the most heartwarming compliment I've ever received. For the first time in a long time, I really *did* feel beautiful, and I hugged her and told her so.

Nowadays I try to remember the wisdom a six-year-old passed on to me: Seen through a filter of love, all people are beautiful.

Father, I praise You for the wondrous gift You've given us, the eyes of love.
                                                    — Madge Harrah

28 | W E D | *"But a certain Samaritan, who was on a journey, came upon him; and when he saw him, he felt compassion."*
— Luke 10:33 (NAS)

"Like for me to drop you off at the mall on the way to my meeting?" my husband Mark asked. It was a thoughtful gesture on his part, but I couldn't help feeling annoyed. Ever since Dr. Shy had told me not to drive until he'd run some more medical tests, I'd received a number of invitations like that. *The only way I get to go anywhere anymore,* I moaned to myself, *is on the way to somewhere else.*

The next afternoon at the hospital where I work as a nurse, my ride home was delayed. To pass the time, I was heading for the library when a frail, elderly woman approached me. "I'm looking for Five South," she said, peering at me through thick, cloudy glasses. "My brother's a patient there. They say it's brain cancer. He probably won't even know me."

"Come with me," I said. "I'll help you find him." *On my way to somewhere else again,* I thought. We took the elevator to Five and walked toward the nurses' station to find out her brother's room number. The next thing I knew we were walking past the elevator again.

"Sis," I heard a man chuckle from the other end of the hall, "you always did walk around in circles." The frail woman all but skipped toward her younger brother, who reached out his arms to her.

"I was having trouble finding you," she said to him, "but this lady, she walked with me." Then she turned and gave me a hug. And in that moment, I felt I really understood that when Jesus changes our plans, He has better plans in mind. Didn't some of the most life-changing events in the Bible take place on the way to somewhere else? Like the transformation of the woman whom Jesus met at the well on His way through Samaria to Galilee. For on the way to somewhere else, the best detours often take you to where you should have been going all the time.

Help me, Lord Jesus, always to trust Your plans, not my "to do" list.
— Roberta Messner

29 | T
H
U | *This is the day which the Lord hath made; we will rejoice and be glad in it.*   — Psalm 118:24

Here's a question for you: If you were given a gift of time — let us say a twenty-four-hour day — what would you do with it?

I ask this because 1996 is a leap year, and the calendar has thrown in a joker, a day in February that hasn't appeared since 1992. What a boon! What an invitation to do something unusual! But what?

"Quite seriously," said my friend Mary Lou, "if I were given the opportunity to do anything I wanted, I'd spend it in solitude."

"I'd spend it outdoors," said Mary Ruth. "I'd try to find the perfect place to wander in nature, to get as close as possible to God and His creation."

"Frankly," said my buddy Harold, "I think the thing should be declared a worldwide, quadrennial holiday. Close the banks, open the pleasure palaces, let's all go to the beach!"

As you can see, it takes all kinds. And that includes those who said they'd go on a museum binge or "clean out my attic at last," or those who told me that they'd look for some unusual way to help others.

So I suppose you're wondering what I would do with this unexpected gratuity. Actually, I made my choice weeks ago: I'd treat February 29 as though it were a day like any other. Why? Because of something I remember my old boss and mentor having written years ago. "Today has never happened before," Norman Vincent Peale said. "It's a glorious opportunity to start all over again."

That's it. A glorious chance to change my attitude, to wipe the slate clean of grudges and grime. That's the real gift I'm being given, time to start over. And I can do that today and tomorrow and tomorrow....

I will use this day as You would have me use it, Lord, and I will be glad in it.
— Van Varner

GIFTS OF LIGHT

1 _____

2 _____

3 _____

4 _____

5 _____

6 _____

7 _____

8 _____

9 _____

10 _____

11 _____

12 _____

13 _____

14 _____

15 _____

16 _____

17 _____

18 _____

19 _____

20 _____

21 _____

22 _____

23 _____

24 _____

25 _____

26 _____

27 _____

28 _____

29 _____

MARCH

If we walk in the light, as he is in the light, we have fellowship with one another....

—I JOHN 1:7 (RSV)

S	M	T	W	T	F	S
					1	2
3	4	5	6	7	8	9
10	11	12	13	14	15	16
17	18	19	20	21	22	23
24	25	26	27	28	29	30
31						

1 | F R I   *We have not ceased to pray for you....*
                                    — Colossians 1:9 (RSV)

I was working late in our Guideposts office in Carmel, New York. It was dark outside, and I was a little worried about the meeting I was about to drive to on some unfamiliar country roads. The phone rang. "Is this Susan Schefflein?" a man's voice asked politely.

"Yes, may I help you?"

The man said joyfully, "I didn't know if I would get you so late. I just wanted to hear your voice." I was mystified as to who my caller was.

"My name is Wilbert Kimmel," he continued, "and I want you to know that I've been praying for you every morning at five-thirty."

Now I was even more mystified.

"I'm eighty-seven years old," Mr. Kimmel said. "I've been subscribing to *Guideposts* for many years. Praying for people is my special ministry." His delight in sharing his story spilled over in his words. "I want you to know of the statement I signed before God. I told Him that I would pray for you every morning at five-thirty till the Lord calls me home."

At Guideposts, we do a lot of praying for others in our Prayer Fellowship. But to have the tables turned, to have someone I didn't know praying for one of us — for *me* — what a surprise!

That night I drove to my meeting as calmly as though I had done it a thousand times before. I must admit I got lost and had to drive up and down the road several times, but still I maintained my sense of peace. Each time I turned around to head back in the opposite direction, I thought, *I am in Mr. Kimmel's prayers. Everything is going to be all right.*

And everything was all right. And will be, Mr. Kimmel. It will be!

Dear Lord, please take particular care of an unseen, but very close friend of mine. I don't have to tell You his name. You've known him well for a very long time.   — Susan Schefflein

2 | S A T   *They that sow in tears shall reap in joy.*   — Psalm 126:5

Grandpa Snicklefritz (that's what my kids called their great-grandfather Ray Tressler) had a low-tear threshold. And as the shadows in his life grew longer, his eyes would often well up with emotion. The memory of an old friend, the singing of a beautiful hymn, giving thanks at mealtime for the blessings God had bestowed were all he needed to shed a tear or two. I know he was embarrassed by such a display of emotions. I smiled indulgently, not fully understanding how such little moments could touch him so deeply.

Now I'm a grandfather, and I catch myself getting a lump in my throat over crimson sunsets, a grandchild's homemade birthday card, a poem that reminds me of my youth. Not long ago, I even found myself wiping away a tear during the singing of the alma mater at a Penn State football game. Why it broke me up, I have no idea. I didn't even graduate from Penn State!

All of this is prologue to a family rite that took place last week, the wedding of my son Steve to Karey Burkholder. The ceremony was beautiful, and I got along fine until the bride and groom each took a candle and lit a central candle, symbolizing their oneness. Before this ritual was halfway over, I was reaching for my handkerchief. When I related my experience to someone afterward, they smiled and said, "You've simply been blessed with good, sensitive tear ducts."

Nice answer. I wish I'd thought of that response when Grandpa Snicklefritz was sniffling. Maybe it would have lessened his embarrassment. Now I understand.

> *Thank You, Lord, for the blessing of tears*
> *That helps us express what the heart reveres.*
> — Fred Bauer

3 | S U N *For God, who commanded the light to shine out of darkness, hath shined in our hearts....*— II Corinthians 4:6

When my son Michael was eleven, he bought for me a large picture of Christ with a light attached just below it. I loved the picture, and we used it for a night-light.

When he was about sixteen, some problems started, the kind that many teenagers have. Michael became rebellious and defiant, and refused to come in at his curfew. I could never go to bed while he was out, and one night he stepped belligerently into the living room to find me up ... again. He looked straight at the picture of Christ. "Why do you always leave this light on for me?" he demanded.

"We've been leaving it on for about five years now for anyone who is out," I responded.

"Well, don't leave it on anymore," he said. "I don't like to walk in here at night and see Him staring at me like that, first thing." I smelled beer on his breath and recoiled in shock.

His father had a long and serious talk with him the next day about his attitude and his actions. I did not wait up for Michael that night, nor did I leave the light on...not for the rest of the week. But I heard him coming in, and he was coming in on time every night now.

Then one evening he said, "I'm just going to the movie, Mama, but leave the light on for me, will you?" At the door, he turned and looked back at me. His eyes met mine with full force. "I've kinda missed Him lighting my way in."

Oh, Lord, please guide our young people through adolescence into adulthood with Your great love and care.   —Dorothy Nicholas

4 MON

Ye all are partakers of my grace.   —Philippians 1:7

When we moved to Waco, Texas, my mother gave my family and me a housewarming present, something I *never* would have bought myself: a bird feeder.

I hung it from the limb of a magnolia tree outside our kitchen window. *A nice, decorative piece,* I thought. And for the first few days each morning, I looked out the window at the birds flocking to the feeder. But there was no food, so they came and went.

I need to fill their feeder with seed, I thought. So that afternoon I bought a twenty-pound sack of birdseed. Wouldn't you know? The warblers and the cardinals and the robins filled our yard with their color and song.

Mother's bird feeder was a rather odd present, but thank God for oddities. Because now I see the very wonderful effect it has had on my life as a point of daily spiritual focus. Feeding the birds reminds me that just as they are dependent on me for food and their lives are made that much easier, so am I dependent upon God in every aspect of my life.

This is a wonderful world, God. Help me to care for the creatures in it as You care for me. Amen.   —Scott Walker

5 TUE

Whatever is true, whatever is honorable, whatever is right, whatever is pure, whatever is lovely, whatever is of good

repute, if there is any excellence and if anything worthy of praise, let your mind dwell on these things. — Philippians 4:8 (NAS)

It's taken me a long time to learn that my "what-if thoughts" can cause me a lot of unnecessary trouble. Thoughts like, *What if my husband doesn't love me anymore? What if my children move too far away? What if the little lump is more than just a little lump?*... Once the thoughts are in, they create havoc with my emotions, control my dreams, produce panic. I can't eat, sleep, think, read or even pray.

One night, after some friends prayed for me and my fears, I received a vivid mental picture that has helped me battle wrong thoughts and keep away fears. I imagine my mind as a junkyard piled high with items to be discarded. A giant truck backs up carefully, and the driver loads every trace of trash and every disturbing thought onto the truck, sweeping my mind totally clean. Finally, he erects a protective, meshlike dome over my mind. Right away, thoughts hover eagerly over the dome, anxious to be admitted. But the dome only has tiny, G-shaped slits in it. Only G-shaped thoughts — those from God — can get through the mesh. Every other thought, especially the what-if kind, bounces off the mesh again and again, rejected.

Today, if you seek relief from tormenting thoughts, perhaps this exercise will work for you, too.

Father, with Your help, I choose to think only God-shaped thoughts. Amen. — Marion Bond West

6 | W E D | *Write the things which thou hast seen, and the things which are....* — Revelation 1:19

Each Wednesday when we visit our favorite restaurant, we chat with Dick, our popular waiter. "Late Friday," he said, "I had a wonderful experience. Twelve high schoolers visited, and I have never met a more appreciative group. When they finished eating, they handed me a huge tip and apologized that it wasn't larger."

Dick smiled and continued. "This morning they were back. When they finished eating, I was in the kitchen. I was called to the door where all twelve were waiting to hand me another huge tip. They're juniors at a nearby school. Today, I'm writing their principal a letter of appreciation."

Dick's words struck home, and I was reminded of the time I ran into a friend of ours, Mrs. Rogers, at a social function. We chatted, and I wondered why she wasn't accompanied by her husband. "John died very suddenly four weeks ago," she said. "Yesterday, I was going through the papers on his desk. There near the top was your letter written in July 1965. He cherished it!"

I blushed and remembered the letter. John was the real estate agent who sold us our home. We were so delighted with it that we wrote him a thank-you note. The letter brought joy to John, but no more happiness than we felt as homeowners. Saying thank you seemed such a small gesture at the time.

Dick's letter will please the school principal. The letter may not remain on his desk, but its tribute will remain in his memory. Gratitude never goes out of style.

Holy Father, good words spoken or written never fail to please You or the person receiving them. Let me say them to someone today.
                                                          —Oscar Greene

7 | T H U | *I will pray the Father, and he shall give you another Comforter, that he may abide with you for ever.*
                                                          —John 14:16

After two years of infertility treatment before conceiving our second child, those months of doctor's appointments, daily injections, blood tests, and emotional swings between hope and despair were taking their toll on me.

One day, after I returned from the lab with bruises on both arms (it took three stabs before they were able to draw blood), the doctor called and said my hormone levels were menopausal. I hung up the phone, put my head in my hands and wept. "Lord, no one really knows what this is like for me. Thank You for my loving husband and supportive friends, but they don't understand my pain."

I do. I know. I am walking through all of this with you.

I knew God understood; I believed He was with me. But have you ever longed for Him to be physically present... so that you could feel His love in a comforting embrace? I poured out my grief awhile longer, then dried my tears and went to pick up my daughter from preschool.

Arriving early, I joined Elizabeth's class on the playground. I barely knew her new teacher Mrs. Stein, a short, older woman with gray hair wrapped in a bun. Today, she walked over to me with a wide smile. "I am so glad to see you," she said, then opened her arms wide and enfolded me in a long, warm hug. Feeling Christ Himself hold me, I almost collapsed in tears in her arms. Somehow I managed just to whisper, "Thank you so much. I needed that today."

Maybe she simply wanted to let me know I was welcome, or maybe she saw a sadness in my eyes or heaviness in my step. Whatever it was, Laura Stein's hug encouraged me in a way nothing else could, that, yes, God would carry me through this ordeal. Through her, He had even granted my desire to physically feel His love.

Dear God, thank You for showing me Your compassion in unexpected ways. Help me remember the power of touch. Please show me someone who may need to feel Your comfort today.

— Mary Brown

8 | F R I *He that is soon angry dealeth foolishly....*
— Proverbs 14:17

When Fran, the owner of a local restaurant, offered to provide food for the opening of our church's day care center, we were only too happy to accept. "Give me a call when you settle on a date," she told me.

I called a month ahead of time and left a message on her answering machine. She didn't return the call, so I called again. Still no response.

Then I began to get angry. She was rude not to call, I decided. If she had changed her mind, why didn't she say so? Obviously, we would have to make other arrangements, and there wasn't much time. I typed out a letter to Fran, expressing my disappointment in no uncertain terms, but I was out of stamps and didn't mail it that day.

The first thing the next morning I had a call from Fran. "I've been calling you for days and getting no answer," she said anxiously. "Then I checked your number in the telephone book and found I was off by one digit. I'm so sorry!"

I looked at the letter on my desk, the one without a stamp, and said a little prayer of thanks. The Bible says we ought to be slow to anger, and I had been in a bit of a hurry. By slowing me down, God had prevented me from turning a small mistake into a big misunderstanding.

When something doesn't make sense, Lord, help me to look for an answer instead of blame. Amen.
— Phyllis Hobe

9 | S A T   *Therefore comfort one another with these words.*
                                    —I Thessalonians 4:18 (NAS)

It was 5:30 in the morning when I slumped into my airplane seat. Two hours earlier I had been awakened by a call from a Scottsdale, Arizona, hospital telling me a dear friend needed me because his wife had taken a turn for the worse. She had slipped on some stairs during a trip away from home and suffered a severe blow on her head. Emergency surgery followed to relieve the pressure on her brain, but now the outlook was grim. Sitting on that plane, I wondered what I could possibly do or say. I wanted more than anything else to be whatever Rocco needed. I prayed and prayed for God's help.

"Thanks for coming," he said as I entered the hospital room.

"I couldn't be anywhere else," I replied. Not much more was said as the doctors and nurses moved in and out, speaking in whispers. Rocco's children arrived from other cities, and as the afternoon stretched out, the surgeon came in to explain the definition of "brain death" and to tell us there was no hope. A family conference was held where everyone agreed, "Mom never wanted to be hooked up to machines." Then Rock turned to me.

"We're going to turn all this stuff off, but the kids don't think they can manage watching. I promised to be there 'till death do us part.' Will you stay with me?"

No, not this, Lord! screamed my brain, but my lips said, "Sure, I'll stay."

It didn't take much for tubes to be clipped, switches to be flipped and dials turned down. Then the doctor touched us both and said, "I'll be outside if you need me," and we were alone. And so, while my friend held his wife's hand and bowed his head to pray and cry, I watched her breathing and then her heart beat ever more weakly, finally stopping altogether. I put my arm around my friend and said, "She's gone, Rock, but don't worry. The angels are about to wake her." And in that moment I knew I shouldn't have worried on the plane about what to do or say. The only thing that mattered was being there.

Father, thank You for being with us through every dark moment and for being all the comfort we need.
                                    —Eric Fellman

10 | S U N | *I was glad when they said unto me, Let us go into the house of the Lord.* — Psalm 122:1

My church consists of fifty friends and neighbors. Each Sunday we spend as much time on "concerns"— who's sick, who's facing troubles, whose grandchild is visiting — as on the sermon. I guess I thought all congregations were as neighborly as mine, so my recent experience in a large city church was a shock. The music was wonderful, the sermon was Christ-centered and inspiring. But not one person smiled or shook my hand or said hello, despite the bright red "Visitor" badge I wore.

"I guess that church is too big to be friendly," I told my friend Elsie.

"Size has nothing to do with it," she said. "One Sunday I took my daughter Julie with me to a tiny rural church where I was guest pastor. We were totally ignored when we arrived. I finally found the nursery, left Julie, then went out and preached. After the service a woman apologized for not greeting us. 'I didn't know you were the preacher,' she explained."

These experiences made me want to examine my own behavior and that of my church. We were warm with one another, but were we as interested in newcomers? The next Sunday, I took the challenge. It didn't matter that the unfamiliar person had no "Visitor" badge or the credentials of a guest preacher. I extended my hand and told her, "Welcome. I'm glad you're here today."

Lord Jesus, let our love for You and for others be evident whenever we meet in Your name.   — Penney Schwab

11 | M O N | *God is our refuge and strength, A very present help in trouble.* — Psalm 46:1 (NAS)

Several years ago, our beloved dog disappeared. Family and friends organized a search to find her, but with no success. Each day, I'd anticipate the affectionate thump, thump of her tail lulling me to sleep in my bed. How could I ever make it without her?

Then, one day, the TV newscaster announced the arrival of some beagle puppies at the local pound. Late one Monday afternoon, my husband Mark and I drove over to check them out. "The beagles went fast," the animal caretaker said, "but you might want to consider one of our other dogs."

Discouraged, I plodded from cage to cage, studying the signs posted on their doors. "Landlord says, 'No pets.' " "Owner too old to care for dog." Above the yelps and barks of at least fifty hopeful adoptees, Mark hollered, "Have a look at this one!"

Cleo was four years old and resembled a giant, double-stuffed Oreo cookie. She didn't come close to being a beagle or a puppy. "Older dogs make such wonderful pets," the caretaker said. "This one's already housebroken." As if on cue, Cleo cocked her head in the most endearing pose and extended a fuzzy white paw.

Searching for a clue to Cleo's past, I read the giant handwritten black letters aloud. " 'PTS Tuesday.' What does that mean?"

The caretaker hung her head, and I strained to hear her speak. "Put to sleep Tuesday."

"We'll take her! We'll take her!" Mark and I pronounced as we scooped a snuggling Cleo into our arms.

"Let's name her Monday," I suggested.

It's been seven years now, and while we didn't actually change Cleo's name, she'll always symbolize Monday to us. In our time of loss, God rescued us both. And, oh, the joys of adopting a loving, older dog! What seemed to be a "PTS Tuesday" was really a brand-new Monday.

How often in my life, Lord, have You turned a "PTS Tuesday" into a Monday? Thank You for Your gifts of new beginnings…always right on time.   — Roberta Messner

12 | T U E | *Let us throw off everything that hinders and the sin that so easily entangles….*   — Hebrews 12:1 (NIV)

I slammed out of the hardware store, burning at the rude clerk who'd brushed aside my question about directions on the paint remover I was buying. "They're pretty plain," he'd snarled, with a nod to the customer next in line. I felt like two cents.

In the car, I opened my wallet to deposit the change in my fist and gasped. He'd given me five dollars too much. Normally, I'd have gone right back in and returned it. But not after that scene, no sirree. I backed out the car. From the dusty corridors of the past, I felt a tap from my fourth-grade teacher Miss Runkel.

I could still smell the old wood and stale ink in that school building. I sat at my desk, staring at a pencil, pretending not to hear the click of Miss Runkel's high heels coming my way. Her hand was gentle on my shoulder. "Lisa started it!" I blurted. "She made fun of my picture."

"That was cruel and wrong," Miss Runkel conceded. "But tearing hers in pieces was wrong, too." She tilted my chin to look in her eyes, while I fought hot tears. "Two wrongs don't make a right," she said. I nodded, shameful tears oozing. From her pocket she pulled a handkerchief, smelling wonderfully of her perfume, to dry my face and wipe away the hurt.

Now decades later, that forthright equation tapped me. *Two wrongs don't make a right.* I pulled back into the parking space and got out of the car to return the money. And as I came out of the store, five dollars lighter, I sensed the wonderful fragrance of God's approval wiping away my embarrassment and hurt.

Dear Lord, when we are tempted to repay a wrong with a wrong, tap our hearts with a reminder. Amen.   — Shari Smyth

13 | W E D   *How were thine eyes opened?*   —John 9:10

For a long time, my thoughts of my father had been clouded by memories of his many angry outbursts during my childhood. Then at a workshop on "Completing Your Past," it was suggested that I write a letter to Dad, even though he died in 1968, to settle this unfinished business.

After expressing my own anger and fear in the letter, I began sorting through memories to see what else I had to say to him. For the first time in my life, I became aware of a tremendous sacrifice Daddy had made for me during World War II. Before being sent overseas by the Navy, he was stationed in Chicago for two years. My parents decided not to put me through the trauma of adjusting to a new school, so Mother and I stayed in Nebraska. Though we did finally move to Chicago the second year, that whole first year my father was so lonely he sometimes called and cried on the phone. *My strong, tough dad did that?* I'd almost forgotten!

Now, fifty years later, as I wrote the letter, I could touch Daddy's pain and identify with him. Awareness of his suffering helped me finally to *see past* the hurtful memories I'd carried with me all those years. Despite his temper, my father truly loved me, even to the point of sacrifice. How good it felt to end my letter by thanking him for that!

What could you say in an unmailed letter to someone from your past? Even if you begin with a complaint, ask God that your eyes be opened to see beyond your pain. It just might heal your heart!

Open my eyes, Lord, that I may see. Open my heart that I may truly love. — Marilyn Morgan Helleberg

14 | THU | *MY GIFT TODAY... THE SCREW HEADS*

"Don't do your good deeds publicly, to be admired, for then you will lose the reward from your Father in heaven."
— Matthew 6:1 (TLB)

I stopped in front of the light switch in our bedroom this morning, grateful for a gift I couldn't see. It was more than twenty years ago that a white-haired electrician left a gift behind him — probably without knowing it.

He'd come to the house to replace some antiquated wiring. We followed him, fascinated, from room to room as he cut through walls, installing wires and switches.

One thing especially intrigued us. Before he closed up the holes in the walls, he carefully lined up the screw heads on the switch boxes. Patiently, painstakingly, he made sure that the groove on each screw was horizontal, exactly parallel with all the others. It was a pleasing pattern, a small work of art really, but who would ever see it?

At last, I couldn't contain my curiosity. "Why are you taking such trouble when it's all going to be covered up? Who's going to know?"

The old man stuck his screwdriver back in his tool belt before turning to look at me. "I will know," he said.

And *I will know* has been a family phrase ever since, reminding us that joy in work doesn't depend on applause. Each little unsung, unseen act today, done with integrity, can affirm like those hidden screw heads that the life "hid with Christ" is the one that counts.

Father Who sees in secret, I will know and You will know everything I do today. — Elizabeth Sherrill

Editor's Note: We'd love to hear what gifts you've found around your home these past months that point to God's love and care in your life. Take a few moments now to review your monthly "Gifts of Light" diary pages and write us about one or two of your "gifts today." Send your letter to: *Daily Guideposts* Editor, Guideposts Books, 16 East 34th Street, New York, New York 10016.

15 | F R I *You ask, "What does God know? He is hidden by clouds—how can he judge us?" You think the thick clouds keep him from seeing, as he walks on the dome of the sky.*
—Job 22:13-14 (GNB)

"A lonely man and a distant God. A lonely man and a distant God. A lonely man...." The rhythmic pounding of my feet matched the repetition of my words, words that matched my mood—heavy.

On this cold March evening, I had felt the need for a run. Winter had been hard and dreary. The sun had shone seldom. I had been grinding out unsatisfying work. My family and I were all busy about our own tasks and had little to do with one another. I saw my children when I delivered them to various functions: hockey, Scouts, Sunday school, Tae Kwon Do. I saw my wife at supper between her work and her various evening meetings. I was buried in accomplishing my duties as duties. Although I was sure all of us loved one another, this winter I experienced little emotional warmth. Spring so far had not been much better.

A lonely man and a distant God.

Somewhere about the fifteenth minute and the third mile, I realized that my tongue had turned the incantation around without my being aware of it. Now I was repeating, "A lonely God and a distant man. A lonely God and a distant man...."

It was true. I was lonely. But it wasn't God Who had been distant. I had pulled myself away from Him ... and from my family.

A lonely God and a distant man? No more. I stopped myself in mid-run and turned toward home.

"I have always known that when you are miserable you withdraw from people, but now I know you withdraw from God, too," my wife commented after I told her about my run. "If you decide to move toward Him, will you put me next on the list?"

"Do you think we still have time to light a fire in the fireplace?" I replied.

Dear Lord, give me the grace to remember that You are ready to embrace me, if I am willing to take one step toward You.
—John Cowan

16 | S A T   *Lord, thou hast been our dwelling place in all generations.*
                                         —Psalm 90:1

It was my mother's eighty-third birthday, and I was not looking forward to visiting her. She no longer could say for sure what year she was born. In the 1950s she had been a quiz show champion. Now you couldn't even get her going anymore on baseball or politics.

On the drive to see her at the group home where my siblings and I had recently moved her, my own memory troubled me. I thought of all the times she had wanted me to visit and I hadn't come: the Easter vacation in college when I went to Key West; the Thanksgiving night I went to a movie rather than help with the dishes; the extra days I couldn't spare after my father's funeral....

I was in a bad state when I arrived at the group home, though the fierce strength of her hug was a surprise coming from the stooped figure who greeted me. "My youngest," she announced to the other residents. We sat quietly together on the screened back porch for a time when, suddenly, Mom said, "Remember my birthday when you played trombone?"

I thought she was drifting into some irritating absurdity, and then a memory fell open. I must have been about nine, and I'd just taken up the trombone. It was a sad time for Mom. We'd lost my brother in a tragic death, my older sister and other brother were off to college, and my father was away that night on business. Just the two of us were celebrating with one candle and a homely little cake.

"Until you came down the stairs playing 'Happy Birthday' on your trombone, it was the worst birthday of my life. Now I think it might have been the best."

As my mother relapsed into silence, my bad state began to turn. *God makes certain memories strong for us,* I thought, *so that when our capacity to remember begins to fail, the best can still prevail for those times we need them the most.* I felt a warm strength flow in the hug that came from my mother's frail and brittle arms. It is the strength of the spirit when the body fails, and of God bringing out the best in us.

God, help me not to dwell on my failings, but to build on the love and goodness in my life.
                                    —Edward Grinnan

17 | S U N   *But I say unto you, Love your enemies....*
                                          —Matthew 5:44

The month of March has major significance for me, because it's the month in which my family went into a Japanese internment camp outside of Shanghai during World War II. We were surrounded by two rows of barbed wire fence and warned that if we were caught escaping we'd be shot on sight by any of the guards patrolling with their bayoneted rifles.

Today, however, one of the facts of St. Patrick's life has challenged me. Around A.D. 405, sixteen-year-old Patrick was kidnapped from Britain and sold as a slave in Ireland. He was ill-treated and held captive for six years, until he finally escaped and went back to Britain. There he continued his education and was ordained a priest. But then he had a dream in which the Irish Celts asked him to come back to Ireland to live with them. In 432, Patrick went. He stayed in Ireland the rest of his life, caring for the people, evangelizing and founding churches.

Since 1945, I have looked upon the Japanese with suspicion, always with the memory of guards and bayonets and semistarvation. But, today, Patrick's renunciation of both hate and indifference toward his former captors speaks to me. He did not let the mistreatment of his captive years prevent him from answering God's call. I have not been called to go to Japan as a missionary. But I have been called to forgive, not to hold grudges, and to live in love as Christ loved me.

Lord, I open my heart now to Your love, not only for me but for anyone whom I have considered an enemy. —Mary Ruth Howes

18 | M O N   *For God did not give us a spirit of timidity, but a spirit of power, of love and of self-discipline.*
                                          —II Timothy 1:7 (NIV)

"Dolphus, we want you to be our speaker in Greenville, at the statewide meeting of the Chamber of Commerce." It was the state president on the phone.

"Who, me?"

"Yes, you! We want you to speak on the subject of working together across racial lines to make our communities a better place to live."

As I hung up the phone, I was trembling. I had no problem with the subject — I'd delivered that very message on many different occasions. But parts of Mississippi, I felt, still didn't want to hear this message. Only twenty years ago, my mentor John Perkins, the founder of our work, had been beaten and thrown in jail in a small town near Jackson, the capital. And Greenville, the site of the meeting, is part of the Mississippi Delta, historically known for its plantations and cotton fields worked by slaves, and the slowest area of the state to change its attitude toward blacks.

"What will people think about me and my message?" I wondered aloud to my wife Rosie. "Will they accept me?"

"You won't just be a speaker," she reminded me. "You'll be representing the kingdom of God. And here's a promise for you: 'God did not give us a spirit of timidity, but a spirit of power, of love and of self-discipline.' "

I drove to Greenville with her words and that promise in my mind. Instead of antagonism, I met a group of people who were open to the challenge of working together across racial and historical barriers. And I found friendship. "Please welcome Dolphus Weary," the president said in his introduction. "We grew up on two different sides of the tracks, but I am glad he is here today as my friend."

Lord, help me to acknowledge fear but not be controlled by it.
— Dolphus Weary

19 | T U E   *In every thing give thanks: for this is the will of God....*
                                                 — I Thessalonians 5:18

It really was about time we bought some new furniture. The old bookshelves sagged under the weight of volumes, the TV cabinet doors never closed, our dinner table wobbled whenever the boys used it for coloring, the chairs had flaking paint. And yet....

"We couldn't replace the table," my wife said. "It always reminds me of Rodney. He gave it to us when he moved out of the city, and I like keeping it in hopes that he'll move back."

"And the bookshelf," I acknowledged. "Nancy and Dominic gave it to us when they had their first child, when their 'office' became a nursery. It reminds me of them."

"The end table has to stay," Carol said. I nodded. An elderly neighbor gave it to us before moving to a retirement home.

"Your dad brought us the TV cabinet when we first moved here," I said.

"The chairs came from your parents' basement," my wife added. "We didn't think we'd need them for long. But it's been eight years now."

"Nine," I corrected. "They've been more permanent than we knew."

"There isn't anything I'd like to get rid of," Carol finally said. "So what if we don't have an apartment where everything matches. We've got something better."

"What's that?" I asked.

"A home," she said, "that makes us think of those who helped us make it one."

Lord, I'm thankful for a life that isn't store-bought. — Rick Hamlin

20 | W *Ye should do that which is honest....*
     | E
     | D   — II Corinthians 13:7

Do you ever stop to wonder how you came to be the person you are? Was it luck? Was it chance? Was it hard work? Was it heredity? Was it environment? No doubt all those things played a part, but they're not the main thing. The main thing is the values you carry around inside you.

Where do our values come from? From our parents, if we're lucky. From sermons, from teachers, from books.

Once in a while, though, we can remember the source. My father had a very clear sense of right and wrong, and I remember his saying to me, "It's no great credit to you if you behave decently only because you're afraid of the penalties that may be enforced if you don't. Obedience to the unenforceable, that's the mark of a truly honest man." And he added reflectively, "It's not always easy, though."

A good many years ago a bracelet belonging to my wife Pam turned up missing. We had an insurance policy that offered protection against "mysterious disappearance," so eventually we filed a claim and were reimbursed. Then months later Pam was astonished to find the bracelet behind some sofa cushions, deep in the upholstery. "Oh, Lord!" she said, and I knew the thoughts that were crossing her mind, because some of them were crossing mine. No one need know that we had found the bracelet. There would be no penalty for keeping it and forgetting about the insurance money. Then like an echo from the past a phrase jumped into my mind: *obedience to the unenforceable.*

"When we send the insurance money back," I said, "let's explain to the children why it's necessary."

Values. If they're good ones, pass them on.

Grant us, Lord, the wisdom to know what is right, and the courage to do it. —Arthur Gordon

21 | T H U   *He restores my soul....*   —Psalm 23:3 (RSV)

I used to dread the hour after work when weariness had begun to creep into my bones. After a day in the classroom, my feet hurt from standing so long, my back hurt from carrying books, my mouth hurt from talking to students. Yet I wouldn't allow myself to rest, afraid that if I once gave in to fatigue, I might sleep the rest of the day away. So I would race from school to my aerobics class, skipping the final "cool-down" period, when the instructor led us in relaxation exercises, in order to race to my next activity. There were kids to take to piano lessons, dinner to make, papers to grade....

"It's unhealthy not to cool down after hard exercise," my aerobics instructor warned one day. Reluctantly, I stayed. And, surprise! The relaxation energized me.

A cool-down convert now, I build a rest period into the going-home hour when exhaustion is at its peak. I flip the radio dial to the station that plays Mozart in the late afternoon, lean back in the driver's seat and, instead of the freeway, take the scenic route that winds through back roads to my tiny village of Pleasantville, New York. I stop at two places when I hit the middle of town: the corner store for my favorite newspaper and the deli for a cup of cappuccino.

At home, the dinner is still unmade. My bag is overflowing with ungraded papers. My body still aches. Yet I plop into an easy chair with my paper and my cup of coffee and, after eight hours of labor, savor ten minutes of cool-down bliss.

Lord, I have labored hard in Your name today. Grant me this moment of well-earned rest. —Linda Ching Sledge

22 | F R I

Do not say, "Why were the old days better than these?"
For it is not wise to ask such questions.

— Ecclesiastes 7:10 (NIV)

Not long after I turned seventy, I got a letter from my longtime friend Flo. Opening it, I found a yellowed envelope addressed, in my handwriting, *For Isabel. Open when you're seventy.* Inside, I read what Flo and I, in our mid-twenties back then, had wanted to be reminded of fifty years later.

"Senior citizens are such bores!" We were complaining about the exasperating habits of several elderly folk we knew.

"Do not talk about your health. Do not repeat the same old stories."

Flo and I had laughed as we dashed off the items.

"Do not offer advice. Do not criticize the choir, pastor, church members, younger people....

"Do not refer to your *Good Old Days*!"

I had put the sheet of paper in an envelope, addressed it and given it to Flo. "Keep this for me," I told her, "and return it to me in 1992." And we laughed again, never expecting to live *that long*.

Now, with the list in my hand, I was hearing myself tell my sons that their children could stand a little more discipline. And that "we *used to* worship as a *family*, remember?" when the grandchildren sat with their peers in church. And how many times had I boasted how good things were in the old days, after reading about all the evils of the present day?

I laughed ruefully, caught by my own words.

Father, help me not only to remember the past with fondness, but to live joyfully in the present.   — Isabel Wolseley

23 | S A T

Therefore shall thy camp be holy: that he sees no unclean
thing in thee....   — Deuteronomy 23:14

I was thirteen the day my mom dropped my best friend Danny Albert and me off at the video store to pick a movie. Danny was going to spend the night, so we decided to get something on the dirty side and watch it after my parents went to bed. I don't remember the name of the movie, just that it had Bo Derek and a rating of R. That was enough for us.

Soon Mom was back to pick us up. "What movie did you guys get?"

We giggled and punched each other in the arm a couple of times. "Aw, Mom, I don't remember," I answered.

"C'mon, Brock, what did you get?" she asked again.

In a desperate attempt to hide our prize, I answered, "Uh, *Bambi*."

"Okay, boys, let me see it." She pulled over, took one look at the video's title, made a U-turn and headed back to the video store.

"Ma," I groaned, "it's just a movie!"

"Brock, you know better. Now you're going to march right back into that store and tell them that in our home we don't willingly feed garbage to thirteen-year-olds!"

I was humiliated. Danny was a year older than I, and I was particularly interested in impressing him. Why was I cursed with a crazy mother? All my friends rented R videos!

At twenty-two, I can still remember the terrible walk into the video store to return that movie. But you know what? Now I know that the crazy mother I was cursed with was really my blessing.

God, I need Your help when it comes to worldly choices. Make me hungry for Your ways.   — Brock Kidd

24 | S U N   *I will not leave you comfortless: I will come to you.*
                                                    —John 14:18

In the days after Norman left us, when I came home from a busy day at the office, the emptiness of the house would hit like a cold draft of air. I did what I could to dispel it. I'd prepare my dinner, set a table by the television and listen to the six-thirty news. In the mornings I'd turn on the radio — there was always a certain comfort in hearing a human voice, even if it just provided a traffic report.

You must find things to do, I'd tell myself. *But I've always had things to do,* I'd reply. As a mother and a minister's wife, when hadn't I been busy? And after Norman's passing, there was much work at the Peale Center and for *Guideposts* magazine. Also, I continued to travel and give talks. I was very busy.

And then it happened. Out of the blue an incident came to mind about a friend I hadn't thought of in years. She was a fine person, an admirable church worker. She was on committee after committee and never seemed to rest, until a discerning friend said something that changed her life. "I've known people," he said not unkindly, "who were so busy in the service of God that they forgot to love Him."

Being busy, I now said to myself, *is that the only antidote I can think of for loneliness?* I began then to use some of my supposedly fallow time for praising God. I took long walks about the farm, thanking Him for the beauty of the hills and the wonder of changing seasons. Or when a wisp of sadness strayed in, I'd just sit at my desk, fold my hands and love Him. Gradually, it seemed to me that love was squeezing out the emptiness.

I have found that the loneliness hasn't disappeared entirely — there are always some little aches waiting in ambush — but when I consciously fill my thoughts with praise, there simply isn't room for both.

I thank You, Lord, that You are here and Your presence heals all our wounds.   — Ruth Stafford Peale

---

POINT OF LIGHT

A room of quiet ... a temple of peace;
The home of faith ... where doubtings cease;
A house of comfort ... where hope is given;
A source of strength ... to make earth heaven;
A shrine of worship ... a place to pray —
I found all this ... in my church today.
                                    — Cyrus E. Albertson

---

25 | M O N   *Remembering before our God and Father your work of faith and labor of love....*
                                    — I Thessalonians 1:3 (RSV)

One morning I picked up the newspaper in the driveway and flipped through it in an absentminded way. Suddenly, I stopped and my heart thumped. There, looking up at me, was a blurry photograph of a Rwandan child, with arms like sticks and skin stretched over his bones. He was crouched over, bent double, wearing only a sweater with a shape and stripes that were unmistakable to me.

"Look at this!" I said excitedly to my sleepy children, who were only interested in Frosted Flakes. But I waved the paper under their noses.

"Hey, Mom," said my son Hilary, "he's wearing one of your sweaters." Then all three crowded round as if I were holding a winning lottery ticket.

I knit. My friends tease me about the fact that I always have a piece of knitting tucked into my bag. I tell them I am knitting children's sweaters for an international relief group. Knitters, adults and children, all around the world have made many thousands of these simple garments. They're all the same shapeless, easy-to-knit pattern, good for any yarn and any degree of skill. The sleeves are knitted as part of the body, making both the back and the front like a woolen T.

I began doing this about ten years ago and must have sent off more than fifty sweaters of every size and color. Lately, I've even lured friends into using up their yarn scraps this way. (That's why the pattern is striped, of course, to use every spare ball of yarn available.)

As I've worked, I've often wondered whether this tiny contribution made any difference, or even whether the sweaters ever reached the children. After a decade of knitting, here was proof.

A special grace, I know, led me to open the newspaper that day. Now, as I sit waiting for a train, clicking my needles, the photo of that little boy is worked into every stitch.

Help me, God, to keep working and giving even when I don't see results — and to thank You when I do.   — Brigitte Weeks

Editor's Note: If you're interested in finding out more about this relief program, you can contact OXFAM America, 26 West Street, Boston, Massachusetts 02111-1206.

26 | T U E   *Surely I have behaved and quieted myself, as a child....*
                                                        — Psalm 131:2

My eight-year-old son Michael recently stood in the middle of the kitchen and kissed a bee. It was about the size of a jellybean, in a yellow and black body.

I've always had such a fear of bees that the very thought of kissing one sent me shrieking. "Michael!" I shouted. "What are you doing? Are you crazy?"

My son gave me a look of hurt and surprise. "I kissed the bee. I showed everyone in school how I kiss a bee."

"But it can sting you," I said with my adult voice of knowing.

"Daddy, the bee is dead. It's cute, too. Look how little it is."

I bent down for a close look at the bee curled in Michael's small palm. It had a certain charm about it, I'll admit.

Children often lead us to simple truths that we sometimes forget. Thanks to Michael, I had seen the beauty of one of God's creatures that previously I had only feared.

Dear God, help me always to see beyond my fears to the beauty of Your creation.   — Christopher de Vinck

---

27 | W E D | *Husbands, love your wives, and be not bitter against them.*   —Colossians 3:19

We had a little spat on Monday, my wife Sharon and I. I said some harsh things, and so did she. Even a good marriage of thirty-one years has its moments.

The next day my joints ached, my eyes swelled with allergies, and my stomach burned—all symptoms I experience when I'm at odds with people I love. "I should ask forgiveness," I told myself, "but…."

By bedtime Tuesday my conscience had won, and I thought about how I could do it. Maybe I would say, "Oh, by the way, I'm sorry if I was a little abrupt yesterday." *No, that wouldn't be genuine.* How about, "We were both unfair to each other. I regret that." *Uh-uh. That would be placing some of the blame on her.* At last, I decided to keep it really simple and straightforward.

Sharon was reading when I sat on the bed and cleared my throat. Our eyes met momentarily. "I need…I need to ask your forgiveness for things I said yesterday."

There, I did it. Years seemed to pass as she stared blankly at me. Then she smiled. "You know, I need to apologize to you, too." She reached for the light switch.

My aches subsided. I slept like a newborn.

Lord, nothing is right when I am at odds with the people I love. Help me not to wait for them to come to me when things are wrong, but to be the first to say, "I'm sorry."   — Daniel Schantz

28 | T H U   *Called.... to be conformed to the image of his Son....*
                                              —Romans 8:28–29

Dutch Slade, a good friend of ours, has a real way with anything that grows. His garden and hothouses are filled with wonderful flowers and greenery. Each time my husband Gene and I visit Linda and Dutch in Griffin, Georgia, we want to see what's been added to their garden spot.

On a recent visit in the spring, I noticed Dutch had some wisteria growing. Wisteria is one of my all-time favorites, reminding me of my childhood and the great, spreading vine that bloomed across my grandparents' porch. But I was astonished at Dutch's wisteria. The color was the same — delicate lavender. The foliage was the same — great bunches of flowers, like bunches of grapes, among light green leaves. But our creative friend had somehow changed the structure and shape of this wisteria.

"Dutch, I've never seen a wisteria bush before," I said. "It stands straight and tall and doesn't spread out like a vine. How did you do that?"

"I pruned back and cut away everything that didn't look like a wisteria *bush*," Dutch said. "Whenever the vine started growing out, I cut it back."

Now, when I pray, I often see that unique wisteria bush in my mind. I believe I know what it means. There's a lot about me that's not truly like Jesus — being short-tempered or impatient or fearful. So I've been asking the Lord to cut away anything that doesn't resemble Him — and keep me growing straight and tall.

Father, help me to remember that pruning may often be drastic, but it brings new, exciting growth. Amen.   — Marion Bond West

29 | F R I   *Pray one for another, that ye may be healed....*
                                              —James 5:16

When my friend Paula learned that she had breast cancer, she became fearful and depressed. She and I called around town looking for a healing service and found that St. John's Episcopal Cathedral here in Albuquerque, New Mexico, holds one every Tuesday morning at ten o'clock. We went together to the service. When the priest spoke of the power of faith and prayer, the presence of Jesus filled the room with an almost tangible force.

Then Paula went up to the altar rail where the priest prayed for her and anointed her head with oil. As he did so, she told me later, she felt strength surge through her body, along with renewed hope for eventual recovery.

Although she did have to have a mastectomy, followed by chemotherapy, Paula said that the continued prayers of that church and of loved ones sustained her throughout her treatment. "I could feel those prayers. I could feel the energy," she says. "They gave me the strength and courage to face some really bad days."

Because of my friend's experience, I've learned to keep on praying, for others and also for myself, even when the body falters and the way looks dark. For the strengthening of the spirit that comes from Christ — that is the true "healing" that can see us through.

Heavenly Father, I offer up my prayers to You, for the power of Your love to lift us up and give us fortitude and hope.   —Madge Harrah

30 | S A T   *Cast thy burden upon the Lord, and he shall sustain thee*   —Psalm 55:22

"I'm going on a hike, Mom," my son Derek announced one clear Saturday morning during his spring break, as he loaded some oranges and a water bottle in his backpack.

"Alone?" I asked warily.

"Yes," he answered, kind of gritting his teeth like any twenty-two-year-old who's trying to be patient with a mom who worries too much.

"But is that safe? I mean, what if you fall, or get lost, or lightning strikes, or a mountain lion...."

"Mom, where do you want me to put all those worries in my backpack? Here in the front by my pocketknife or in the back by these sandwiches?" he asked, half-teasingly. "Because, Mom, I'm going to carry your worries all the way up the mountain with me."

"*Hmm,*" I said, long and slow, like a mom who has just heard something important and needs time to think about it. His words reminded me of some parenting advice I once learned: *If you worry out loud, you give your child a worry.*

"I have something better for you to carry," I said as he hoisted the backpack over his shoulder.

"What's that, Mom?"

"How about my prayer that God will protect you and be with you every step of the way."

"Thanks, Mom," Derek said with a grin. And he was gone.

Jesus, forgive me for telling my fears to the wrong person. May I remember to tell them to You, and always send my loved ones out the door with a prayer instead of the burden of a fear.
— Carol Kuykendall

THE SURPRISES OF EASTER

During Holy Week, Keith Miller looks at the many surprises Jesus' coming created both for the people of His time and for us. Through His life and teachings, His death and Resurrection, Jesus challenges our view of God, our standards of success, our feelings about love and about the way we live. During this Easter season, join Keith as he invites all of us to recommit ourselves to God's loving family. —The Editors

31 | SUN *LOVE OR TERROR?*

Rejoice greatly, O daughter of Zion!...Lo, your king comes to you...humble and riding on an ass, on a colt the foal of an ass.
— Zechariah 9:9 (RSV)

"Da-a-a-d-dy!" a little girl's voice called out on a cold winter night. I got up, stumbled into my daughter's room and carried her like a limp cotton doll against my chest into the bathroom, where I sat her on her little potty seat. In the red glow of the gas wall heater, I saw the softness of her face, her closed eyes and the long, slightly tousled blond hair. I was filled with the most amazing sense of love and gratitude for that little girl. *Someday,* I thought, *we can talk together about this night when she is grown.* But as I tucked her back in bed, it struck me that she would never remember this midnight closeness — because she had been asleep the whole time I was holding her and loving her.

The people in Jesus' day were like my little girl — asleep and unaware of God's love surrounding them. In fact, their view of God was sometimes terrifying. When they asked Jesus how they should pray to this awesome God, Jesus told them to pray, "Father — *Abba* — Daddy." God was a loving Father.

When He entered Jerusalem on a donkey, rather than a horse (symbol of war), Jesus was reminding the people again of God's love. It was as if the Hebrew nation had been asleep to the loving, fatherly care they had received from God as He had held them and comforted them through the many long, scary nights in their history. Jesus was trying to wake them up to experience God's love once more.

Lord, thank You for making Your way into our frightened, lonely hearts in a way that wouldn't scare off the child part of us — on a little donkey.   — Keith Miller

GIFTS OF LIGHT

1 _____

2 _____

3 _____

4 _____

5 _____

6 _____

7 _____

8 _____

9 _____

10 _____

11 _____
12 _____
13 _____
14 _____
15 _____
16 _____
17 _____
18 _____
19 _____
20 _____
21 _____
22 _____
23 _____
24 _____
25 _____
26 _____
27 _____
28 _____
29 _____
30 _____
31 _____

"I am the light of the world; he who follows me will not walk in darkness, but will have the light of life."

—JOHN 8:12 (RSV)

APRIL

S	M	T	W	T	F	S
	1	2	3	4	5	6
7	8	9	10	11	12	13
14	15	16	17	18	19	20
21	22	23	24	25	26	27
28	29	30				

1 | M O N *REALITY OR SUCCESS?*

And Jesus entered the temple of God and drove out all who sold and bought in the temple, and he overturned the tables of the money-changers and the seats of those who sold pigeons.

— Matthew 21:12 (RSV)

Some years ago, my Christian ministry was going better than I could have ever imagined. I was faithful in church attendance, I tithed, I read the Scriptures, I prayed daily. I had helped to start many Christian fellowship and study groups and had written several successful books about living for Christ.

So when I read about Jesus' overturning the tables and seats of those who were exchanging money for the purchase of the sacrificial animals used in temple worship, I cheered Him on — never realizing that the cleansing of the temple had anything to do with me.

But one day, Jesus walked into the inner temple of my life and turned over my delusion that I was a good, unselfish, Christian husband and father. Suddenly, the things that had seemed so stable in my life began going out the window, including my marriage and my sense of myself as one of the white knights of the faith. Eventually, I was divorced, wound up in a recovery program and was rejected by many of those who had read my books.

Because I had focused so intently on myself and my ministry, I had fouled up my relationships and was far from the closeness with God that earlier had changed my life and given it purpose. And I hadn't even seen the change taking place, because I *felt* sincere.

I am grateful that Jesus came into my inner life and overturned the tables of my complacency and success. My failures forced me to take an honest look at my life, and with His help — and forgiveness — I began once more to focus on loving God and my family.

Lord, I'm glad You didn't pass by and leave me in my religious unreality. May I always be ready for Your cleansing touch.

— Keith Miller

2 | T U E | *CARING OR TALKING?*

"Truly, I say to you, as you did it not to one of the least of these, you did it not to me." — Matthew 25:45 (RSV)

Bill and I were sitting alone at the breakfast table the morning after his wife's funeral. She had died of lung cancer, leaving two small children. I've known Bill most of his life, and over those thirty-odd years I've given him lots of advice, spiritual and otherwise, from my vantage point of age and experience. Often, though, I had sensed his anger at me. Now he began to speak a little hesitantly about his pain, and then went on to tell me what he planned to do about his financial obligations, and about setting up an educational fund for his small children.

As in the past, all kinds of advice flooded my mind. But this time, something told me to be still and let him talk out his feelings and plans. After almost an hour, he looked up and there were tears in his eyes. "You really heard me!" he said in surprise. "Thank you! I know that you *do* care because you're not just talking to me about religion and what I *should do*. You're listening to me and caring about what's happening to me."

It had taken me thirty years to learn what Jesus was teaching His disciples during His last week. Being on God's side isn't a matter of behaving religiously, or knowing the Bible and being able to give a lot of spiritual advice. To be part of God's kingdom, Jesus said, involves giving people what they need: food for the hungry; cold water for a thirsty traveler; clothes for the naked. *And,* I heard Him say to me, *a loving ear, rather than advice, for someone in emotional pain. Because, whatever you did not do to love one of the least of these, My brothers and sisters, you did not do for Me.*

Lord, help me not to miss meeting You where You want to meet us — in the lives of the hungry, the poor, and all Your lonely brothers and sisters in pain. — Keith Miller

3 | W E D | *WEAKNESS OR POWER?*

But he said to me, "My grace is sufficient for you, for my power is made perfect in weakness." — II Corinthians 12:9 (RSV)

A few years ago, I went into the hospital to have a bladder examination for a suspected malignancy. After the exam, the urologist said, "Well, Keith, there's good news and bad news. The good news is that you don't have cancer." He paused.

"What's the bad news?" I asked quickly.

"The bad news is that you have an incurable disease called interstitial cystitis. But if you can learn to live one day at a time and follow the prescribed diet and exercise program, you may be able to keep this from getting worse."

"What happens if I don't respond?"

"Well," he said, "ultimately it could be fatal."

I went home feeling very helpless, angry and afraid. I've always hated not being in control of my life. But when I prayed that day, I got the clear sense that God was telling me, "I have some things for you to do, and I want you to get about doing them."

So I began a journey of *having* to trust God one day at a time in my weakness. I did exactly what the doctor said about diet and exercise. Each morning I would surrender my powerlessness, my life and the disease to God. Then, paradoxically, I began to feel free and clearheaded. Although I felt powerless over the disease, I felt a different kind of power that enabled me to accomplish a number of creative projects.

A year later, I went back to the doctor for a checkup. At the conclusion of the examination, he said, "I can't find any evidence that you still have the disease. You may be the first person who has been cured of it."

As I drove home, I could hear Jesus telling me again to follow His example to love and serve others, to do God's will, not my own (John 6:38; 13:14–16). I don't know what tomorrow will bring, but I now know that I am not to control the outcome of my life. I am to live for God one day at a time.

Lord, Your strength grows out of my admission of powerlessness. Help me to keep trusting Your love and care.   — Keith Miller

4 | T H U ACTION OR FEELING?

"My Father, if it be possible, let this cup pass from me...."
          — Matthew 26:39 (RSV)

I was sitting on my front porch one day when my children were small, thinking about the love Christ showed us when He went to the cross, and what it might look like if I were acting with the same kind of love…. In my mind, I saw my daughter pedaling her tricycle down the driveway straight into the path of a huge truck. With no time to think, I vaulted over the iron railing, ran into the street and shoved her out of the way, just in time to hear and feel the awful crunch as the truck ran over my back!…

Though it was only a daydream, I was covered with perspiration. *That was really an act of love!* I thought. But then the scene started replaying itself…. Except now the tricycle rider was the mean little boy from down the street, the one who teased and threw rocks at my daughter. And he was heading right into the path of the truck. This time, I did not want to risk my life for that kid. But I couldn't stop myself and I vaulted over the iron railing, pushed the kid to safety and was killed myself….

Which of these two actions was the greater act of Christian love? I wondered. Any father might risk his life for his own child. But to do that for someone unworthy— or an enemy, even — that was more like Jesus' actions. In His humanness Jesus did not want to go through with the loving act of dying on the cross. Three times, Matthew tells us, He prayed in great distress to be spared from the ordeal. At the end of His praying, He said in effect, I still don't want to go ("Let this cup pass from me"), but if You won't change Your mind, I'll do it out of obedience to Your will ("My Father, if this cannot pass unless I drink it, thy will be done," Matthew 26:42, RSV).

If that is true, then to love as Jesus did, I don't have to have warm, loving feelings. My job is to do loving acts for others, out of obedience to Him, no matter how I feel.

Lord, help me not to sit around waiting to feel loving before I agree to be Your loving representative. Help me always to act in loving ways.   — Keith Miller

5 | F R I | *ACCEPTANCE OR FEAR?*

Father, into thy hands I commend my spirit….   — Luke 23:46

One thing in particular strikes me deeply every Good Friday: Jesus' surrender to God and His silent acceptance of the total and humiliating defeat His enemies won over Him. Often, then, my mind goes back to the time when I faced the reality of death—in great terror.

I was twenty-eight years old. My mother had died, leaving me the last of my family. After the funeral, I went to our family home in Tulsa, Oklahoma, where the personal belongings of my father, brother and mother were stored. I hauled everything into the big basement room, sat down in the midst of them and cried like a very sad, lonely little boy. I had no idea what to do with their precious keepsakes.

That night I dreamed that I had died and had been put in a coffin. But as they were nailing down the lid, I realized I was still alive, and was helpless. I woke up sweating, terrified of my own death. All my abilities and accomplishments seemed like nothing. For several days and nights after that, I lived in fear as I buried, burned or gave away the rest of my family's possessions, keeping only a few mementos.

One night, I held up a large, very old family picture of relatives. *They are all dead,* I thought. *No one gets out of here alive! And what happens after that is up to God.* Almost exhausted with sadness, I said to God, "Lord, I don't even know for sure if You're there. All my childhood supports are gone. But I'm going to *bet my life* that You are real and trust that You'll be with me in the future—whatever it brings. And as for death, well, what was good enough for them"—and I looked at the family picture—"is good enough for me."

And the fear of death lifted like a fog from that now-clean basement in which I stood.

Lord, help us to trust You as we walk through the Good Fridays of our lives, believing with Jesus that You do have a future for us.
                                                — Keith Miller

6 | S A T *LONELINESS OR PRESENCE?*

But all those who knew him, including the women who had followed him from Galilee, stood at a distance, watching these things.
                                                —Luke 23:49 (NIV)

As I have read through the Gospels' accounts of Jesus' death, I have come to identify most with Matthew. What follows are the thoughts I might have had the day after Jesus' crucifixion if I'd been walking in Matthew's sandals.

Saturday was probably the worst day of my life. I'd never known grief like this. All of us just kept out of sight. There wasn't anything we could do for Jesus, or for ourselves, or for anybody.

I'd watched his crucifixion from a distance, heartsick. *This was not the Messiah!* I thought. Nothing that looked as pitiful as he did could possibly be from God. He didn't call down the angels to help him, as he said he could. He failed completely in what he'd come to do. And he failed me. I felt sorry for him, but more, I was sorry for myself. I felt more alone than I ever had in my life.

In the past three years, as we ate and laughed and sang and prayed together, Jesus filled the empty loneliness in our lives. Never again would that emptiness be filled.

Then I began to cry. Because I didn't care what Jesus was. I didn't care if he was a fraud. He was the only man in my whole life who ever really knew me, who saw the misery, the selfishness and guilt behind the mask I wear. He let me know that God loved me — that he loved me. And now my life was going to be totally lost without him.

In that moment I knew that I loved him. And I wished with everything in me that I'd died for him. I just sat there and ached inside.

O God, thank You for the haunting hunger we call loneliness that drives us to find love. Help us to accept You, even before we understand how You come to us in Jesus. —Keith Miller

7 | S U N *THE INTIMATE KINGDOM*

"Do not be afraid.... he has risen...." —Matthew 28:5–6 (RSV)

For many years I used to think about God and wonder if He were real, and if so, what He was like. As a child, I'd heard He was like Jesus, but the Sunday schools I was exposed to seemed to picture Jesus as a sissy no one would want to be with, or a father, which meant that He traveled a lot and didn't have much time for me, or as a giant policeman in plain clothes who was "on my case."

Over the years my picture of Jesus changed. But it wasn't until I read the Gospel of Matthew and put myself in Matthew's place that I really found Him. Here is what I imagine Matthew must have experienced on Easter Sunday....

I have seen Jesus alive! Suddenly, He appeared right in the

midst of us. I've never been so confused. But I touched Him. So I have to believe.

Yet what did His dying on the cross mean? What was this stuff about being raised from the dead? When and where was God's kingdom coming? And then it hit me. We'd misunderstood! We were not to look for a political king who would take over the government. Jesus was trying to tell us that God's rule was going to be a personal kingdom within ourselves, which would reach clear across the world! What Jesus had done when He walked into my experience, and John's and Peter's, was to put down a bridge from God to us, a bridge into the inner loneliness and fear in which I lived. "Listen," He had told us, "God loves you and you're never going to be alone again! He's with you and I'm with you."

Now, as His follower, I am to put my life down as a plank across the separation into other people's lives, so that God can somehow walk across my vulnerability into their fear and loneliness. God can lead them out of their caves of hiding and put their hands in the hands of other lonely little children. They, and we, will form a new and intimate community, the family of God, the church of Jesus Christ.

Lord, thank You for reminding me this Holy Week that You have come as an intimate friend, and that through Your Spirit You whisper Your love to each of us so that we can be Your love for others.
— Keith Miller

8 | M O N   *"He has risen, just as he said...."*   — Matthew 28:6 (NIV)

It was Easter Sunday, twelve noon. My Sunday school classroom of three- and four-year-olds was empty, except for the cluttered aftermath: dripping paintbrushes; half-finished puzzles; juice cups; cookie crumbles; the burned-out candle tipped over on our altar. I was burned out, too. The weeks of preparation, the sudden letdown.

The felt story pieces were still on the Velcro board. *How many years I've told this same story!* I thought, as I folded each piece — Mary Magdalene, the disciples, the empty tomb — and put them in the cardboard box till next year.

Suddenly, I felt a presence in the room. Turning, I saw four-year-old Brendan Fox grinning mischievously in the doorway. A born ham, Brendan spread his arms wide and dramatically mimicked the angel's words he'd heard from me earlier. "I just came to tell you, Jesus died, but He didn't stay dead. He's alive." Then Brendan was gone, his footsteps pitter-pattering back down the linoleumed hall.

I looked down at the box I was still holding. The figures might be packed away, but the story wasn't. In the cluttered, tired silence, I heard the words echo: *Jesus died, but He didn't stay dead. He's alive!*

Lord Jesus, may Your living presence always be a reality to me.
— Shari Smyth

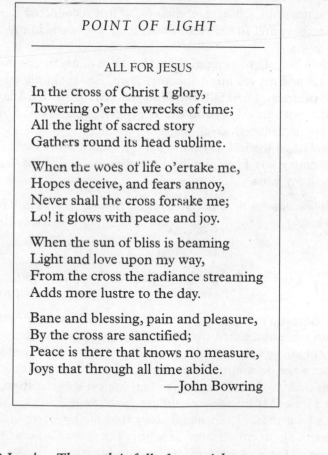

POINT OF LIGHT

ALL FOR JESUS

In the cross of Christ I glory,
Towering o'er the wrecks of time;
All the light of sacred story
Gathers round its head sublime.

When the woes of life o'ertake me,
Hopes deceive, and fears annoy,
Never shall the cross forsake me;
Lo! it glows with peace and joy.

When the sun of bliss is beaming
Light and love upon my way,
From the cross the radiance streaming
Adds more lustre to the day.

Bane and blessing, pain and pleasure,
By the cross are sanctified;
Peace is there that knows no measure,
Joys that through all time abide.
—John Bowring

9 | T U E | *O Lord....The earth is full of your riches.*
— Psalm 104:24 (TLB)

I stepped out on my deck Easter Sunday morning a few years ago in

Nashville, Tennessee, and looked out over the woods below just beginning to turn green. But not even the welcome signs of spring could make me ignore the untidiness below me. The boy across the street hadn't come to mow the grass when he said he would. So the grass in my sloping backyard seemed at least a foot high and was beginning to go to seed. I had wanted the lawn to be neat for Easter, and I was provoked at him that it wasn't.

Just as I turned to go inside, something bright blue in the tall grass caught my eye. *More untidiness*, I thought with annoyance. *Something one of the neighborhood dogs dragged over and left.* Just as I started down the stairs to pick it up and dispose of it, I recognized it. A bird! An indigo bunting! In *my* yard. Feeding on the seeds in my uncut, untidy grass.

I had been hardening my heart because of my neighbor boy's negligence and my resulting unkempt lawn. Easter should be celebrated with neatness, I had felt. But God was telling me that He celebrated Easter with new life, and life is prolific, abundant, not carefully boxed, landscaped, arranged.

I watched the indigo bunting and its more sober mate feed on my abundant seeds. How grateful I was that the boy across the street had *not* cut my grass.

Help me always to thank You for all things, even before I see You at work.
                                                    — Mary Ruth Howes

10 | W E D *They that deal truly are [the Lord's] delight.*
                                                    —Proverbs 12:22

Tax time again! As always, I spread my records out on the dining room table and asked myself which expenses were deductible. *Was the purpose of that luncheon business or personal?* If business, I could claim a tax deduction; if personal, I could not. Again and again, I went over my records trying to find logical ways to stretch the facts just a little. My business could use the savings.

As I sat there, I recalled a story told me by a friend from Texas where I spent much time as a boy. There was a pond behind the house where Richard grew up, and his great ambition as a small boy was to catch a fish there. He had no luck from shore. Perhaps he'd do better nearer the middle. So at age seven, Richard decided to build a boat. He found some lumber and located a saw. The saw was warped, but Richard used it anyhow, and in time he had himself a rectangular boat with wobbly sides. He dragged his creation down to the lake and pushed it out from shore. It took on water and sank in less than a minute.

"As I stood watching at my boat settle into the mud," Richard told me, "I realized what had happened. I'd tried to saw straight lines with a crooked saw. The edges of the planks were not flush, so my boat went down. You cannot build properly if your tools are warped."

Of course! I was trying to work with some warped tools. I scooped up a handful of questionable receipts and tossed them into the wastebasket. Along with them, I tossed the money I would have saved in taxes. But that was okay. Records are a business tool; if my record-keeping is less than straight, how can my business float?

Help me to remember, Lord, that when I need to stretch my resources I should do so in a manner that is pleasing to You.   —John Sherrill

11 | T H U   *"Greater love has no one than this...."*
                                        — John 15:13 (NAS)

It had been a long day, and I was tired. When the telephone rang, I answered and heard Red's chipper voice. "Scott, why don't you ride out to the farm with me? I've gotta check on some things, and I'd like to show you the place."

My first thought was *I need to go home, collapse, take a nap.* But I heard my voice say, "Sure, Red, I'd love to. Drop by after work and we'll go!"

Red came by in his pickup and soon we were bouncing down a country road. Before long I was laughing, cracking jokes and having a good time. The pressures of the day began to lift in the midst of humor and good friendship.

Red is a doctor, and the farm is his hobby. As we walked through the barn and over his acreage, I could tell that this was his place of solace; a retreat where he could place his surgeon's hands into rich soil and sweat away the wear and tear of a stress-filled life.

An hour later, as we prepared to leave, Red said, "I want you to come out here any time you need to rest or get away. This farm has saved my life, and it can save yours, too."

As I stumbled with words to express my appreciation, Red showed me that, more than naps or farms, pastures and rivers, the generosity of friendship can restore our souls.

Dear God, may I give to someone today my friendship. May I let them rest in my love and care. Amen. — Scott Walker

12 | F R I | *They that wait upon the Lord shall renew their strength....* — Isaiah 40:31

As I registered for the weekend retreat at Canyon Meadows in the Southern California mountains, I was handed a small package wrapped in a dainty floral print. "When you get to your room," the young woman told me, "please unwrap this and read the label first thing." Her eyes danced as she looked at my quizzical expression.

I did as she said — first thing — and found a small baby-food jar filled with grains of rice and one fairly large walnut. The label read:

> The walnut in this jar represents the time we spend with God. The rice represents the time we spend doing other things. If you pour the rice into the jar first, then try to insert the walnut, it will not fit. If you put the walnut in first, then pour the rice around it, there is a perfect fit.
>
> Likewise, if we spend time doing other things first, we will never find time to spend with God. If we spend time with God first, there will always be time for other things.

No wonder my week had been so frantic and out of whack. I had filled my hours with errands, phone calls, housework and paperwork, until there was no room for time with God. There and then I made a new commitment: "Every single day, dear Lord, the walnut goes in first!"

Truly, Lord, the greatest thing in the world is loving You! Let my pleasure be to serve You with joy and gladness. — Fay Angus

13 | S A T | *The inspiration of the Almighty giveth them understanding.* — Job 32:8

I know nothing about baseball. As a kid, I hated to play. In school, I was always one of the last ones picked on a team and then was relegated to right field where I trembled lest the ball came my way.

Then I became a father, and with complete bewilderment I watched William, when he turned seven years old, fall in love with baseball. He read about all the games in the newspaper. He collected cards with a relish. He spent hours tossing a ball up and down in his mitt. And he wanted to play on a team. It was too late in the season to sign up for Little League, and father-son catch and toss hardly did the trick. "Lord," I prayed as hard as I had once prayed in right field, "help!"

Then one evening I got a quick answer to my prayer. I was reading a book to Willy about kids who played games in their local playground—the sandlot, they called it. *The perfect thing!* I thought. I called some fathers in the neighborhood who knew more about baseball than I did and asked them to join us for a game in our local park. "Saturday at ten o'clock."

To my amazement, ten kids and a handful of parents showed up on a cold morning in April. The rules were established: no strikes, parents pitch and everybody gets to hit. We played all spring and summer long, kids coming and going, runs made, and Willy's batting average getting better with every game. "You know, Dad," my son said at summer's end, "if I do Little League next year, let's still have our sandlot league."

Thanks, Coach, I thought. Sometimes it takes a Father to show a parent the way.

Lord, continue to guide me through any unknown territory I face today.
                                                        —Rick Hamlin

14 | S U N   *"Lord, teach us to pray...."*   —Luke 11:1 (NAS)

One Sunday, the teacher of the Sunday school class my wife Barbara and I attended asked us to pray for his son-in-law who was facing critical brain surgery the following day. "He has the best brain surgeon in the area," he said, "but unless he also has the prayers of those who care, we don't feel that we have the whole team in the game. Will you be a team player with us?"

A year later, in the hospital for a coronary bypass, I remembered his words. Yes, I had the best surgeon in the area. But as I looked around the walls of my room the morning of the surgery, I had proof of something else: Those who cared for me were also praying for me. Our daughter Nancy had covered my walls with colorful, handmade posters from the children of the church. And Barbara was holding a stack of prayer cards written and signed by the adults. By their cards and posters, they had demonstrated their commitment to pray. They had all joined the team.

Dear God, make me a team player in this game called life.
— Kenneth Chafin

15 | M O N   *MY GIFT TODAY...*
THE SAND BARREL

The desert shall rejoice, and blossom as the rose.   —Isaiah 35:1

I found my gift today when I went to take the car out of the garage. Our garage is dark, even in daytime. I have to switch on the light to make my way around the lawn mower and the garbage cans and the bottles waiting to be recycled.

I was about to get in the car when something in the darkest corner caught my eye. We keep a plastic barrel back there, filled with sand for use on our almost perpendicular driveway during the winter. Each spring my husband takes a wheelbarrow, a broom and a shovel and laboriously salvages the used sand, returning it to the barrel for the next winter.

He'd completed this yearly ritual a few weeks earlier, and now I stared incredulously at what I saw. In the gritty sand, a little garden was growing. Without water, in the near darkness, in the most inhospitable soil I could imagine, a score of pale-green shoots had thrust their heads into the air. I bent down and counted... twenty-six.

I thought about the errand I needed the car for: I'd run out of the Blackwing pencils I write with. A particular kind of pencil, a special place, just the right light — what a lot of external conditions I thought I needed before I could be productive.

But true productivity, genuine creativity, my gift-garden suggested, comes from within. Radiant poetry from blind Milton, soaring melody from deaf Beethoven, the charter of Christian freedom from Paul's prison cell. I looked again at the valiant seedlings. Then I switched off the light and went back upstairs to work.

Take my eyes off externals today, Father, and onto Your limitless life within.
— Elizabeth Sherrill

16 | T U E | *Thou shalt have joy and gladness....*   —Luke 1:14

"Wow, your fortieth!" my friend Melanie exclaimed. "How will you celebrate?"

"I just want to ignore it," I replied. Desperately longing for a second child, I dreaded this birthday, seeing it as a dark curtain drawing my childbearing years to a close.

"Oh, Mary," Melanie protested, "you don't want to miss this chance to celebrate! Let's make it a wonderful occasion!"

Melanie delights in creating festive celebrations. She was already planning for her husband's fiftieth birthday next year. She and her two preschool boys planned to put a big sign in the front yard proclaiming, "Nifty, Nifty, Our Dad's Fifty!"

Her enthusiasm was contagious. Could I rejoice in forty years of God's goodness? Could I put aside my longing for more and celebrate all He had already given? Could I stop waiting for life to be perfect? I decided that I could.

Once the word went out that I no longer resented the day, I was royally feted. Friends took me out to lunch. One gave me a sign to wear: "Yes! I'm really forty! I only look like I'm twenty-nine!" My daughter Elizabeth, coached by Melanie, declared, "Lordy, Lordy, Mama's forty!"

Yes, I thought, joining in the laughter, *I will treasure this time of my life, whatever shape it takes.* And as I learned to rejoice in being forty, God gave me even more reason for joy—the birth of my son Mark a year later.

Dear Lord, God of joy, help us celebrate Your goodness in all seasons of our lives.   —Mary Brown

17 | W E D | *I treasure your word in my heart, so that I may not sin against you.*   —Psalm 119:11 (NRSV)

My reconversion was not instantaneous. I was much too stubborn to come back to God that easily. My first prayer to God after fifteen years of silence was a challenge, something I can only describe as holy *chutzpah!* First, I told God what the rules were going to be: *You don't have any of me now, so You'd better be pleased with anything I offer You!* Then I started to read the Bible like any other book. I was starting from a basis of total unbelief, and I told myself that I didn't have to believe anything I read.

Somewhere within the first two weeks, God's Word started to get a hold on me. I was fascinated. I couldn't wait to wake up at 5:30 each morning to read more. With time, I found God's Word reactivated in my heart. It was no longer a matter of the sins I was willing to give up. There was nothing I had that was worth holding on to.

I don't tell you this to recommend either my prayer or my own path back to God. I share them simply to show you how loving and patient God is and how powerful is His Word.

Your Word, O God, breathes life and light into all those dark corners of my heart.
— Diane Komp

18 | T H U *Cast all your anxieties on him, for he cares about you.*
— I Peter 5:7 (RSV)

I've been doing a lot of worrying these days — about my career, about a possible move to Canada, about finances. Each morning I pray for a calm spirit and a trust in God that doesn't waver. I list my blessings like the old hymn tells us:

> Count your blessings,
> Name them one by one,
> Count your many blessings,
> See what God has done....

But the next thing you know, I'm fretting. I start to list my blessings one more time, but again the worry rises. *Why can't I pray and trust God once and for all?* I wonder. *Why do I have to keep working at it?*

This morning when I went to wash my hair, for some reason I noticed the directions on the shampoo bottle: "Wet hair. Lather well. Rinse. Repeat if necessary."

"Repeat if necessary." There's my answer, I thought. *Shampooing isn't a once-in-a-lifetime thing. And neither is prayer.*

As I dried my hair, I thanked God for His message from a shampoo bottle. And I began to pray again: "Here are my worries, Father.... And here are the blessings I thank You for: my three teenagers; my work; my family and friends...."

Dear God, it's comforting to know that prayer is "repeat if necessary," and that I can come to You daily, hourly, whenever I need to.
— Brenda Wilbee

19 | F R I | *Nothing is secret, that shall not be made manifest....*
                                            —Luke 8:17

After a busy day at work yesterday, I parked the car in the driveway, noticed something in the bushes and then entered the house. The children greeted me at the door.

"I've got a secret!" I announced.

"Are we going to the shore?" Karen asked. She often equates secrets with a surprise trip.

"Are we gonna have pizza?" Michael asked.

My teenage son David just rolled his eyes, thinking, *Another of Dad's great secrets.*

"Follow me," I whispered as I walked back out to the driveway. We gathered before the forsythia, and I pointed to a nest deep within the green bush. "There's a nest," I announced.

David rolled his eyes. Karen was disappointed we weren't going to the shore, but she was interested in the nest. Michael asked, "Is there an egg?"

I lifted Michael up, and he pulled back a few green branches. "Nope. No egg."

This morning, just before I climbed into the car, I had a thought. I walked back up the driveway and stood before the forsythia. I pulled back a few branches, stood on my toes and peered in. One blue egg.

Tonight, after work, I entered the kitchen with the newspaper under my arm as the children called out, "Daddy's home!"

As I stooped down among my three children, I whispered, "I've got a secret!"

What a delight to share the things you discover in your life with those you love. So cut out an article in a magazine or newspaper and mail it to someone you think would enjoy the piece. Or perhaps you might read about a good program on television tonight; so call a friend and tell him or her about it. As we share our discoveries with other people, we can grow together.

Psst, *I've got a secret, Lord. I love You with all my heart!*
                                            —Christopher de Vinck

20 | S A T | *And God created... every living creature that moveth....*
                                            —Genesis 1:21

My grandfather and I had just finished helping a cow through a difficult birth. It had taken quite awhile, and we had been fairly certain the large calf would not survive the delivery. In the end, however, when we dropped the heavy, wet bundle down into the clean straw we had spread for its coming, the bundle struggled feebly. While the cow was being taken care of, I pulled the calf into my lap, and with a wisp of straw, wiped his face clean. Within minutes, he had struggled to his feet and was walking hesitantly toward his mother.

I walked out of the barn into the dusky West Virginia twilight, slowly wiping the palms of my hands on the legs of my well-worn blue jeans. The moon was shining, and several softly glowing stars had joined it. I leaned against the white, peeling barn door, enjoying the impressive quiet and the sweet smell of the hay. The miracle of birth had been played out in front of me.

I started to wonder about all the miracles that God performs that I accept — like the calf — as everyday occurrences. I stood outside the barn for a long time. In awe.

I am overwhelmed with gratitude, Lord, for the miracle of my own birth.
                                                              — Hollie Davis

21 | S U N *He that dwelleth in the secret place of the Most High shall abide under the shadow of the Almighty.* —Psalm 91:1

One Sunday, Pastor Carl preached on the Cross. "The Cross is the *crux* of the matter," he expounded. "We need to make the Cross — Christ's death for us — the center of our lives."

How can I do that? I wondered.

Later that day, my husband and children and I went to Nyack, New York, a town on the Hudson River near where we live. As we walked down the pier toward the water, five-year-old David began climbing atop a large refuse container covered with a wooden board. I pulled David up on the board, standing him in the middle. "I'm so big!" he shouted in his childish exuberance. Then instead of staying where I put him, he began to move toward the edge.

"David, stay in the center," I told him. "That's the safest place for you to be." As I spoke, the words seemed to speak to me on another level. In that moment, I saw the Cross as my place of safety. Because Christ gave Himself for me, I don't have to fear whatever may come — financial woes, my children's future, even death itself.

Now, if I sense fear inching its way into my heart, or if I feel worry straying into my thoughts, I see it as a warning that I'm off-center. I know what I need to do — stop everything and confess it to the Lord. Then, I ask Him for a Scripture, a piece of the Word that I can hold on to. Finally, I thank Him for His willingness to help me.

As gospel vocalist Larnelle Harris sings, "When the storms of life are all around me raging, I am safe in that secret place"—centered in Christ.

Lord Jesus, help me to keep You as the focus of my life.
                                            — Robin White Goode

22 | M O N   *And God said, Let us make man in our image, after our likeness: and let them have dominion over...*
all the earth....   — Genesis 1:26

When I was a young girl, I dreamed of becoming a space traveler. I would explore the universe and discover uncharted worlds. I'd be the first to see a new, beautiful planet covered with majestic mountains, sparkling waterfalls, multihued flowers, exotic fruits, towering trees and skies with drifting, multicolored clouds.

Then one day, I described my dream planet to a friend. "Madge," she exclaimed, "you've already found it! That's earth!"

Startled at the vision of earth as a new, beautiful planet, I was even more taken aback when she added, "Too bad we're destroying it with all this pollution. I don't think that's what God intended when He gave us humans dominion over all the earth. Do you?"

That's when I quit dreaming of finding a new world and began searching out ways to help this one, like recycling my trash and carrying my groceries in reusable canvas bags. I've also joined an organization called Keep New Mexico Beautiful. Together we work for litter control and recycling, graffiti prevention and beautification. The organization gives grants to communities for the planting of trees and wildflowers. In addition, we have an education program that aims at instilling a sense of personal responsibility in adults and schoolchildren for the preservation of our environment.

Today is Earth Day, a good day to ask what else I can do — what else you can do — to protect this beautiful planet, our precious trust from God.

Father, today I resolve to become a better steward of our world.
                                            — Madge Harrah

23 | TUE

Let brotherly love continue.   —Hebrews 13:1

Every morning before work I like to sit in the clouds. I mean, I sit in the men's steam room at my gym.

You hear amazing things in the clouds of steam: men's voices bragging or complaining about work; bragging or complaining about their wives; bragging or complaining about their children. There's something therapeutic in sitting in a room where you can barely see your hand in front of your face, like sitting in white darkness and sounding off about life.

Today there were just three of us, three dim, fleshy outlines. Perhaps because he felt comfortably anonymous, the man on my left suddenly said, "I haven't had a drink in over a week."

I sat wondering what I was supposed to say to this, or if I was supposed to say anything at all, when the man on my right volunteered, "I haven't had a drink in five years."

"How do you do it?" the man on my left asked softly. "It's the hardest thing I've ever tried. But I know if I keep drinking I'm gonna lose everything. I saw my dad go through it, saw him lose it all. Still, I want to drink."

Then the man with five years of sobriety told an amazing story of how his life was nearly destroyed by alcohol. He talked about his recovery, the faith that he had found and the life that he rebuilt. His voice flowed with gratitude. When he had finished, he asked the man on my left which way he was going when he left the gym. "Uptown," the man replied.

"I'll walk with you," the man said. "Maybe we'll grab a cup of coffee."

With that they were gone. Later, as I dressed in the locker room, I wondered who they were. But I couldn't tell, and it didn't matter. What did matter is that I had seen God working in a most unusual place, as is so often the case.

You never know what you'll find in the clouds.

Make me ever vigilant, God, for signs of You at work.
                                        —Edward Grinnan

24 | W E D | *Let all bitterness, and wrath, and anger, and clamor,*
and evil speaking, be put away from you....
—Ephesians 4:31

It was a beautiful spring day, with a clear blue sky, a few fluffy white clouds and a lively breeze. A perfect day—except for people like me with allergies. Pollen was blowing in the wind, I had the runny nose and swollen eyes to prove it, and I felt miserable.

I was walking my dog along our road, eager to get back home, when I saw Don Evans, a teacher friend, out for his morning jog. As he approached, he grinned, waved and said, "Great day, isn't it?"

"Not if you can't breathe," was what I was going to say, but I hesitated. Don was in a happy mood. Why spoil it with a sour remark? Somehow, I didn't want to be the kind of person who would do that. So I grinned back and said, "Have fun!" Immediately, my own spirits lifted.

I can't count the times I have allowed my bad moods to spill over into other people's lives. But when I do that, I don't like myself. My brief encounter with Don showed me that I can choose the kind of person I want to be. When I'm in a bad mood, I can try a little harder to consider the feelings of those around me. I can ask myself, *Do I want to spoil their day or make it nicer?* It all comes down to a pretty simple choice: What kind of a person do I want to be?

Lord, help me to choose, even in the hard times, to be a spirit-lifter.
—Phyllis Hobe

25 | T H U | *Be strong and of a good courage, fear not, nor be*
afraid....   —Deuteronomy 31:6

A little bit of courage—that's what I prayed for each morning. I needed some to calm the butterflies in my stomach during the first days I worked at Guideposts way back in 1977. Fortunately, at midweek, a fellow worker asked me to join her for lunch. It was a beautiful April day, so we took our sandwiches down to the edge of Lake Gleneida, a short walk from our company headquarters in Carmel, New York. We settled in close to a large bronze statue of a young woman on a horse.

"Who's that?" I asked my new friend.

"Sybil Ludington," she told me. "Sybil's rather famous around here."

I walked over for a closer look. There was a fierce gaze on the rider's face, and she was obviously driving her charge at a furious pace. "Why is she famous?"

"She rode all night to warn the militia that the British were attacking Danbury. Some say she rode farther than Paul Revere. She was only sixteen at the time."

As I munched on my sandwich, I kept looking at Sybil, picturing the dangers she faced riding through what was then wilderness. *If a sixteen-year-old could do that*, I said to myself, *I ought to be able to cope fearlessly with a new job.* I went back to the office with a new spirit. I'd been sent a message by horseback!

There were two hundred years exactly between the April of Sybil Ludington's heroic ride in 1777 to the April afternoon of my lunch. I think of that odd coincidence every time I pass Sybil and her horse Star. But mostly I think of the wonderful and surprising ways that God can find to answer our prayers.

Grant me a fearless spirit, Lord, knowing that You are on my side always. Amen.   — Susan Schefflein

26 | F R I | *Train up a child in the way he should go....*
                                            — Proverbs 22:6

"What do you want for graduation, Derek?" I asked our twenty-two-year-old son as our family ate lunch together in a campus cafeteria. I expected a sensible answer like "a watch," or something silly and extravagant like "a million dollars." I wasn't prepared for his real answer.

"An ice ax," he said, without hesitation, as if he'd already thought about it. Immediately, I pictured him climbing the mountains he loved, spearing his ax into the ice of a glacier just before he started to slip.

"But that's not what I had in mind," I objected. "Mothers like to give their sons things like a new suit for job interviews, or an electric razor, or a trip to Washington, D.C., to visit museums."

He kept eating, as if maybe he hadn't even heard me. So after lunch, we headed off to the store, where Derek began examining a variety of axes. I shuddered just looking at them, but I was curious about the different sizes and shapes.

"What's the difference?" I asked Derek.

"Some are mountaineering ice axes and some are climbing axes, so it depends on the use and height and weight of the climber," he explained.

Surprised, I looked at him with a new sense of respect. How did this child of mine know so much about something so unknown and scary to me?

Finally, Derek selected one, and I held it as we stood in line to pay for it. Not because I liked this ice ax so much, but because I wanted to ask God to bless it and use it as a tool to protect and anchor Derek on all his future adventures.

"Happy graduation!" I said, when I handed it over to him.

"How'd you know this is just what I wanted?" he grinned.

Father, may I have the faith to allow Derek to grow into the person You created him to be.   — Carol Kuykendall

27 | S A T

...Growing in the knowledge of God.
—Colossians 1:10 (NIV)

"When will the well-drillers be here?" I asked my husband as he hung up the phone.

"Toward the end of the week. They're being delayed by equipment breakdowns," Harry replied.

"That's the same thing they've told us for the last three weeks," I complained as I heated a pot of water for washing the breakfast dishes.

"Look," Harry said, "this is going to get the best of us. What can we find in this situation that's good? What do you think God might want to teach us here?"

As we explored it together, it didn't take long to see that this was a great opportunity for us to practice patience. That's not one of the things I'm famous for. I realized that I could continue to complain, or I could accept the situation and ask God to "grow" patience in me, and maybe even a cheerful attitude about the inconvenience. And so it was that Harry and I went to work at being patient.

The well-drillers finally did come, and we were grateful to find good water at a reasonable depth. Now we're getting into the serious house-building stage, and I can almost see our heavenly Father saying with a smile, "Just look at all these opportunities I'll be giving you to practice that patience thing: delays in the building permit process, waiting for the concrete truck or the plumber or the electrician...."

Thank You, Lord. We can hardly wait.

Loving Father, help me to recognize, and even welcome, these lessons in patience.   — Mary Jane Clark

28 | S U N *I remember the days of old; I meditate on all thy works; I muse on the work of thy hands.*   —Psalm 143:5

After flying into Kansas, I picked up my mother at her retirement home, then drove my rental car to the area where I'd spent my childhood. We parked and looked over our former property at the edge of McPherson's city limits.

"This land was bare when we were newlyweds," Mom, now ninety-eight, told me. "Nothing to it but earth and sky. Back then our eighty acres were enough to raise chickens, cows, lambs, plus grain and hay for them, too."

I reminisced also. "I remember taking our milk to Silver Springs Creamery in glass bottles. And how you and Dad exchanged eggs and homemade butter for flour and sugar and other staples at Rothrock's Grocery or Swanson's Market."

Mom quickly added, "Don't forget that some of those eggs and chickens went to church, too. It was about the only way Dad and I could tithe back during Depression days. We ladies put on dinners. And we worked and prayed. We prayed a lot."

How could I forget? Each Sunday morning back then we sat together as a family in the rich, walnut pews of the church at the end of Euclid Avenue. We drove to it and stopped. There it was, exactly as I remembered it, standing firm.

Many other things have changed in seventy years, but I also stand firm in what I learned back then—things like faith, doing things as a family, tithing, working, praying and seeing God provide.

I'm thankful, Father, for the values rooted in me during childhood. Keep me ever faithful.   — Isabel Wolseley

29 | M O N *Grace be with thee....*   —I Timothy 6:21

Some of life's best gifts have come to me in small, undramatic moments, like the words that came shortly after I began my first job from a woman whom I never saw.

"I hear you are working with the old folks at the county home," said a voice on the phone. "I want to help. Write down my phone number and when one of those dear people has a need, you are to call and let me know. In the meantime, I'll be checking back with you."

And she did check back. At least once or twice a week my morning would begin with one of her calls. If I knew someone who needed a new coat or a special book or the comfort of a soft stuffed animal, all I had to do was ask. She was a self-appointed link between local churches, civic groups, caring individuals and people in need. Requests made to this woman were always fulfilled within a few days.

We had many phone conversations before I learned that she was an invalid, confined to her bed. I was astounded. "How can you think of others, when you have so many problems yourself?" I asked her one day when I was feeling a bit down myself.

"My dear," she answered, "in the first year of my confinement I spent all my time feeling sorry for myself, until a very wise friend said to me, 'What's happened has happened. You can face it with bitterness, or you can face it with grace.' I knew he was right, so I gathered my courage and chose the latter.

"Moving the center of attention from myself to others, I found I could use the telephone to perform at least one useful act each day. One act of kindness blossomed into two, then three," she continued, "and now my days are full. So each morning when I wake up, I say these words, 'This is a new day. Face it with grace,' just to remind myself what I'm about."

Today, her words continue to bless me. To face the day means no regrets from the past, no resentments in the present, no fears of the future. It is to say each morning:

What can I do for You today, God?   — Pam Kidd

30 | T U E *At the end of ten days their countenance appeared better and fatter in flesh than all the young men who ate the portion of the king's delicacies.*   — Daniel 1:15 (NKJV)

"Would you be willing to make some fund-raising phone calls?" our college's financial aid administrator asked me awhile back.

"Let me get back to you," I hedged. "I'm not comfortable talking to people about money. That job just isn't right for me."

When I told my wife Sharon about the request, she reminded me of how the biblical Daniel responded when he was asked to do something not right for him. As a captive student under King Nebuchadnezzar, he was asked to eat rich foods to build up his strength. But they were foods his religion forbade. So Daniel proposed an alternative. "Let us eat our vegetables for a week," he told the king's steward. "Then examine us and see if we're as healthy as the king wants."

Daniel's alternative plan worked. He knew he couldn't reach the king's goal in the way the king expected, but by being diplomatic, he didn't offend the king. And he ended up as healthy as or healthier than the other students.

"I've used that technique myself," Sharon told me. "When they asked me to be on a calling team at church, I volunteered instead for the cooking-baking team. My motivation for that is much higher."

So the next day I volunteered to write letters instead of making fund-raising calls. "I express myself more easily on paper," I said. "The phone makes me very nervous." My offer was accepted, and I was pleased to see later that my letters had raised some money.

If you're ever asked to do something that you find uncomfortable, think of an alternative task that opens up your best energies and volunteer to do that. In the long run, you'll do more good.

Father, I want to be cooperative, but sometimes I need to take another track. Help me to find the way I can contribute best.
— Daniel Schantz

GIFTS OF LIGHT

1 _____

2 _____

3 _____

4 _____

APRIL 1996

5

6

7

8

9

10

11

12

13

14

15

16

17

18 _____

19 _____

20 _____

21 _____

22 _____

23 _____

24 _____

25 _____

26 _____

27 _____

28 _____

29 _____

30 _____

M A Y

*You will do well to pay attention to this
as to a lamp shining in a dark place,
until the day dawns and the morning
star rises in your hearts.*

—II PETER 1:19 (RSV)

S	M	T	W	T	F	S
			1	2	3	4
5	6	7	8	9	10	11
12	13	14	15	16	17	18
19	20	21	22	23	24	25
26	27	28	29	30	31	

1 | W E D   *Always try to do good to each other....Always be joyful.*
                                    —I Thessalonians 5:15–16 (TLB)

I had the grumps. The whole world looked "tattletale gray" in spite
of the sun. Today was my day to get at all the old mundane chores
that had been piling up. Run a dozen errands. Do the laundry. Dust
the living room ... the bedroom ... everything.

What's more, it was trash day. Lugging a sack of garbage to the cans
at the sidewalk, I felt put out.

An unexpected glint of color on the hood of the car caught my eye.
Is that paint? No, it was spring flowers — homegrown daylilies,
daisies, bright blue periwinkles and tiny pink tea roses — carefully
arranged in a small basket tied jauntily to the hood ornament. *Of
course! Today is May Day!*

I didn't know where or whom it came from, but no matter. I found
myself singing and whistling on the way back up the drive. The gray
mists blew out of my heart. Mundane became fun-filled. I ran my errands with the perky basket wobbling on the car's hood, and got many
smiles and waves from pedestrians and other drivers.

I know now that it was my good friend Millie who crept around at
dawn to touch my day with wonder, and I am grateful. This year I
am passing along Millie's blessing. Early this morning I will fill my
own small baskets with flowers from my garden, then hurry around
the neighborhood to place one on the doorstep of each house. Nancy
and Jack, Lennie and Jim, dear Goldie way up the hill...won't they
be surprised!

> A sweet surprise from the heart of a friend
> Blesses our day with radiant joy!

*Thank You, Lord, that a blessing shared is a double delight! Help us
to send one on its way — to gladden a heart and brighten a day.*
                                    — Fay Angus

2 | T H U   *A friend loves at all times....*   — Proverbs 17:17 (NIV)

I once heard someone say that you are lucky indeed if you have a
friend you can phone and say, "Hi, it's me," and then launch into a
conversation without having to identify yourself. I have such a friend.

Chris and I met on the steel steps of the "Up" staircase in a school
crowded with more than one thousand students trying to find their
way around a building they'd never been in before. It was my very
first day of high school, and until a blonde girl with a friendly smile

asked, "What subjects do you have?" I didn't know a soul. But as we compared crisp new program cards, we were astonished to learn that we had all the same subjects, from English, to Spanish, to math and music—and we both had chosen to learn the flute. By the time we got to the top of the staircase, I wasn't lonely anymore.

Chris and I have been through much more than high school together. We've been through college graduation, career changes, life changes, learning to drive and my move to another coast. But we still talk on the phone at least once a week and send each other news clippings. And almost thirty years later, I know I can say, "Hi, it's me," and Chris will know immediately who it is.

Today, on this National Day of Prayer, I'm reminded of Chris. Because I have another Friend Whom I can call at any time — and do. And this is what I say: "Hi, God, it's me." And He knows who I am — always.

Dear God, thank You for Your closeness to us through prayer.
— Linda Neukrug

3 | F R I *Give thanks unto the Lord, for he is good....*
—Psalm 107:1

"Attitudes," a great American psychiatrist once said, "are more important than facts." I thought of this the other day when I went to see a longtime friend in the hospital. Jack had been a marvelous athlete as a young man and an energetic civic leader in the years that followed. Now the sudden onset of a serious kidney disorder had left him dependent on dialysis machines just to stay alive.

I knew how difficult this drastically curtailed existence must be for him and tried to express the sympathy I felt. But he waved my words aside. "We all go through stages in life," he said. "Here I am, and I can't say I enjoy these surroundings. What I try to focus on is the fun I've had getting here. The Lord gave me so many good times that there's no end to the happy memories I can summon up. When I do, this hospital room just fades away."

The fun I've had getting here. I wish I had a calendar with that phrase inscribed at the top of every page. Even on dark days, it would be a reminder of how many sunny ones there have been. A reminder, too, to be grateful to the One Who made those happy times possible.

Lord, in all my attitudes, keep me facing toward You.
— Arthur Gordon

4

S
A
T

"The Spirit of the Lord is upon me...."

—Luke 4:18 (GNB)

Early in the month of May, I was suffering from a thorough case of fear. June was coming with no work schedule and, therefore, no pay. I headed over to the barbershop for a beard trim and haircut, hoping for some distraction from my concerns. I was greeted by Stacy as I entered the door. "What can I do for you?" she asked.

"A haircut and a beard trim," I said. "What else would anyone want when they enter a barbershop?"

"Well," she said, "you might have wanted directions."

That said, I sat down next in line waiting my turn. Then, on a sudden inspiration, I said, "That is precisely what I want. I want directions. I want directions for the next ten years of my life." Stacy laughed and returned to cutting hair.

A couple of minutes later her partner called me for my haircut. As I sat there, lulled by the click of the shears and the rumble of the clippers, I became aware of a presence eight to ten inches from my right ear. I opened my eyes. There stood Stacy, silent, looking directly at me and waiting for my attention. "Here," she said, handing me a slip of paper, "are the directions for the next ten years of your life."

It read, "Enjoy every precious moment!"

I accepted the message with gratitude, and wondered if when she got up that morning, Stacy knew she was a vehicle for the Holy Spirit.

Lord, may I daily realize that You would speak to me always in the voices of my friends and neighbors if I would but listen.

—John Cowan

5

S
U
N

Make a joyful noise unto God....　　　　　—Psalm 66:1

My twenty-seven-year-old son Jon is the strong, silent type—almost never complains. He also never discusses "heavy stuff" with me. I'm always trying to get him to open up when we talk. I haven't had much success, yet he called recently and asked right up front, "Are you praying for me, Mom?"

Thrilled over his question, I replied, "Oh, yes! Daily!" Then getting my voice back to a normal, nonpushy tone, I asked softly, "Do you ever pray for yourself, son?"

"In a strange kind of way. Sometimes when I don't know how to pray or even the words to use, late at night in bed I, well, I sing old hymns to God." He hung up abruptly.

But the next Sunday he showed up at church. It had been a long time. He towered above me as we stood to sing and share a hymnal. I listened to him singing out, "Amazing grace, how sweet the sound/That saved a wretch like me." I stared straight ahead, singing softly and my heart thumping loudly.

So Jon doesn't open up to me a lot. He's not vulnerable with me. Maybe there's a lot of wonderful stuff about him that I don't know. Like right now, he's not just singing the opening hymn in church. He's communicating with God. He's talking to his heavenly Father, and I just know that God is listening! He hears Jon now, and He hears his songs in the night.

Dear Father, I feel so much better knowing that Jon is talking/singing to You. I believe one day he'll talk to me, too. Amen.
— Marion Bond West

6 | M O N | *And Jesus said to them, "Follow me...."*
— Mark 1:17 (RSV)

When I met Joe, he was eighty years old and firmly shaking my hand at the church door. Still tall, strong and virile, he had a handsome face and a twinkle in his eyes. I remember thinking, *I'd like to get to know that fellow. There's a lot of depth there.*

I did not discover until months later that Joe Dawson was a war hero. During the fiftieth anniversary commemoration of D-Day and the invasion of Normandy, Joe's name and picture popped up everywhere. He was even selected to introduce the President of the United States at the anniversary ceremony.

Digging into my history books, I learned why Joe was such a hero. When American forces landed on Omaha Beach, they were hopelessly pinned down by German machine-gun fire and faced annihilation. The Allied commanders were considering evacuating the survivors and aborting the invasion. It was at that moment that a young Army captain named Joe Dawson stood up amidst the carnage, led the first American troops to the top of the bluff in that area of the beach and penetrated the German line. It was a turning point of D-Day.

Joe Dawson has helped me to believe again in the power of one individual. Too often I feel that I don't matter, that my example is inconsequential. But all it takes is for one person to stand up in the
midst of great odds and do what is right. All it takes is me ... and you.

Father, may I remember that Your Son, Jesus Christ, forever changed
human history through His singular life. May I have the courage to
rise up and follow His example. Amen.   — Scott Walker

7 | T U E *[A virtuous woman] looketh well to the ways of her*
household, and eateth not the bread of idleness.
— Proverbs 31:27

Mama was the best doughnut maker in the whole wide world, and
she made them frequently as I was growing up. But I remember one
time in particular when she made a huge number of doughnuts. She
put an especially beautiful red cloth on the table and lit two red
candles. That evening she smilingly told us that she had decided to
give us a "doughnut party," and we got to eat as many doughnuts as
we wanted. There was nothing else for supper except freshly churned
buttermilk.

Her smile and gay spirits were infectious, and I remember she was
wearing a bright red apron and her coal black hair was gleaming.
There was a high intensity about her that was almost flamelike.

Later, I happened to step quietly out onto our back porch, and
I heard Mama saying to our father, "John, I do pray to God that
we can sell some of that corn tomorrow, so that I can feed these
young 'uns right. I just can't give them doughnuts again without truly
making them sick."

So often over the years, I have thanked God for giving me a mother
like that — one who made the best of what she had with a smile and
who in adversity always used her God-given imagination to pull us
through. She never acknowledged defeat under the most trying circumstances. Instead, she used things like a pretty red tablecloth, a
couple of red candles and a bright red apron to create a scene that
would never be forgotten by her children.

Dear Lord, I thank You for the mother You gave me. May there be
many more like her in the future.   — Dorothy Nicholas

8 | W E D
"Do you truly love me more than these?"
—John 21:15 (NIV)

My seven-year-old son and I enjoy a bedtime ritual of "love exchange." "I wouldn't trade you for all the boys in the world," I tell him.

Andy enjoys being creative in his responses. "I wouldn't trade you for forty motorcycles," he'll reply. Or, "I wouldn't trade you for Hollywood, or Elvis' Cadillac. I wouldn't trade you for Aunt Judi's pool if it were filled with cash and I was swimming in it!"

I cherish all these comparisons, but one that has really touched me was when he simply said, "I love you with all the pieces of my heart."

Yes, sometimes my heart, too, seems to be all in pieces, pulled every which way by things to do, needs to fill, people to care for. Then I remember Andy's words. And I pray:

God, I want to love You with all the pieces of my heart.
—Joan Rae Mills

9 | T H U
A mirror reflects a man's face, but what he is really like is shown by the kind of friends he chooses.
—Proverbs 27:19 (TLB)

David was leaving the Thursday morning breakfast group that he and I had started. Five years earlier, we had been having breakfast at a coffee shop when we began talking about spiritual things. Then he said, "We should get together and talk like this more often."

Now, after countless Thursday mornings at the coffee shop, where we — and the other men who joined us — had talked about our prayer lives, our work, our frustrations with bosses, our wives, our children, our parents, our thankfulness for the great beauty of life, David was leaving. He had received an irresistible job offer, and he and his family would be moving a thousand miles away. The group would go on, of course. New challenges would be faced, the mystery of God working in our lives would continue. But how could I thank David for what never would have happened without him?

Fumbling for words, I finally stumbled on the right ones. "You know, David, I never knew how much I knew about faith until I started talking to you."

"Funny," he said, "I was going to say the same about you."

Sure, we had given each other a lot of advice over the years, but the best thing we had done was to listen to each other. When a good friend listens carefully, prayerfully, there is no end to the wonderful things you will learn about yourself.

God, may I be a good listener today, helping by hearing.
— Rick Hamlin

10 | F R I

"But whoever would be great among you must be your servant."
— Matthew 20:26 (RSV)

I once heard another woman describe motherhood in three words: "Laundry, laundry, laundry!" I had to laugh because, having given birth to four children in four and a half years, I always had such a huge pile of clothes beside the washing machine that I called it my "mountaintop experience."

Over the years, I've managed to pull some amusing — and heroic — memories from my laundry basket. There was the time, when the children were small, that I got so far behind on the washing, my husband packed me off to my mother's while he stayed home with the kids and did *sixteen* loads of clothes. (Now that's heroic!) One time we had a mouse in our basement, and I would load the clothes in a flurry, stamping my feet the whole time and singing at the top of my lungs! When the kids grew into teenagers, the big joke was the record ninety-eight socks without mates that we counted one day! Plus, my son and I kept up a running debate over whether his favorite shirts were lost in the laundry or lost in his room.

My clothes-washing days are on slow spin now as the kids go out the door much the way they came in — one after another. And one place where I particularly feel their absence is the laundry room. I miss those wash-and-wear traces of their nearness — the loud green socks, the Class of 1994 T-shirt, the number nine volleyball uniform, the handmade blue skirt.

My laundry room view may have seemed a little hazy some days, but having those kids around to love in everyday ways truly was a "mountaintop experience."

Lord Jesus, brighten my desire to love others in everyday ways.
— Carol Knapp

11 | S A T *If any of you lack wisdom, let him ask of God, that giveth to all....*
                                                     —James 1:5

How I loved those evening baseball games at our high school field in Williamstown, Massachusetts. It was 1933, I was fifteen and I dreamed of becoming a baseball star.

Our town team was composed of high school athletes, players from Williams College and local men. Some of the players were of major league caliber, but African Americans weren't allowed in the major leagues, and the Depression and the scarcity of farm teams in the Negro leagues reduced opportunities to play ball professionally.

Then the Philadelphia Black Giants came to town for an exhibition game. The team's star was Will Jackman, an underhand pitching wizard and the team's first-base coaching comedian. Before the game, a town official visited our home, seeking accommodations for the team. They would be playing in Bennington, Vermont, the next afternoon, but local hotels would not rent to them. Our fifteen-room home was ideal, so Father agreed to put them up. I was thrilled to think real, live baseball stars would be staying with us!

The game was exciting as a Giant player hit the longest home run ever. Jackman pitched one inning and kept the crowd roaring with laughter. But that evening as I waited tables, I noticed Jackman was not his humorous self. He was concerned with salaries, traveling expenses and accommodations.

I was not allowed to fraternize with the guests. The next morning, however, I was in the backyard when Jackman approached. Soon we were locked in conversation. I peppered him with questions about baseball and shared my dream of becoming a ballplayer like him. He listened, rose, shook my hand and said, "Get your education, young man. That's the only thing others can't take from you!"

I never saw Will Jackman again, and I never became that baseball star. But I remembered his words, which opened my mind and helped me to see that life was filled with opportunities. It still is!

Teaching Savior, all knowledge comes from You to be passed on to others. Help me to do this.   —Oscar Greene

12 | S U N

Honor thy father and thy mother....   —Exodus 20:12

When I was nine, the boy next to me in our Sunday school class asked the teacher what honoring thy father and mother meant. "It means obeying your parents," the teacher replied, "and respecting them." The commandment was clear to me then, yet in recent years and on this Mother's Day it has taken on deeper meaning.

My mother is in her mid-eighties, and I'm finding it more complex to honor her than I had anticipated. Her needs are constantly changing, and our mother and son roles are shifting. Mom still lives alone in her own house in northern Illinois. She is relatively healthy, independent and skilled in a host of ways, yet her arthritis is bothering her more, and I am faced with questions that have no easy answers. *Should I urge her one more time not to renew her driver's license? Should I tell her that the time has come when she should give up her house and living alone? How do I preserve her dignity?*

For now, the answers I've come up with are these: I stay in close touch by phone and talk longer. I visit her more frequently. I tell her of my gratitude for what she means in my life. I pray for her. And out of my prayers has come a definition of honoring my mother even greater than obeying and respecting. It is *loving* her.

Lord God, there are parents everywhere who need a Father's love. Watch over them now. Be their guide.   —Kenneth Chafin

13 | M O N

Always pray and not give up.   —Luke 18:1 (NIV)

I believe in prayer and in what God can do through prayer. But sometimes my faith grows tired when my prayers don't seem to be answered. That's what happened back in 1974 when our health clinic here in our little town of Mendenhall, Mississippi, lost its doctor after only a few months. Our ministry is an outgrowth of Mendenhall's Bible Church, and we exist to meet the spiritual and physical needs of the poor and disadvantaged. Up until we opened our clinic, poor folk had little or no access to medical services.

We didn't have another doctor on hand, so we wrote our friends and asked that they pray with us for God to send us a Christian doctor. We wanted someone who would be committed to Jesus Christ and to our ministry, and who would be willing to be part of our community. "Doctors who will work in rural areas are so scarce," some of our friends wrote back, "that maybe you need to quit praying for a Christian doctor and just pray for a doctor."

But we believed God would provide for our special needs. For a whole year we kept looking for just the right person—without success, so that at times we were very discouraged. Then one day, the staff decided to spend time in fasting and praying together for a doctor. A few days later we received a letter from Dr. Eugene McCarty. "Dolphus," he wrote, "I understand that you need a doctor, and I am willing to move my family from Colorado Springs to Mendenhall for two years or until you get another doctor."

At that moment, my faith took a leap. Jesus had told us always to pray and not give up, but sometimes I had had doubts. Now I had seen God answer. Dr. McCarty proved to be God's doctor for us in Mendenhall, for two and a half years, until God provided us with a permanent doctor. God had again proved His faithfulness to us.

Thank You, Lord, for the people You place in our lives ... answers to prayers.   —Dolphus Weary

14 | T U E | *MY GIFT TODAY...* *THE SEEDLINGS*

Let us not become weary in doing good, for at the proper time we will reap a harvest if we do not give up.   —Galatians 6:9 (NIV)

Last month, the sand barrel in the back of our garage held a gift for me—new life springing from what looked like hopeless conditions. Today, that same barrel offered another gift at a time when I needed it most.

I hadn't checked on the hardy little plants for a while. I'd been racing to meet a deadline at work, juggling family demands and a travel schedule. When I happened to glance into the barrel this morning, the plants had begun to droop.

No wonder, I thought, bending over them. Back here in the corner, deprived of light and water, they could hardly sustain themselves for long.

My husband John came downstairs, and together we wrestled the barrel to the front of the garage. As I poured water over the parched seedlings, I recognized my own condition. I, too, had been trying to produce in a dry and lightless corner. Too busy for prayer, Bible reading, the sacraments, Christian fellowship.

Plants need light and water, but so, the seedlings reminded me, do people. Didn't Jesus say, "I am the light of the world" (John 8:12), and "Whosoever drinketh of the water that I shall give him shall never thirst" (John 4:14)? Once more the little plants sent me back upstairs — this time to seek that Water and that Light.

Keep me close to You today, Lord, that I may bring the seeds You have planted to the harvest.   — Elizabeth Sherrill

15 | W E D *Without having seen him you love him; though you do not now see him you believe in him and rejoice with unutterable and exalted joy.*   — I Peter 1:8 (RSV)

When I was growing up, it was unusual for mothers to work outside the home. My mother did, partly out of financial need, but also because she enjoyed her career as a legal secretary. I realize now how difficult it must have been for her to juggle motherhood and a job, but somehow she managed to do it very well.

For instance, I was in a lot of school plays, and most of the performances were held in the afternoon. That was a challenge for my mother. It meant giving up several lunch hours to make up for the time it took to catch a bus, ride five miles to my school, see the play and catch a bus back to work.

"Will your mother be here?" one of the other kids would always ask me a few minutes before we went onstage.

"Sure," I would always say. I never had any doubt about it.

Once onstage we couldn't see the audience beyond the footlights, so none of us really knew where our mothers were sitting. Afterward they would come backstage to congratulate us, but my mother had to skip that and run for her bus. Sometimes one of the kids would say, "How did you know your mother was there if you didn't see her?"

"She was there," I would answer. "I could feel it."

Then one afternoon, my homeroom teacher came to me at the end of a play and said, "Oh, Phyllis, I just met your mother on her way out. She said to give you a big hug." With that, she hugged me right in front of everybody. Never again did anyone ask me how I knew my mother was in the audience.

When it comes to love, we don't always have to see it. We can feel it. We just know it's there — like knowing God is there.

We thank You, Father, for Your constant presence in our lives. Amen.
                                                              — Phyllis Hobe

---

POINT OF LIGHT

STAY THY HEART ON ME

I am the God of the stars,
They do not lose their way,
Not one do I mislay,
Their times are in My hand,
They move at My command.

I am the God of the stars,
Today as yesterday,
The God of thee and thine,
Less thine they are than Mine;
And shall Mine go astray?

I am the God of the stars,
Lift up thine eyes and see
As far as mortal may
Into Eternity;
And stay thy heart on Me.
                                    —Amy Carmichael

---

16 | THU

Ye shall be witnesses unto me….   —Acts 1:8

A friend, Carol Gipson, told me a story recently about her father and a German business colleague. Over years of association, the two men formed a deep friendship. One day Carol's father was shocked by a call from his friend. He was dying and had a final request. "I can't be there for my daughter's graduation," he said. "Will you stand in for me?" On graduation day in Germany, the daughter looked into the parents' section, and there Carol's father stood, cheering for her.

Stand in for Me. That is what Jesus asked His disciples to do just before He ascended into heaven. *I am going to My Father in heaven.*

Be My witnesses. Your hands must take the place of My hands. Your feet must carry you where I would go. Your voice must say the words that I would say. Stand in for Me.

Today, I am privileged to stand in for Jesus right where I am. He summons me to collect the names of poor children at a nearby rural school. He is risen, but I know perfectly well what He would do — see that they receive needed clothes and shoes and school supplies. Jesus welcomed the homeless; my church offers a place for them to sleep in safety and warmth. I have the honor to stand in for Him, welcoming them, serving them dinner, providing clean linens for their bed.

On this Ascension Day, Jesus' invitation comes again to each of us. Do My work. Feed the hungry. Welcome the stranger. Care for the sick. Love each other as I have loved you. Forgive seventy times seven. *Stand in for Me!*

I want to represent You, Jesus, and make You proud. Point the way!
                                                    — Pam Kidd

17 | F R I | *"But when you pray, go away by yourself, all alone, and shut the door behind you and pray to your Father secretly, and your Father, who knows your secrets, will reward you."*
                                        — Matthew 6:6 (TLB)

It's seven o'clock on a May morning, seventy degrees in Oak Creek, Wisconsin. I'm sitting in a very comfortable yellow rocker on my deck with a large mug of Earl Grey tea. Two squirrels are dining on the ear of corn attached to the "squirrel diner" at the end of the deck, and a dozen birds are singing their way through breakfast, also provided by the management.

This deck is my place and time for prayer. No newspapers, books, people or phone calls. Just me, the birds, squirrels and God.

Morning prayers were part of my life as a child. From first through twelfth grades, the Sisters of Loretto orchestrated morning prayers at school. But then in college and into marriage and motherhood, my morning prayers fell by the wayside. Twenty-five years passed.

Then one spring, I discovered how quiet and peaceful it was on my deck in the early morning, and I began to pray. I thanked God for this place of beauty and this hour of quiet and for this wonderful chair I found at a yard sale. I praised Him for the trees … and asked Him for many favors.

Do you have a specific place and a definite time for morning prayer? Believe me, it's an amazing way to start your day. It calms you, keeps your life focused, reminds you of what's truly important and begins each day on a positive, happy note. Promise yourself thirty minutes alone in your favorite spot every morning. Bring a cup of tea or coffee and perhaps the book of Psalms to get you started.

Today, Lord, bless this place and time that I've set aside to be with You. And bless all those I pray for in my yellow chair on the deck.
— Patricia Lorenz

18 | S A T | *Taking the five loaves and the two fish he looked up to heaven, and blessed, and broke and gave the loaves ... to the crowds. And they all ate and were satisfied. And they took up twelve baskets full of the broken pieces left over.*
— Matthew 14:19–20 (RSV)

When my children were younger, I often worried about the permanent effects our near-poverty might have on them. My daughter Heather remembers being forced to sit alone in a classroom because she didn't have enough money to buy pizza with her classmates. I remember her cutting the labels off her friend's cast-off Keds and gluing them onto the heels of her cheap imitations. She also remembers missing social events because my illness or work prevented my driving her to them. All I could do was pray for God's blessing on my children, and that He would keep all of us from bitterness.

This past Mother's Day, I began to see how God was answering my prayer. The first evidence was a lovely bouquet from Heather, who was away at college. It spoke to me of her love and understanding. The other, oddly, was a bill that arrived the same day. It was Heather's monthly reminder from an international charity. *How can she afford to do this,* I wondered, *when she needs every penny she earns for school?*

It was then I realized that her painful memories had not been a burden but a blessing! Hard times had taught my daughter the joy of giving to someone less fortunate than herself! I forwarded her bill, grateful that my children were turning out fine. Exceptional, in fact. And I breathed a prayer of gratitude.

Dear God, thank You for all of the abundance You bring when we trust You to turn our very little into so very much.
— Brenda Wilbee

19 | S U N | *We shall be satisfied with the goodness of thy house, thy holy temple!* —Psalm 65:4 (RSV)

I confess. I've been known to miss church on occasion due to: (a) sleeping in; (b) watching football play-offs on TV; (c) just not feeling like it.

I used to think it didn't really matter if I skipped now and then, but this year I'm in the grip of an attitude adjustment for two reasons. First, I heard a grandmotherly pillar of the congregation say, "I don't always feel like being in church either, but on those days I go anyway as an encouragement to the pastor and the others who attend. I never know, until I get there, how I might be needed." One Sunday I was able to welcome someone I knew who had never come before. On other occasions troubled friends have needed a listening ear or a prayer together after the service.

Secondly, I'm rethinking my commitment to being in church because of the mixed message I'm sending my kids. Now that my son Phil is out on his own, his attendance Sunday mornings is less than spectacular. Why? Because he is often sleeping in...just like his mom.

And if these two considerations fail to motivate me, there's a third. God has opened the doors to His house, and especially invited me to come in and commune with Him. Sure, there's a football game on, but the most it can offer is a few hours of fleeting entertainment. What God has to offer lasts a lifetime.

> *Every week You are there, Lord, ready to greet me.*
> *Surely, that is me, Lord, running to meet Thee.*
> —Carol Knapp

20 | M O N | *Thou holdest fast my name....* —Revelation 2:13

I'll have to admit at the beginning of May I was suffering from chronic "big head disease." I was the only one of my close friends who was graduating from the University of Tennessee within four years' time. I took the opportunity to rub it in as often as possible. But all of that changed five days before graduation.

"Brock, I've been trying to call you," my adviser said, worried. "There's been a goof-up. You're two hours short of meeting graduation requirements."

"What? How could this possibly happen?"

"Listen, I'm going to meet with the department head and see if we can work something out. Just wait for my call."

Back in my room, I called my parents. "There's nothing you can do until your adviser calls back," my father said. "We'll be praying for you." I hung up the phone feeling a little better.

Then my adviser called. "Our only hope is last summer's internship. If you could write a paper relating it to your major, there's a possibility the university will give you the hours you need."

For two days I lived in the library. The only breaks I took were to eat and to update my family. "You're going to make it, Brock!" my sister Keri said.

On the eve of graduation, the call came. "Congratulations, Brock. You did it." I never felt so relieved. I made the call to my family.

"We're packed and ready," they laughed.

The next morning in cap and gown, I walked into Thompson Boling Arena. Sure, I worked for this day, but it was a caring adviser, a supportive family and, most important, a God Who answers prayers that finally got me here.

Through my foolishness, through hard times, hold my name close, Lord. Never let me go.   — Brock Kidd

21 | T U E *Walk humbly with your God.*   — Micah 6:8 (NIV)

I had circled around the mall food court a third time when my friend Barb rushed in the door. "Sorry, I can't walk today. Got called in to work." We agreed to walk Thursday, and she raced out.

Disappointed, I plodded along the mall. Ahead of me, two moms chatted behind strollers. An older couple passed me, engaged in animated discussion. Longing to talk with someone, I thought, *It's so hard to do this stint alone!* I even envied a woman sporting headphones, singing along with her unseen companion. *Oh, I wish I had a tape player!*

Wait. Why couldn't I walk with my unseen Friend today? Pumping my way past store after store, I "talked" a steady stream of concerns to God. I confided my sadness about my sister Carol's battle with lupus and asked for her healing. Even when things like the aroma of freshly baked cinnamon rolls coming from the bakery interrupted, I used the distraction: "Lord, You know I'm worried about the weight I'm gaining with this pregnancy. Guide me in my eating."

Thursday, Barb was back. "Sorry you had to walk alone on Tuesday," she apologized.

I didn't set her straight. I just smiled.

Lord, it is so good to walk—and talk—with You in a very special way. Every day.   — Mary Brown

22 | W E D   *...God, namely, Christ, in whom are hidden all the treasures of wisdom and knowledge.*
— Colossians 2:2–3 (NIV)

The mailbox is full. Very full. But I'm used to it. What else can I expect since I began sharing it with a turtle?

Not just any turtle, of course. I am partners with Wally the Turtle, the wise, advice-giving reptile who writes an advice column for the magazine I edit, *Guideposts for Kids*. Admittedly, he gets a lot of help from me and my staff. And, in an odd way, I get a lot of help from him.

Today's mail is the usual, poignant, problem-filled narratives: "I don't like spinach, but my mom puts it in lasagna!" "My pastor at my church committed suicide." "My best friend in the whole galaxy is having trouble; her dad isn't living with her mom anymore." "I just moved into this new neighborhood and everybody calls me names." "My dad just lost his job." "I might have to get braces — and that means NO MORE GUM!"

Problems. Everyone has them, even children. And their problems are just as big, just as important, just as daunting as any I am facing today. Yet in their letters I sense not despair, but rather expectation. They believe Wally the Turtle can help them. They expect things to get better. They are waiting by the mailbox for his answer.

I bow my head over the stack of letters, humbled and strengthened by the courage of these kids. I go to my Divine Advice Giver — taking a few problems of my own. Asking for His wisdom. Believing the answer is on the way. Then I pick up my green pen ... and Wally begins to write.

You, O God, are the Source of all solutions — whether we're eight or eighty-eight. Thanks a lot!   — Mary Lou Carney

23 | T H U | *The word is very near to you; it is in your mouth and in your heart for you to observe.*
—Deuteronomy 30:14 (NRSV)

Long before I was a medical student, I was one of those "Bible whiz kids" who memorized so much Scripture that I won every contest I entered. When I went to medical school, though, I turned my back on God. Faith in God didn't make sense in a world where innocent little children died of diseases they were too young to pronounce. By the time I became a doctor, my head was crammed full of the Krebs cycle and other things that were supposed to save lives. I put away the Bible, and I put away my feelings as well.

But the day finally came when the things my head could not comprehend came spilling out of my heart. One day I had no words of consolation to offer a family, so I sat quietly with them at the bedside of their dying child. It was in that quiet of my heart that I heard it—the Word—in *my* heart, so near: *Let not your hearts be troubled. My peace I give to you, not as the world gives* (John 14:1; 14:27). God had never removed His Word from my heart. It was all there, stored up for the time when I could hear with more than my ears.

Today I go through the Bible and note the hundreds of verses I learned as a child. I write them on cards to refresh my memory. And then I sit back—and listen.

Let me never be too old to hear Your Word, God, and store it in my heart.
—Diane Komp

24 | F R I | *Who through faith... out of weakness were made strong....*
—Hebrews 11:33–34

I was in my early teens before I knew about one of my imperfections. I'd just appeared in a school play and believed I'd done pretty well because several people said so. That included one woman who told my mother authoritatively that I showed great potential as an actor, but, of course, something would have to be done about "his lisp."

There are two things I'd never thought about: (1) becoming an actor; (2) my having a lisp. Nobody had mentioned it to me before. But from then on I was always aware of it. I tried to make fun of it, taking derisive pleasure in telling friends, "I lithp exthept when I thay Ithaca," or laboring for hours on making a translation of the

Gettysburg Address without the letter *s* (don't try it). In our daily chapel at school, I'd often ask God to do something about it. The best He seemed to do was to have people tell me they hardly noticed it. I didn't believe them.

God did do something, however. Some years ago, forced to make a speech I'd tried to avoid, I began my talk with an attempt to disarm my listeners by saying, "The terrible thing about a lisp is you can't *say* it without *doing* it." Later, a man came up to me — I still don't know who he was — and said, "You haven't accepted that lisp of yours, have you?"

I was so surprised by his directness that I could only nod. "A wise man once told me," he went on, "if you accept your limitations, you go beyond them. Think about it."

Think about it I did.

So today, if there's anybody reading this who'd like me to come and speak, I'm available. But fair warning: You, too, will have to accept my limitations.

Forgive me for bothering You about that speech problem, Lord. It seemed important at the time.   — Van Varner

25 | S A T   *We all come in the unity of the faith....*
                    — Ephesians 4:13

I am interested in the spiritual beliefs of everyone, because I want to know how other children of God reverence Him. Over the years I've worshiped in churches of many denominations and have never found the name on the door to be a deterrent to prayer or my worship of God.

I shared my feelings once with the late Bob Benson, a publisher, writer and speaker out of Nashville. He was as proud of his Nazarene roots as one of my old United Brethren friends who used to joke, "When we get to heaven, we will all be united brethren."

Bob was a great storyteller. One of my favorites was about a Sunday school picnic he attended as a kid. Bob recalled arriving late with a dried-up piece of baloney between two stale pieces of bread. He sat down at a table covered with all kinds of delicacies — Southern fried chicken, baked beans, potato salad, homemade pies. Self-consciously, he unwrapped his sandwich. And then the mother of a large family saw him and suggested he join them. "Let's put everything together and share," she said. Bob protested, but only half-heartedly, and in a minute, he later said, he understood what the miracle of loaves and fishes was all about. His baloney sandwich had been transformed into a feast.

God promises a feast for all who come to His table, too. He doesn't ask for our denomination or our attendance records or character references. Only that we come seeking forgiveness. His grace does the rest.

> *Teach me, God, Your heavenly art*
> *Of listening to others with my heart.*
>
> —Fred Bauer

26 | S U N   *They saw what seemed to be tongues of fire that separated and came to rest on each of them.*
—Acts 2:3 (NIV)

Do you know why the color red has special significance on Pentecost Sunday?

Last year, when my husband Lynn and I were on a business trip in Pennsylvania, we went to a Presbyterian church in Harrisburg on Pentecost Sunday. There we learned about the color red when the assistant pastor, wearing a bright red dress, gave the children's sermon.

"I always wear red when I need to feel brave," she told the children. "Red reminds me of Pentecost, which is the anniversary of the day when God sent His Holy Spirit to live within the disciples who were feeling afraid about what might happen since Jesus had left them and gone to heaven. The coming of the Holy Spirit was made more real that day by the appearance of bright red flames of fire that seemed to touch each person.

"When the Holy Spirit came to dwell within the disciples, they grew braver and went out and told others about Jesus. Today, the color red reminds us of those flames that announced the coming of the Holy Spirit Who lives within you and me and gives us courage when we feel afraid. So that's why I wear red when I need to feel brave."

I carried her words all the way back to Colorado with me, and intentionally added some splotches of red to my life as reminders of God's presence through the Holy Spirit. I purchased a pot of bright red geraniums for our front porch. And when one of our children faced a tough new challenge, I purchased a red leather journal "to give you confidence in God's indwelling presence as you write down your thoughts and prayers."

Father, now when I see the color red, I remember that we live on this side of Pentecost and are indwelt with Your courage-giving presence through the Holy Spirit. Thank You.   — Carol Kuykendall

27 | M O N | *A man who has friends must himself be friendly....*
— Proverbs 18:24 (NKJV)

I was feeling sorry for myself the other day, so I went down the hill for a walk in the meadow. *I wish someone would call and invite us over for dinner, or just for an evening of conversation,* I thought. We had just moved to Colorado — our fourth move in seven years, and I was longing for someone to talk to. *I'd enjoy getting to know Ann better, that woman I talked with at church the other night.* But having done this moving stuff before, I knew that most people here probably already had their quota of friends.

My wandering brought me to a sunny place near the juniper trees. As I watched the wildflowers waving in the warm summer breeze, I was remembering a vase of flowers offered in friendship after another move. We had just come to Tanzania, and a few days later I met Meredith, a young missionary wife, who appeared on my doorstep, her two toddlers in tow, and handed me a small vase of flowers. "I'd like to be your friend," she said. And she was.

Well, shoot, I thought, *what am I waiting for? Why can't I take the initiative, even if I am the new person? Maybe I'll give Ann a call and see what she's doing for lunch?*

Heading back up the hill, I stopped to pick a handful of bright yellow sunflowers — a lovely bouquet for a new friend.

Thank You, Father, for faithful old friends. Give me courage and confidence to reach out to new friends.   — Mary Jane Clark

28 | T U E | *"You have told many a troubled soul to trust in God and have encouraged those who are weak or falling, or lie crushed upon the ground or are tempted to despair."*
— Job 4:3–4 (TLB)

For several years, I'd felt the need for an advanced degree. As director of a ministry for Mexican Americans in southwest Kansas, I raise funds, oversee a medical clinic and social service programs, work with churches and a board of directors, and make certain the agency meets requirements of state regulatory agencies and private funders. The job is complex, and I knew further education would help me do it better.

After considerable thought and prayer, I enrolled in a Master of Science program. After the second class period, though, I was ready to quit. "I can't do it!" I wailed to my friend Glenda. "I have to read a hundred forty pages, write a five-page paper and do a survey of my workplace — all before Wednesday night! I can't handle two years of this!"

"You can't quit," she said matter-of-factly. "I've already bought a card for your graduation."

I didn't quit, and every step of the way I was helped by friends, family, classmates and instructors. Virginia shared her notes when I missed two classes following Mother's death. Jerie explained residual profits and transfer pricing in words I could understand. Dr. Friesen let me postpone the completion date on my thesis when my computer crashed. My husband Don ate frozen dinners without complaining...much. And when I was really discouraged, Glenda reminded me about the card.

The card finally arrived—after I received a master's degree in business management in May 1994, an accomplishment made possible because others believed I could succeed. Their words and acts of encouragement have nudged me to strive for another goal: "Master of Encouragement." This time around, it shouldn't be too difficult. After all, look at my teachers.

Lord Jesus, thank You for the encouragement I've received from others and from You. Keep me ever ready to pass that encouragement on to others.   —Penney Schwab

29 | W E D   *We are more than conquerors through him that loved us.*
                                              —Romans 8:37

As I left the dentist's office, the receptionist asked me how things were going. "Pretty well," I said, "under the circumstances."

Actually, those circumstances were awful. Our basement had recently flooded, the car had broken down, our school taxes were being raised again, and I'd just spent four hours in the dentist's chair. But as I walked to my car that day I met my friend Josephine Burchell — and began to change my attitude about circumstances.

Josephine lives alone. She has no phone and no automobile. She walks to church, to the grocery store, to her job. She takes much pride in her work as a draftsperson for a local surveyor. During the recent recession she was laid off from work, but she appeared at the surveyor's office building anyhow to rake leaves.

"A wonderful thing just happened to me," Josephine said. Her unemployment checks had run out, and she had been preparing to move from her small apartment near the railroad station. "My landlord lowered my rent. I hadn't said one word to him, either."

I've never known Josephine to complain about her life; she's too busy finding things to be grateful for. I am certain that such an attitude comes from her faith. She doesn't talk a lot about her beliefs. It just shows in the way she walks, as if she can't wait to get where she's going, and in her smile, and in the volunteer work she does at church and around town.

Josephine doesn't live "under" her circumstances, but "over" them. Her trick is gratitude, and that morning I began trying to apply the art. Our basement flooded, but only some old newspapers were ruined. Our car broke down, but the mechanic came late at night to help us. I'd spent hours at the dentist, but I didn't lose a single tooth. There's always much to be thankful for, and that, I am sure, is Josephine's secret for living *over* the circumstances.

Lord, help me to see each tough patch of my life as one more opportunity to become a conqueror of circumstances.

—John Sherrill

30 | T H U *Put on a heart of compassion....*
—Colossians 3:12 (NAS)

When my younger brother Dexter went off to Vietnam in 1969, I was newly married and living far away from my family. And far away from knowing how he felt about going off to war. During our childhood, he always seemed invincible and fearless. His idea of fun was jumping off a seventy-five-foot cliff into the ocean or wrestling a bear at a sideshow when a traveling circus came through town. So I assumed he approached this challenge with a similar attitude of confidence that he would survive. I was thankful he did. He returned home, married and had three daughters. Life has moved so far beyond that war that at our noisy family gatherings, no one mentions it.

But, recently, I started wondering about the feelings of a young soldier going off to war. So I dug out some of Dexter's letters from Vietnam, which my mother had copied and sent to each member of the family.

"I pray a lot now," he wrote. "Sometimes I wake up in the middle of the night. I hear the sounds of mortar shells in the distance. I think to myself that they could well be landing around me. The thought of death being near is terrifying."

He described other hardships, such as sleeping in a mud puddle with huge red ants crawling all over him, or growing delirious from dehydration while on ambush patrol in the scorching sun.

As I read these letters now, I realize that I never acknowledged Dexter's fears. Worse yet, I never acknowledged his sacrifices or even said a simple "thank you." For as awful and confusing as war is in our imperfect world, I enjoy freedom in America today because of soldiers like my brother. So, on this Memorial Day, I'm going to write him an overdue thank-you note, because this holiday honors not only the Americans who sacrificed their lives for their country, but also those who sacrificed their comfort and safety.

Do you know a living veteran you can thank?

Father, I thank You for soldiers like my brother who know what it means to make sacrifices.   — Carol Kuykendall

31 | F R I | *I thank my God every time I remember....*
                                     — Philippians 1:3 (NIV)

Lately, I have been reading about people who have had near-death experiences, and I must admit that I feel envious, almost cheated. You see, when I was seventeen years old, I had open-heart surgery. I had been born with a hole in my heart, and it wasn't discovered until I started college.

But with my experience, I hadn't seen any angels or heard any harp music. All I had seen was Dr. Torres, who explained to me what the operation would entail. My boyfriend at the time came to visit me at the hospital every single day; so did my closest girlfriend and my mother. Six girls from a school club that I belonged to had taken the club dues and, instead of going out for a big lunch, bought me a delicate gold locket with "Love" engraved on the back. And while I got cards from friends of mine, I still remember how touched I was when a girlfriend's parents — I'd met them only once and was surprised that they even remembered me — sent me a get-well card signed "Fondly," with their names.

A friend whom I related this to just chuckled. "Sounds like you had something better than a near-death experience. You had an open-heart experience. You got to see that you had friends who cared enough to send you cards and come to see you, relatives who rallied around you, and a caring doctor who took the time to explain every-thing to a frightened seventeen-year-old girl."

After a moment, I touched my friend's hand. "And I have a friend who cares enough to remind me to focus on what's important in life — my blessings!"

Dear God, today let me open my heart to the blessings I have all around me—for those who show me they care for me are surely the "heart" of life.   — Linda Neukrug

GIFTS OF LIGHT

1 _____

2 _____

3 _____

4 _____

5 _____

6 _____

7 _____

8 _____

9 _____

10 _____

11 _____

12 _____

13 _____

14 _____

15 _____

16 _____

17 _____

18 _____

19 _____

20 _____

21 _____

22 _____

23 _____

24 _____

25 _____

26 _____

27 _____

28 _____

29 _____

30 _____

31 _____

J U N E

The Lord is God, and he has given us light....

—PSALM 118:27 (RSV)

	S	M	T	W	T	F	S
							1
	2	3	4	5	6	7	8
	9	10	11	12	13	14	15
	16	17	18	19	20	21	22
	23	24	25	26	27	28	29
	30						

1 | S A T

Light rises in the darkness for the upright....
            —Psalm 112:4 (RSV)

My husband and I live in a split-level home in upstate New York. It's modern and very comfortable, and yet there is something about our house that I miss: a front porch.

I think often of the Ohio farmhouse where I grew up. It was built in 1907 and had a generous veranda with doors that opened out to it from the living room and the dining room. After a rough day of work, our farm family would go there to sit and relax. There was no television then, so we'd talk, which drew us closer together, I think. We felt closer to our neighbors, too—less shut off—as we waved to them when they passed by on our county line road.

The front porch was a place for the casual airing of the day's little problems and for praying out loud to God the way we did when Grandpa Harman was so ill. For me, as a teenage dreamer, it always had its moments of enchantment, especially in the quiet of a cool June night. I can picture us there now, my dad sitting on the porch steps, Mother in her wicker rocker, my brothers swaying back and forth on the old creaky swing. The long twilight fades, the night takes over, and the fireflies rise up out of the wheat fields.

"Fireflies," I say dreamily, "are like little messengers of light."

My mother nods. "Perhaps so," she says, "but wouldn't it be nice if they were prayers, just like the ones I say for you, all lit up for God to see?"

Tonight in upstate New York, I recall these fanciful things because this is a June evening and the fireflies are out just as they were back in Ohio. But, truth to tell, I miss a front porch.

Things change, I know, Lord, but thank You for the richness of memory.
            —Susan Schefflein

2 | S U N

Blessed is the man who refuses to work during my Sabbath days of rest, but honors them....   —Isaiah 56:2 (TLB)

Two summers ago I contracted to write a book for teachers about how to teach well. School over, I plunged into writing without taking any time to recuperate from the classroom. I worked feverishly. Two weeks later I had finished all of two pages. I broke pencils, kicked the wastebasket, and my eyes were popping out of my head. "I'm not getting anywhere," I confided to my wife Sharon one day. "I know my topic well, I just can't seem to say it."

"Okay," she fired back, her red hair flashing. She had seen me struggle long enough. "That's it! We are going on vacation."

"What? How is vacation going to get this book done?"

Nevertheless we went, spending a budget week in Bardstown, Kentucky, doing less than nothing. We sat in front of our motel, reading magazines. I rode a bike around shady streets, stopping to admire flowers and talk to children. One night we enjoyed the Stephen Foster play, then snacked ourselves to sleep, watching the late shows. No itinerary. No goals. We just did what we felt like doing or did nothing at all.

Back home in Missouri, rested and relaxed, I wrote four chapters in four days, and finished the book ahead of schedule!

Rest. What an amazing cure for what ails you! I wonder if many of the problems of our world could be caused by tired people who just will not take time off. Even God, Who never tires, rested on the seventh day after creation (Genesis 2:3).

So my wife was right. And if you know what's good for you, you will listen to her, too. Can't possibly take a day off? That's a sure sign you need one.

Lord, I try to do too much. Help me to remember that sometimes doing a little is more than enough.   —Daniel Schantz

3 | M O N   *Lord, how oft shall my brother sin against me, and I forgive him?...*   —Matthew 18:21

The manager of the supermarket around the corner drew me aside and with accusing eyes said, "I expect you to pay for the milk you stole."

"Stole?"

"We caught you on camera."

Slowly, it came to me what he was talking about: the quart of milk I'd purchased last week. When I discovered it was sour, I returned it to the store, told the Spanish-speaking clerk about it, then went back to the refrigerator and exchanged it for a fresh quart.

"Didn't the clerk tell you that the milk I'd bought was sour?" Apparently not. Perhaps she had misunderstood my English? As the manager shrugged his shoulders, my temper flared. I sputtered out a series of righteous protestations, paid for the milk and left.

Then the boycott began. From that time on I'd walk four blocks farther to a store where I wasn't known as a shoplifter, a thief. The hurt of being falsely accused was too great to face — until the day I told my goddaughter about the experience.

"Why didn't you shop there again?" Valerie asked. "You were innocent. Why didn't you act like it?"

That was several months ago. Today, because Valerie's kids are dropping by for a visit, I've just returned from the corner store with a box of Popsicles. The manager was there, but the accusation in his eyes has disappeared. I myself can't forget what happened between us, but I no longer hold it against him. So I have learned something about allowing for the human failings in others — and how much better it can feel to forgive than to be forgiven.

Father, help me to walk with the dignity that You have made my inheritance, if I will but claim it.

— Van Varner

4 | T U E *When you call, the Lord will answer. "Yes, I am here," he will quickly reply....*   — Isaiah 58:9 (TLB)

It was one of those months when Murphy's Law prevailed in my household. The TV and stereo both broke within two days of each other. Before I could take them in to the repair shop, my computer died. Two of my children were sick, and when I tried to go for medicine the garage door broke. Then a friend called in tears to say her father had died unexpectedly.

"God, why? How can You dump so much on us at once?" I asked. I felt my faith wavering.

The next day a friend at the radio station where I was copywriter dropped a piece of paper on my desk. It said:

> God is like Ford® — He has a better idea.
> God is like Coke® — He's the real thing.
> God is like Pan Am® — He makes the going great.
> God is like Alka-Seltzer® — Try Him, you'll like Him.
> God is like Bayer aspirin® — He takes the pain away.
> God is like Tide® — He gets out the stains that others leave behind.
> God is like Frosted Flakes® — He's grrreat!
> God is like Hallmark Cards® — He cared enough to send the very best!

My friend's list changed my thinking and lifted my spirits. Soon I decided I could be a little more like Timex®: Take a lickin' and keep on tickin'.

Lord, when things go wrong and stress piles up, help me to remember: You love me, no matter what!   — Patricia Lorenz

5 | W E D   *...Upholding the universe by his word of power....*
                                        — Hebrews 1:3 (RSV)

Some of us were sitting on the beach in a happy seaside trance, watching the waves roll in. One of the older grandchildren, an eager student of high school science, was not above demonstrating his new-found knowledge from time to time.

"Look at all that water," he said. "Millions and trillions and zillions of gallons. Hundreds of thousands of square miles. How can it possibly stay in one place? The earth is whizzing around the sun. It's spinning on its own axis at a thousand miles an hour. Why doesn't all that water just fly off into space, or maybe roll up this beach and drown us?"

I think perhaps he planned to answer his own questions with a lecture on the mysteries of gravity, but he never got a chance because his four-year-old cousin looked up from a sand castle she was building. "Because God won't let it," she said serenely.

And that took care of that.

Father, thank You for the protection You have built into the scheme of things for us, Your children.   — Arthur Gordon

6 | T H U   *Lay up for yourselves treasures in heaven....*
                                        — Matthew 6:20

At breakfast, I pore over my *Wall Street Journal*. "How are your stocks today, Brock?" my mother asks.

"Great! Just think, Mom, if I work hard and invest wisely, in about ten years my portfolio will be worth a fortune. You'll be the first one to ride in my new Mercedes."

My mom has heard all of this before. "*Mmm*" is her response as she wipes the crumbs from the counter. Stocks and bonds, the highs and lows of the market have been a passion of mine since high school. Mom knows that all too well. Now she's smiling her secret smile....

Later that day, Mom, my sister Keri, and I are at the mall. I'm chattering away about options and futures and how my portfolio will someday be in *Investment Business Daily*. All of a sudden, a boy who has to be six feet six inches walks up to us. "Hello, Mrs. Kidd!" the boy grins.

"Hi, Bo!" my mom replies. She asks about his mother, his math grades and basketball camp. Before he leaves us, Bo bends over and hugs Mom, practically lifting her off the ground.

"Mom, who was that?" I had never seen the boy before and was a little confused. "How do you know him?"

My mother was answering, "Oh, just a friend..." when Keri interjected, "Brock, you know, he's the one I told you about. Mom was tutoring him and found out he didn't have the money to go to that camp last summer, so she and Dad paid. But it's kind of a secret. She bought his high school yearbook, too."

My parents will never get ahead financially, I thought. "Mom, how could you afford the extra expense?"

My mother looked at me, smiled her wonderful smile and said, "Don't you see, Brock? I have my own portfolio. It's just that your dad and I sort of lean toward people investments."

I had to laugh at myself then. Mom had just handed me the investment tip of a lifetime.

Lord, help me to remember the investment You have made in each of us, so that I won't forget to reinvest in others.   — Brock Kidd

7 | F R I   *Thy sins be forgiven thee.*   — Matthew 9:2

I must have been seven or eight when I knocked my father's expensive camera off the table in his "off-limits" basement darkroom. When I picked up the camera, the lens fell to pieces. *Uh-oh! What in the world am I going to do?* I was scared to death of my father's loud voice and angry words, but most of all, I was afraid of losing his love. I decided not to tell him.

That night I prayed, "God, please don't let Daddy find out I broke his camera." It didn't help a bit. I still felt like a terrible child. Then God's answer came with the urgent thought: *Go tell him.* I fought it as long as I could, but then I forced myself to get up. Daddy was sitting in his big chair by the fireplace reading a book. When he finally looked up, my knees were shaking and tears were running down my face. "I broke your camera!" I blurted.

He stared at me, then lectured me about disobeying him and grounded me for the weekend. Next, he did a surprising thing. He reached into his pocket and handed me a nickel (a fortune to a child in the thirties) and said, "This is for telling the truth." Then Daddy lifted me into his lap and held me tight until I fell asleep in his arms.

Even now, whenever I feel guilty, I think of that nickel, that soft lap, those loving arms. And I remember that when I confess my faults to my heavenly Father, He also rewards me — not with nickels, but with a peaceful heart and His loving arms.

Loving Father, please forgive me for _____.
—Marilyn Morgan Helleberg

8 | S A T   *It is good to be zealously affected always in a good thing....*
—Galatians 4:18

The plan was a family trip down the shore for the afternoon. Eighty degrees. Suntan lotion. Picnic lunch. But I do not like sitting in the sun. It hurts my eyes when I try to read. It burns my skin.

"Roe," I called to my wife as I began walking out the door, "I'm going to see if I can buy a beach umbrella." At the third store I went to, I finally found the umbrella at the price I liked—one with blue and yellow fish. When I returned to the house, everyone was ready to pack the car and be off.

An hour and a half later Roe and the children were carrying towels, buckets, blankets and picnic cooler along the hot sand. I carried my blue and yellow umbrella. I dug a deep hole, jammed the umbrella rod into the ground and packed the sand around the base. Then I sat in the shade with my newspaper, prepared to enjoy the next few hours reading. But the problem with the New Jersey shore in early summer is the wind.

Suddenly, the wind lifted the umbrella out from the hole and carried it off several yards down the beach, while I ran to catch up with it. The children laughed and laughed. I did a little dance with it, and they laughed some more. I held the umbrella high over my head and asked them to follow close behind as we played "Follow the Leader." Over the dunes, around the snack stand, into the waves they followed me and my umbrella, still laughing.

That night, after the children were asleep and Roe and I were in bed, I whispered, "Great umbrella."

How wonderful to find something bright to liven up our world a bit, even a blue and yellow umbrella.

Thanks for the reminder, Lord, to have fun and to enjoy our days.
— Christopher de Vinck

9 | S U N   *We are fools for Christ's sake....*
— I Corinthians 4:10 (NAS)

It's Sunday morning and I'm sitting on an old tub in the furnace room of our church, wearing an orange and purple clown suit. I am to make a surprise appearance in the sanctuary to promote Vacation Bible School. This is my very first time at clowning, and I am struggling with stage fright. My bifocals are steaming up under my plastic mask, the ends of my yarn wig are scratching my neck, and perspiration is dampening my striped socks and polka-dotted shoes.

But what is worse is the niggling question about propriety: Will a middle-aged deacon's wife who dares to breach long-established ideas of decorum in our conservative church alienate the very people she hopes to reach?

Filtering down through the air duct comes the hymn "Take Time to Be Holy." By no stretch of the imagination can I expect certain church members to equate a ridiculous clown with holiness.

But wait! There are words in that hymn I have never really heard before: "Make friends of God's children." Isn't that what I intend to do by pantomiming in my colorful costume while the minister introduces me as Rosco, the Vacation Bible School mascot? Saying a quick prayer, I gather my props, adjust my huge bow tie and waddle up the stairs into the sanctuary.

For a moment the congregation is silent. Then, one by one, wide-eyed children begin to giggle and somber adults cannot suppress amused grins. At the suggestion that perhaps nobody has time for Vacation Bible School, Rosco cries with disappointment, dabbing at his eyes with a huge, red handkerchief. "So who will come and make Rosco happy?" asks the minister. Much to my surprise, everybody in the congregation raises a hand, and Rosco merrily exits, stage right.

Father, give me courage to use new and creative ways to attract people to You.
— Alma Barkman

10 | M O N *Therefore let us leave the elementary teachings about*
          Christ and go on to maturity....   —Hebrews 6:1 (NIV)

"Mom, would you and Dad mind if a few friends road-tripped home
to Boulder with me for a kind of final celebration together?" Derek
asked in a phone call about two weeks before his college graduation.

"Sounds great!" I said enthusiastically, because we've always
welcomed the opportunity to meet our kids' friends. "How many is
a few?"

"I think we're up to about twelve," he said.

Over the next several days, my enthusiasm began to wilt as I considered the scenario: me, a person who likes regular routines and
clean kitchen counters, hosting a dozen new members of the
"twentysomething generation," known for their resistance to the
responsibilities of growing up. How would this work?

They began arriving on a Wednesday with their sleeping bags and
backpacks. I tried to memorize names while telling myself not to get
uptight about the piles of clutter around the house. By Friday morning, I could hardly find space at the kitchen counter to read the newspaper, and the family room was littered with bodies everywhere.

For the next several days, these young men climbed mountains,
ate trillions of tortilla chips, played cards and sat up late into the
night, talking about their futures. One was headed to Mexico to help
people with their water purification system. Another was off to
Romania on a mission trip, and two others were going to work with
troubled adolescents in outreach programs. They seemed enor-
mously grateful for the food we served and genuinely interested in
our opinions and activities.

On their last day, they vacuumed, carried out the garbage and even
mowed the lawn before saying good-bye. They left an immaculate
house. No clutter and a clean kitchen counter, except for a thank-
you note I'll always cherish, because it is signed by a bunch of wonderful representatives of the "twentysomething generation."

*Father, in getting to know some of Your "twentysomething
children," I got to know something about stereotypes: They're not
all true. Thank You.*   —Carol Kuykendall

11 | T U E

Since I know it is all for Christ's good, I am quite happy about "the thorn"...for when I am weak, then I am strong.... — II Corinthians 12:10 (TLB)

"It's endometriosis, Fay." The doctor's voice had been kind, but firm. "Pretty far gone. Looks like you need a hysterectomy."

"What other option do I have?" I had asked grimly.

"Pain...increasing pain."

Standing on top of 11,000-foot Mammoth Mountain in the Sierra Nevada, I winced, remembering the doctor's reply. It was pain that had taken me to him in the first place. "I wish we didn't have to go back down," I whispered to my husband John. He knew what I meant, and I felt the strength of his hand covering mine with an understanding squeeze. Going down the mountain meant going in for my scheduled surgery.

Looking around for one last picture-perfect memory to take me through the next few weeks, suddenly I noticed that for all its beauty, nothing was growing on this mountaintop. *Why, if we lived only on the mountaintop experiences of our lives, our souls would be barren!* I thought. It is in the valleys, the deep and low places, that we cultivate understanding, sympathy, kindness, courage and all the sweet fruits of the spirit, which enable us to put our arms around one another and say, "I know because I, too, have walked there."

Standing there on the top of Mammoth Mountain, I felt the quiet assurance of the Holy Spirit, the *One Who walks beside us.* Then, looking down into the valley to which we would soon be descending, I said to John, "Let's go. I'm ready!"

Blessed Holy Spirit, be close to me today. When fear ices my heart and shrouds me in darkness, be my guiding light. — Fay Angus

12 | W E D

"Your heavenly Father knows that you need all these things." — Matthew 6:32 (NAS)

Two years ago, my wife Barbara and I decided that we were in a position to give ourselves a vacation at sea. I cleared three months — June, July and August — in my schedule, we read endless brochures from freighter lines, and finally we decided to travel on a freighter out of one of the Gulf of Mexico ports. We'd touch a part of South America, cross the Atlantic to several ports in South and East Africa, go to Bangkok, Thailand, and several ports in Indonesia, and then come back via the same route to Norfolk, Virginia.

There was one problem. Since the ship carried fewer than twelve passengers, there would be no doctor on board. Consequently, the line required a complete physical and a release from our physicians. My doctors said, "Kenneth, we will not make the decision for you, but at the present time you shouldn't be that far away from good medical facilities." We postponed the trip.

On the afternoon of June 12, I suffered a mild stroke and was placed in the hospital less than ten minutes from our house. A skilled team of physicians and nurses stabilized my condition, did extensive tests and began rehabilitation programs. My neurologist says that I will fully recover the losses the stroke created.

When I was stable enough to reflect on my condition and to be thankful for the wonderful care I was receiving, it suddenly dawned on me. Had we carried through with our freighter plans, on June 12 we would have been halfway between Venezuela and South Africa— more than a week away from a doctor or a hospital.

God really does look out for His children, often when we're not even aware of it. This time His message came to me through my physicians.

Dear God, help me to be more sensitive to all the ways You communicate with me.   — Kenneth Chafin

13 | T H U *MY GIFT TODAY... THE TOTE BAG*

Behold, I will do a new thing....   —Isaiah 43:19

God's gift to me today was originally a gift *from* me, a needlepoint tote bag I made for my mother-in-law. Nothing remarkable, except that I had never before (or since) done anything with a needle. Knitting, embroidery, sewing of any kind in my fingers became a hopeless snarl.

But Mother Sherrill loved handmade things, so when my friend Mavis Hart found me this simple kit, I started in. It was a matter of stitching colored yarns through a plastic webbing of big, kindergarten-size mesh. I labored on it month after month, picturing Mother's surprise when her daughter-in-law presented her with this proof of domestic skills.

It took me three years to complete. And by then tragedy had come to our family. My brilliant mother-in-law, a lecturer and writer, was in an institution, diagnosed with arteriosclerosis, living in an unreachable private world, her memory gone. When her son, my husband John, would fly down to Louisville, Kentucky, to see her, she'd mistake him for the doctor. Family, friends, her long distinguished career, all forgotten.

John took the tote bag to her anyway. "Tib made this for you, Mother," he told her, using my nickname, though of course she wouldn't remember me.

Mother turned the bag over and over in her hands. "Tib made it?" she asked. "But Tib doesn't sew!"

It was a flash of real contact, a momentary connection, brought on no doubt by the shock of the totally unexpected. From that day on, nurses reported, each time a visitor came Mother would hold up the needlepoint bag. "Tib made this!"

Since Mother's death, the bag has hung on a hook in my closet, where it caught my eye this morning. Welcome surprises, it told me. God connects with us through the unexpected, too!

Father, what surprise has Your love in store for me today?

— Elizabeth Sherrill

14 | F R I | *Render therefore to all their dues: tribute to whom tribute is due…honor to whom honor.* — Romans 13:7

I must buy another flag for my car. I miss the one that was tied to the aerial, to beckon me back to my parking place. It made me feel safe, like the big flag that flew over the schoolhouse when I was a little girl — waving encouragement as we came running, afraid we'd be late. And the flag that was always in our classroom, where we pledged allegiance to it every morning, hands over our hearts.

Even when we didn't pay strict attention, it was a wonderful way to start the day. Just to think about God a minute. And to see Old Glory there, proud and strong, weaving its beautiful colors into my being, making me want to sing. And my heart would forever beat a little faster just to watch it going by in a parade.

My children were raised in a time when many people were opposed to some of our government's policies. Some of these protests went too far: Flags were actually burned in the streets and disappeared from some public schools. I protested repeatedly and joined a crusade of other parents to urge schools to continue flying their flags. If children are taught to love their country, then even when they feel a need to protest something, they will do so with respect.

Today, my two grandsons assure me that they do say the Pledge of Allegiance at school.

Let's all fly more flags, not only for holidays and to help find our cars, but to show how grateful we are to live in America.

Dear God, grant our children faith and pride in this wonderful land that You have so richly blessed.   — Marjorie Holmes

15 | S A T | *To him that is joined to all the living there is hope....*
— Ecclesiastes 9:4

For a couple of energetic dogs living in a New York City apartment, Sally Brown, our three-year-old cocker spaniel, and Marty, our two-year-old yellow Lab, are pretty well-mannered. But they can be a handful, and then some.

Taking advantage of the weather one spring Saturday, my wife Julee, Sally, Marty and I piled in a cab and headed up to Central Park. We were stalled in traffic when a horse pulling a carriage full of tourists stepped up and inclined its huge white head to the rear window of our cab. Marty came unstrung, howling and thrashing around the backseat. The terrified cabbie threw us out. I apologized and gave him a generous tip to make amends. He was smiling as we left him.

In the park, we took our eye off Sally just long enough for her to snatch a hot dog out of a little girl's hand. I bought the little girl another hot dog while Julee apologized to the mother. Meanwhile, the little girl gleefully fed her second hot dog to Marty. "She's always been afraid of dogs!" the mother said, laughing.

We then took the dogs to the lake near Bethesda Fountain for some swimming and fetching. That went fine until a wedding party, resplendent in white, came down the path. Naturally, Sally and Marty emerged from the murky waters to investigate the new arrivals and, of course, they had to shake out their sopping coats, splattering the bride and her maids with tiny dots of mud. Out of the corner of my eye, I saw Julee's lips moving in panicky prayer. All was well, though, and Marty and Sally ended up getting their picture taken with the bespattered bride. Somewhere, in some couple's wedding album, are two wet, grinning dogs, delighted to be part of the action.

A smiling cabbie, a slightly braver little girl and an unusual wedding photo — not such a bad afternoon at that. Maybe God was teaching us, slyly using our two gregarious pets, to hone our skills as humans.

I am grateful, Lord, when You reach into my day and train me how to handle life's stickier situations. —Edward Grinnan

16 | S U N | *He shall turn the heart of the fathers to the children, and the heart of the children to their fathers....*
—Malachi 4:6

For Father's Day, I was well prepared to receive the usual silk tie (bought at the store with Mommy's guidance and cash), crayon sketch, pencil holder, clay sculpture and construction paper card. But in addition, Timothy and Willy, at ages four and seven, had another present in mind.

"We're going to give you something special," Willy promised with a big smile at dinner, and Timothy had to be reminded several times to keep it a secret for a few more minutes.

After dinner, I was sent to the bathroom. I was instructed to take a bath and get ready for bed. "Be sure to brush your teeth, Dad," Timothy said. Clean, scrubbed and dry, I sat in bed for fifteen minutes while they read me two of their favorite books. Then they hugged me, kissed me, tucked me in, heard my prayers, sang a good-night song and turned out the lights. "No talking, Dad."

Only when they were safely settled in their room and fast asleep did I rouse myself. "That was a nice present," I whispered to Carol, lest I wake them up.

"They wanted to find the perfect thing," she whispered. "They wanted to give you back some of the good things you give them."

A bath, a good book, a prayer, a song and a hug good-night — the perfect things to be remembered for. How else to honor a father — in earth or in heaven?

Father God, turn our hearts to our children. —Rick Hamlin

17 | M O N | *"His mercy is for those who fear him from generation to generation."* —Luke 1:50 (NRSV)

Some years ago I became interested in my family's history. At times, when I was researching a missing relative, I felt I was participating in a grand mystery story. Other times, as I rummaged through ancient graveyards, it seemed that something dynamic was still happening that had never died.

One year, my travels took me to Colchester, England, from whence came Samuel Pupplett Carr, my great-great-grandfather. In a churchyard close to the family home of the eighteenth century, I found the headstones I sought. Then I asked the vicar of the church what he knew about my ancestors. He invited me into his vestry and showed me a silhouette painted on the wall. "He was one of my predecessors here as vicar, Samuel Pupplett Carr's uncle." The next day he kindly introduced me to one of my distant cousins, also a vicar in Colchester.

A lengthy saga began to unfold. My newfound cousin told me of Flemish Huguenots, exiled during the Reformation for "Gottes Worde," and martyred Quakers. The path then led me back to America and the Indiana cornfields that overshadowed the last resting place of Henry Komp, my other great-great-grandfather. Reading through mid-nineteenth century newspapers from the tiny town, I learned that one of Henry's sons became a circuit-riding preacher.

Not everyone in my generation is a believer. For many years, neither was I. But the heritage is there that we all share, and I've put it together for the rest of them in what I call our "Komp-endium." When they are ready, they can read of the mercies of the Lord in our family from generation to generation.

Do you know who your ancestors are? I would challenge you to do some research. I suspect you, too, will find God's finger traced through your family tree, passing the blessing along from generation to generation.

With those who came before me, I will sing of the mercies of the Lord forever.
—Diane Komp

18 | T U E | *When Jesus looked up and saw a great crowd coming toward him ... he already had in mind what he was going to do.*
—John 6:5–6 (NIV)

Each summer, our Mendenhall Ministries operates a youth leadership development program. Twenty junior-high and high school students are chosen to help run recreation and enrichment activities for children ages three to twelve who come from black communities all over Simpson County, Mississippi, usually through the churches that network with us. They are divided into small groups, so each youth leader works with only three or four children, and they learn Bible stories and songs, read, play games and get to spend time with computers.

"We're planning on sixty children in the program," our director told me last summer. But a few days after the program began I noticed the panic in his face.

"What's wrong?" I asked.

"We have more than one hundred children in the program," he replied. "We're out of space, and the young people are stretched to the limit. What should we do?"

If we planned for sixty, I wondered to myself, somewhat exasperated, *why do we now have more than a hundred? Someone should have said no somewhere along the line. We need to be practical.* But I didn't say anything, only listened.

Just then, one of the young people ran up to me in great distress. "Please, Mr. Weary, can you come help me with one of the three-year-olds? I don't know how to handle him."

Entering the room with the young leader, I saw that she had too many children in her group. As I worked with the frightened child and his helper, I saw how much this child needed our help. And so did all the others. My anger at the poor planning disappeared. Yes, our program was being stretched to the limit. But what a challenge! What a chance to find out how we could be stretched.

Jesus stretched five loaves and two fish to feed five thousand people. With His help, our twenty youth leaders would take care of a hundred-plus children.

Lord, help us by faith to meet the challenges You send us, and to listen to Your voice as we serve You daily.   — Dolphus Weary

19 | W E D *See that ye love one another with a pure heart fervently.*
          —I Peter 1:22

My father was not a demonstrative man. I saw him give my mother a quick peck of a kiss each morning as he left for work, but I don't remember ever seeing his arms about her.

I was sure Daddy loved my two sisters and me, but he never told us so. Nor did he hug and kiss us. He was patient, gentle and totally dependable. There were times when I was tempted to throw my arms about his neck, but something always held me back.

After his death, I helped my mother go through his personal possessions. In the "secret pocket" of his wallet, we found newspaper clippings of each of his daughters in their wedding gowns.

"He loved his girls so much," Mother whispered, holding the pictures in her hands.

Why didn't he tell us? my heart cried.

At that moment, I determined that love would hold a high priority in my family and that it would be expressed openly and often. Before Emily — our only child — was born, Bob and I pledged to build a strong bond among all of us. And what a delight our life together has been! Emily shares many happy memories of trips, school plays, festivals, camping excursions and ball games, as well as serious discussions, all enriched by the presence of obvious love and affection.

Recently, Emily sent us a clipping from the newspaper. It was a cartoon of two people, one in bed, the other standing beside, with a caption that read, "Love is a good morning kiss." She remembers well!

Love is a wonderful thing, Lord; Your gift of it, the perfect example. Amen.
                                                        — Drue Duke

20 | T H U   *Do not provoke your children, lest they become discouraged.*   — Colossians 3:21 (RSV)

"I'm *not* coming to dinner!" yelled Daniel. "I'm *not* hungry!"

I am not a strict parent, but one thing I've always felt strongly about is having our family spend dinner together, at a table set with a cloth and candles — even if we are having only grilled cheese sandwiches. My children have always accepted this maternal eccentricity, so I was dismayed by Daniel's sudden point-blank refusal to conform.

"Why won't you come to dinner?" I kept asking. No answer.

Finally, after several weeks of eating out of the refrigerator, one day he growled, "I can't stand it, Mom. Those candles remind me of church."

I was horrified. At one fell swoop he had undermined two precious parts of daily life: our evening meal and our Sunday churchgoing. But I rallied: "Okay, dear, I won't light any candles. Will you come to dinner then?"

"I s'pose so," he allowed reluctantly. So our life went on with candleless dinners and churchgoing under protest. This wasn't my idea of a happy family. There were plenty of things to pray about that year, but every so often I'd ask for help in unraveling this tangle of angry rebellion. I knew prayer and patience were my best hope.

About six months went by. Life was not going too smoothly for me, and my family was outdoing itself in being supportive and extra kind. One evening as I was setting the table, Daniel slouched into the room. "Mom, you can put on the candles. It's all right," he said. I looked up in amazement. "I don't want to be a rat when you're miserable. Go on, light 'em up."

The teenager, that difficult and unpredictable member of the human family, had amazed and humbled me. I asked no questions, but when I looked around the table that evening at the faces in the candlelight, I felt a serenity and inner peace that had been missing since the candles had been put out.

O God, help me to trust You as I pray for my children and for all young people growing up in these stressful times.   —Brigitte Weeks

21 | F R I *O Lord, You have searched me and known me.*
                                        —Psalm 139:1 (NRSV)

On the June morning thirty years ago, when my son was put into my arms, I waited until the nurse was out of the room and then, my eye still on the door, I pulled loose the deftly bound blanket and began to examine the tiny person it had hidden.

He seemed perfect to me, even the crooked little toes, so like his father's large ones. I marveled, as any new mother might, that this wonderful child had grown for these past nine months inside my body.

And I wasn't the only one. Everyone thought he was beautiful. Why, the first words the nurse had said in the delivery room were, "Look at those eyelashes! Wouldn't you know? Wasted on a boy."

Someday, I thought, stroking his silky cheek, *someday, he's going to have to shave.* I laughed aloud at the thought.

The psalmist remembers that same wonder over the creation of a person when he says in Psalm 139:13–14 (NRSV): "For it was you who formed my inward parts; you knit me together in my mother's womb. I praise you, for I am fearfully and wonderfully made."

As I read the Psalm this morning, I see the Parent of us all bending in love over me. And I see that the marvel we share in God's creation is nothing new. Yet it is new for every parent at every birth. God not only made me, God loves me, searching me with the eyes of a love-struck mother marveling over her newborn child.

Let me know, O God, Your tender, searching love that awakens in me the desire for You.   — Katherine Paterson

POINT OF LIGHT

FIREFLIES

Intermittent stars
Floating flower high,
Nearer to earth and us
Than to the sky —
Minor luminaries
Permit a child to stand
Breathless, holding golden
Stars in her hand.
                    —Jane Hess Merchant

22 | S A T   *Behold, this stone shall be a witness unto us....*
                                    —Joshua 24:27

When we built our house twenty years ago, my husband Gary placed a huge rock at the end of our driveway. The kids would climb on it while they waited for the elementary school bus. The rock towered over the tiny shrubs and bright pansies I planted at its base. Recently, a friend who hadn't visited me in several years stopped by. "What happened to that big rock you used to have at the end of the drive-way?" she asked.

"Oh, it's still there — only now the shrubs are bigger than it is," I replied.

She walked to the window and looked down the driveway. "It used to be a lot bigger."

No, I thought after she left and I stood looking at the rock myself, *it used to seem bigger.*

In my own life, too, things have often seemed large and over-whelming. Brett's speech difficulties when he was small. Gary's work the year housing starts were down. My own health when my anemia worsened. Now those problems are memories—all of them manageable in size. All of them dwarfed by the solutions of patience and prayer and appropriate action.

Is there something in your life today that seems daunting? Why not let my "shrinking" rock remind you that time and trust can often turn giants into dwarfs.

Father, You see the end from the beginning. Help us trust Your vision.
— Mary Lou Carney

23 | S U N | *For your perseverance and faith in the midst of all your persecutions and afflictions which you endure.*
— II Thessalonians 1:4 (NAS)

Just across the road from our church in Monroe, Georgia, is Mt. Vernon Service Station. It's a neat, white, very small gas station operated for more than fifty years by Ossie Mobley and her son. Donnie is in his late fifties and has spent his life in a wheelchair. He helps his widowed mother run the station and really enjoys the folks who stop by. The station has long been Donnie's window on the world.

Recently, because of some red tape, the people who fill the huge buried gas tanks have refused to fill Ossie's tanks any longer. Ossie can't sell gas now. She fought a long, hard battle and lost.

Early each morning Ossie and Donnie still arrive at the station from their house next door. A few cars stop by for a paper, soft drink or candy. Donnie has never been able to speak clearly, but his bright eyes, winsome smile and quick hand motions enable most folks to understand him. Often Donnie manages the station alone and signals his mother (with a buzzer) when she is needed. Ossie is a small, frail woman, always in a neat cotton dress. Inside their station are two ageless straight chairs and a marvelous little heater. On the coldest day of the year, it's snug in the minute station. Ossie and Donnie make anyone feel special and welcome. She still carefully, even lovingly, washes down the empty gas pumps and faithfully sweeps away the leaves.

They don't complain — ever. Each Sunday, Ossie and Donnie are in church in their regular places singing praises to God and asking me after church, "How are you? Is everything all right?"

Oh, Father, teach me about endurance and perseverance. Amen.
— Marion Bond West

24 | M O N *Lord, I have called daily upon thee, I have stretched out my hands unto thee.* — Psalm 88:9

While visiting our son Chris in Anchorage last year, Shirley and I got to see some of Alaska's most beautiful scenery — Denali National Park (Mt. McKinley), Resurrection Bay and Prince William Sound, for starters. But it was on a boat trip at the latter that I saw something more memorable than all the glaciers, grizzly bears, mountain goats, caribou, moose, bald eagles, kittiwakes and horned puffins.

The incident pitted a giant eagle against a tiny mother murrelet, a mottled brown waterfowl, and her brood. The diving bird of prey swooped down again and again on Mama and the four chicks that paddled behind her. Dozens of us watched from railside, riveted by the David-and-Goliath drama. On each pass I held my breath, sure the eagle would snag one of the babies with its lethal talons. But every time the eagle dove, the intrepid mother signaled impending danger and in unison they went submarine. Then like corks they popped up and swam on. Eventually, the frustrated eagle gave up and flew off.

I applauded Mother Murrelet's courage. But it took more than courage to save her chicks. It took discipline. Sometime earlier she had taught her offspring to obey her. I could imagine that in quiet bays and eddies she had schooled them to follow her instructions. Because they did, they lived to swim another day.

I need to remember this lesson when I grow inconsistent in my spiritual pilgrimage, forgetting to pray and study God's Word. It is that discipline in good times that prepares me for bad, which will come to all of us as surely as the seasons. The difference is that in adversity, I'll know Whom to call on and — with absolute certainty — Who will answer.

Teach us to hear Your voice, O God, and obey it,
To heed Your will at once and not delay it.
— Fred Bauer

25

T
U
E

I write this to you who believe in the name of the Son of God, that you may know that you have eternal life.
—I John 5:13 (RSV)

Yesterday, my Auntie Grace died. I fell asleep last night hugging Tinsy Winsy, my cherished sock monkey she made me when I was very small.

I was twelve when she noticed Tinsy Winsy getting shabby, as were my two sisters' monkeys Bimbo and Suzannah. "I say we go buy some new stuffing and new socks and fix them up like new," she said, holding up our monkeys with their floppy arms and legs, the stuffing long gone.

"But they won't be the same!" we cried.

"They will," Auntie replied, "because we'll keep their eyes"—those special little black sparkling buttons that had made our monkeys come alive. "Girls, you don't think I'd throw out Tinsy Winsy, Bimbo and Suzannah's old bodies and not let them keep their souls, do you?"

How well I remember the summer afternoon she handed me Tinsy Winsy, all plump and new, his limbs fit and fat, his eyes sparkling ... the old miracle of creator and creation. And remembering that, I see I've not lost Auntie. Because, though we all have to throw out our old bodies sometime, we have a Creator Who never throws away our souls.

Dear Father in heaven, thank You for all my departed loved ones. Help me keep their gifts and spirit alive for others to enjoy. Amen.
— Brenda Wilbee

26

W
E
D

But Jesus said, "... Do not hinder them [the children] from coming to Me; for the kingdom of heaven belongs to such as these."
— Matthew 19:14 (NAS)

Recently, my six-year-old daughter Jodi gave me a Father's Day present that she had made. It was a cigar box spray-painted gold with small seashells glued to the top. Inside this treasure box was a note in her large, first-grade handwriting: "Dear Dad, if you will get some Rollerblades, I will Rollerblade with you."

I chuckled. I could just see myself with a pair of Rollerblades skating down the street. People would think that I'd lost my mind, that I'd finally flipped out and was having a midlife crisis. Laughing, I hugged my daughter.

But Jodi's words stayed with me. What was she trying to say? In her own little way, I think that she was saying, "Dad, I want to spend some time with you. I want you to be a daddy who has fun and plays with me."

I don't know about the Rollerblade idea. But the message is clear. I'd better spend some time having fun with Jodi. And I'd better do it now. Before I know it, she'll be sixteen and asking for a car!

Dear Father, help me always to listen to what my children are saying and to respond to them in love.   —Scott Walker

27 | T H U   *Behold, thou desirest truth in the inward parts....*
                                                —Psalm 51:6

Some months ago, my friend Jeff LeSourd told me that his wife Nancy was still in pain three years after the birth of their second child. The delivery had been by cesarean section; there were complications and a second operation. "A nerve was cut," Jeff said. "Nancy has been in pain ever since. Still, there is reason for hope."

One of the marvels of the human body, Jeff explained, is that a severed nerve will slowly grow back on its own. The bad news is that on occasion, even though regeneration has taken place, pain continues. We are healed, but don't "know" it yet because the message has not been accepted by our brain. When perception comes in line with fact, the pain will normally disappear. That is what the LeSourds are hoping.

I suspect that a similar pattern exists in the healing of our emotions. Years ago, for instance, when I'd dropped a fly ball during an important high school game, my coach informed me in the hearing of all, "Sherrill, you're hopeless!"

For decades that word *hopeless* kept popping up to undermine my confidence. Then a few years ago I decided to do something about the painful memory. I took it to God and asked Him to forgive us both: the coach for his put-down and me for holding a grudge. Nothing changed. But Jeff's phone call about Nancy started me thinking.

Today, every time the old hurt catches me by surprise, I not only use the occasion to pray for Nancy's pain to subside, but I also take hope from Jeff's description of regeneration.

The damage to my confidence has been repaired! The message has just not yet been accepted by my brain. But it will! I know it will.

When we pray for healing, Lord, help us believe that perception of health will soon catch up with fact.   —John Sherrill

28 | F R I *Therefore do not be anxious for tomorrow, for tomorrow will care for itself....* — Matthew 6:34 (NAS)

Last summer, worry over college finances had me in a funk when my youngest son Jon and I started on a houseboat fishing trip with seven other relatives. My dad and uncle had planned this trip to Rainy Lake on the Minnesota-Canada border for several months. I didn't want worry to spoil it, but I couldn't get my mind off the seeming impossibility of getting three boys through college, with Jason starting in just a year. Even the beauty of the majestic Voyageurs National Park wasn't working any magic on my nagging fears.

Then, one afternoon, we tied up to shore just as a powerful thunderstorm swept down the lake. Sitting under the canopy over our bow, we watched the brilliant lightning flashes and listened to the cracking thunder. Noticing a seagull in the middle of the bay, I muttered, "Stupid bird...can't even figure out where to go in the rain."

"It knows it's raining," my uncle replied. "It just doesn't care!"

"Yeah, Uncle Eric," said one of my nephews, "it's built for the rain. Besides, it knows the rain won't last forever."

As the conversation dropped and the rain drummed heavily about us, that "stupid" seagull started me thinking. *If you live in a lake and have feathers, you're built for the rain,* I reasoned. *And if you live in a family and have kids, hasn't God built you to handle the challenge of college? Besides,* I told myself, *any storm involved will end eventually.*

Before I knew it, my bout with worry was over. And, just then, the rain stopped and the sun came out.

Lord, help me to remember that, through You, I am prepared for whatever You have planned.
                                                    — Eric Fellman

29 | S A T *Bodily exercise is all right, but spiritual exercise...is a tonic for all you do....* — I Timothy 4:8 (TLB)

As we crest yet another hill on our fifty-mile bicycle "Tour de Sweat" on Route 45 in Orland Park, Illinois, a gas station appears to hover above the pavement, floating on the wavy undulations of ninety-five-degree heat. I point ahead and rasp, "Mirage, Uncle Ronny?" My voice seems detached and distant; my feet pedal mechanically.

"Nope, no mirage, Jen," my uncle replies. "Cool drinks and junk food await. Let's go!" Effortlessly, he sprints ahead, and I begin to resent the sight of his tanned and well-muscled back—thirty years older than I and not even breathing hard!

"He's probably dead already," I mumble to myself miserably. "That's why he's not gasping for air!"

Dismounting in the welcome shade, I crumple helpless and limp against the cool bricks while "Super Boy" flashes inside. Moments later he buzzes out holding two bottles of orange soda. I grab one greedily and swallow, reveling in the cold liquid. Between gulps I watch Uncle Ronny. He doesn't drink. He slowly presses the cold glass against his temple, raises his eyes, then the bottle skyward, orange against azure, smiles and whispers contentedly, "Nice."

"Aren't you even thirsty?" I finally snap, maddened by my uncle's self-control. "Why aren't you drinking your pop?"

"Thanksgiving, my quizzical little puppy," he smiles. "Thanksgiving."

Now, as a delicious glow washes over my tired muscles, I begin to understand. I, too, raise my bottle skyward in salute and amen, "Yeah, nice, very nice." We drink deeply and savor the moment.

Lord, may I learn to appreciate the joy of this life in even its simplest forms.
                                                      —Jenny Mutzbauer

30 | S U N   *Let your conversation be as it becometh the gospel of Christ....*   —Philippians 1:27

About noon one Sunday, I glanced out the kitchen window and noticed my twenty-one-year-old daughter Lindsay lying in the sun on the trampoline in the backyard. She'd recently come home from college for the summer, and I still seized every opportunity to spend time with her. I stepped outside and jumped up to join her on the trampoline.

I intended to stay only a couple of minutes, but soon we became involved in a deep mother-daughter discussion. Lindsay is part of the generation that believes in talking through your feelings, and I'm part of the generation that usually grins and bears it and moves on. So there we were, lying on the trampoline, our faces turned toward each other, working through some issues I wanted to forget and she wanted to discuss. It was hard work, but about two hours later, we reached a mutual understanding. We ended with a prayer and a hug and then climbed down off the trampoline.

I didn't realize the price I paid for our conversation until Monday morning when I stood looking in the mirror. Half of my face was bright red with sunburn. Just then Lindsay came into the room, and we both burst out laughing. Her face was just as sunburned, but on the opposite side.

"How will I ever explain this face to the people at work?" I asked.

"Tell the truth," she said. "That you and your daughter had a *great* talk."

I wore my sunburned face that day like a badge of honor.

Lord, may I keep learning how relationships — like children — grow and change.
— Carol Kuykendall

GIFTS OF LIGHT

1 _____

2 _____

3 _____

4 _____

5 _____

6 _____

7 _____

8 _____

9 _____

10 _____

11 _____

12 _____

13 _____

14 _____

15 _____

16 _____

17 _____

18 _____

19 _____

20 _____

21 _____

22 _____

23 _____

24 _____

25 _____

26 _____

27 _____

28 _____

29 _____

30 _____

JULY

"*Let your light so shine before men, that they may see your good works and give glory to your Father who is in heaven.*"

—MATTHEW 5:16 (RSV)

S	M	T	W	T	F	S
	1	2	3	4	5	6
7	8	9	10	11	12	13
14	15	16	17	18	19	20
21	22	23	24	25	26	27
28	29	30	31			

1 | M
  | O   *He saw the spirit of God…lighting upon him.*
  | N   —Matthew 3:16

To celebrate my retirement, my wife Ruby and I took a trip to Honolulu. Our second night there, I was still on Boston time. At two in the morning, Ruby was sound asleep, but I was wide awake, wondering what I should do with the rest of my life. Coming from the very structured existence in engineering, I was frightened by the unstructured life of retirement. What would I do with all my time? Who was I now that I was no longer an engineer? Did I have any other gifts?

It seemed the ideal time to pray. Someone had given me a plan of prayer involving twelve steps — from confession to praise — but I had never taken the time to go through them all. Maybe in the quiet and away from everyday cares and concerns, I would make progress.

I was partway through step one, confessing my sins and failures, when something happened. I may have fallen asleep, I don't know. Suddenly, the room was filled with a great light more brilliant than any I had seen. Yet, despite the power and intensity, there was no blinding glare — I could see clearly. As I marveled, it was gone. I have never seen it again.

Except for the wonder, I didn't feel any different. But the wonder remained. God had used His light to break through my scientific mind, telling me that He was with me and would lead me to His plan for my retirement. In the months that followed, though I never talked of the experience, I began to discover gifts that could be used for God, to help others — by writing, listening to people, being positive.

Not everyone needs a vision of light to let them know that God is with them and will guide them. Perhaps God knew that I did. And now, fourteen years later, I share my experience with you to encourage you to believe that you are not alone. God is going with you into the future and will light the way.

All-knowing Father, thank You for listening to my prayer, and for sending the light of Your Spirit. May I always follow that light.
                                    —Oscar Greene

2 | T
  | U   *But I was free born.*
  | E   —Acts 22:28

Soon after college graduation, my friend Ben and I were walking through the ancient streets of Prague in the Czech Republic. I had been saving for this trip to Europe for years. It didn't take us long to see that there was more to this city than we could pick up on our own, so we booked a tour with a local agency. The next morning our guide appeared in our hotel lobby. Tiny in stature and in her mid-thirties, her name was Dana. While we visited the castle and other local landmarks, we began to ask Dana about herself.

"Before becoming guide," Dana explained in her self-taught English, "I was teacher." With no decent textbooks, she had spent years translating German texts for her students. Encouraged by our interest, she told poignant stories of family members who had stood up for the rights of the local people, only to be taken away by Communist soldiers and never seen again.

"In 1989 came the Velvet Revolution when my country was freed." Looking at me with sweet eyes that had seen more pain than I would ever know, she continued, "Brock, you are from America, so it is not possible for you to ever understand what it was like before the revolution. It was choking." She explained how the public expression of religion and other freedoms that we Americans have were not even options for her as she grew up. I felt shamed. Here was a woman who had spent the majority of her life struggling for a chance to worship God, and I came from a country where my fishing excursions often took precedence over Sunday school and church.

Back home in time to celebrate the Fourth of July, I watched the fireworks burst red, white and blue. I couldn't help but think of Dana, and I began to weep. I was never so proud to be free. "I won't forget," I whispered to the tiny lady in a country far away. "And when I have children, I'll pass on your lesson."

"God bless America, our home, sweet home."   —Brock Kidd

---

3 | W E D | *How clearly the sky reveals God's glory! How plainly it shows what he has done!*   —Psalm 19:1 (GNB)

The *Humming Bird*, my small sailing sloop, left Pepin, Wisconsin, with time to spare. And then, as frequently happens to sailboats, a couple of things did not work out exactly the way I had hoped. I had promised my wife Edith and a friend that we would watch the Lake City fireworks from the boat. But then rain and contrary winds appeared.

"We can stay in the marina until the rain passes," Kathy said.

"Nope! I plan to be there at the first rocket. I am not losing time by ducking out of the rain."

"Why don't we use the motor to make headway against the winds?" suggested Edith.

But I prided myself on my sailing ability, so I put every ounce of my skill and concentration into moving that boat down that lake. The more difficult and unlikely the prospect of arriving on time, the more determined and single-minded I became.

And then, "Oh, oh, oh, you must look!"

Both Kathy and Edith were focused on what was taking place behind my back. The setting sun had turned the hills a phosphorescent green and left the lake itself pitch black. First a single, and then a double rainbow bridged the hills from north to south, creating an amphitheater for the silent and distant lightning in the east. My destination forgotten, I allowed the boat to bob along at a gentler pace as we drank in this unexpected majesty.

We were late for the fireworks. No one complained. Even I was at peace. Once again, God had fooled me by working His wonders not according to my plan.

Lord, when I am desperately focused on a task directly in front of me, will You remind me that the wonders You are working may be happening somewhere else?
—John Cowan

4 | T H U *He that keepeth the law, happy is he.* —Proverbs 29:18

My father was a man who loved words and enjoyed finding new meanings in them. One Fourth of July, I remember, he was talking about that famous phrase from the Declaration of Independence: *life, liberty and the pursuit of happiness.*

"I suppose we all do chase after happiness," he said. "But sometimes I wonder if it isn't the other way 'round. Maybe happiness is pursuing us. And if it never catches up, it may be because something is wrong in the way we're conducting our lives.

"I think the Lord wants us to be happy," my father went on, "and so He created a universe of mighty laws, both physical and spiritual. I've observed that a person is happy in proportion as he or she is in harmony with those laws.

"This means that if you want happiness to overtake you, you have to try to get rid of selfishness and dishonesty and anger and guilt and all the other roadblocks that keep it from catching up. When you clear those things out of your life and keep them out, you're giving happiness a chance to come right up and tap you on the shoulder."

The pursuit of happiness. Is it catching up with you? Or is it falling behind? Something to think about now and then, I do believe.

Lord, make us wise enough to see that happiness comes when we follow the paths You showed us.   — Arthur Gordon

5 | F R I   *Let us lay aside every weight....*   — Hebrews 12:1

The big event, my husband's fiftieth high school reunion in Vancouver, British Columbia, has come and gone. I could not go with him because of an engagement made far in advance, so our son took my place. "Make sure your dad has a good time," I told Ian.

But when John and I went over his senior yearbook before they left, I wondered whether he would have a good time. "Here's Colleen," John said wistfully. "I was sweet on her but couldn't get up the nerve to ask her for a date. And this fellow here," John's voice was tense, "he belonged to a club they wouldn't let me join."

"Where's your picture?" I asked, puzzled.

"It's here at the end, with the tagalongs. I wasn't sure I could cough up the extra money for a picture until the last minute."

His picture didn't show up in any other section of the yearbook except with the air cadets. "I wasn't one of the popular bunch," he explained. "If Ian wasn't coming, I don't think I'd go."

Three days later the fellows returned, loaded with pictures and autographed programs. "Honey, I wouldn't have missed it for the world!" John said excitedly. "Colleen was there at our table. She said she always liked me and would have dated me if I'd asked! The chaps who I thought had shut me out — turned out they thought I was a brain and knew I would do well without the group's help.

"I've spent a lifetime brooding about what I thought was the rejection of my classmates. Turns out that every ounce of that burden I put on myself. This week at the reunion, I threw the weight of it off!"

"Thanks be to God," I said as I kissed him.

Dear Lord, help us to throw off the weights from our past that we have carried all our lives, and to forgive ourselves and others.
                                                              — Fay Angus

6 | S A T *And by you and your descendants shall all the families of the earth bless themselves.* — Genesis 28:14 (RSV)

I had been home from college for about a month when my fifteen-year-old twin sisters Stephanie and Lauren got ready to leave for camp. As they both drove off with my father and brother, I enthusiastically waved good-bye. *Ah, peace and quiet,* I thought as I headed inside to set the table for dinner, for four this time, not six.

My mother was bustling around the kitchen and for a few moments we worked quietly, until my mother broke the awkward silence. "Oh, my goodness," she sighed, "the girls have just left and already it's too quiet."

I replied with a mischievous grin, "I know, isn't it nice?"

"Don't be silly," my mother quickly retorted. "You kids should feel lucky you have one another!"

For a moment I was surprised at her outburst, until she continued. "Your Uncle Mark died when he was only thirty-six, leaving behind your aunt and two little cousins. And now I no longer have a brother." She turned away at that point, and I bit my lip guiltily, thinking about how I would feel if I ever lost my sisters or brother. A reply was unnecessary.

The week dragged by, and I found myself missing the sounds of my sisters: the *thumpity-thump* of Lauren's tap-dancing shoes; the *whish* of water as Stephanie took her twenty-five-minute showers; the sounds of their laughter at a kitchen table that looked incomplete without six people.

Suddenly, they arrived home in their typical chaotic fashion, looking healthy and tanned. Our family came alive once again as we laughed at the stories Stephanie and Lauren told about camp. And as I helped set the table for dinner, I marveled at the complete circle we made—for we were no longer four, but six.

Help us to remember the value of togetherness, Lord, for our closest companions are the ones we miss most when apart.

— Jennifer Thomas

7 | S U N *Blessed are the dead which die in the Lord…their works do follow them.* — Revelation 14:13

During one of my weekend visits to my ninety-four-year-old father's retirement home in Pennsylvania, Daddy kept gamely trying to stay upright, independent and awake. The afternoon that I left to drive back to New Jersey we had a time of prayer as we usually did. Daddy, as always, asked for a safe trip for me, and then added, "Lord, please help me to catch up on my work. I've gotten so far behind."

I chuckled a bit to myself as I drove home, wondering, *What work is he talking about?*

In the next weeks, I discovered what he meant. He was behind in his prayer schedule. For him, prayer was his work. Every day, every week, he had gone through his overflowing loose-leaf notebook filled with letters and prayer requests from friends, missionaries and missions around the world. As he prayed over every person, every request, he would mark the date.

One reason Daddy had been willing to give up his independence and move to the retirement home was to have more time to pray. But now, he didn't have the energy to go through the book or even to read the new letters that came. Yet as his strength waned and his tongue thickened, he would phone friends to find out how they were and what he could pray for as he sat immobilized.

"How much your dad's prayers and interest in us have meant" was the comment that came again and again after his death. "He was a true prayer warrior."

What a legacy!

Lord, thank You for those who have prayed for us over the years. May we take up the work they have laid down.

— Mary Ruth Howes

---

8 | M O N | *Let them give glory unto the Lord, and declare his praise in the islands.* —Isaiah 42:12

Just before my husband Don and I left Kansas for our vacation in Hawaii, I slipped a little brochure called *The Traveler's Commandments* into my suitcase. I read it each morning, and following its instructions made our trip the best ever.

1. Thou shalt not expect to find all things precisely as they are at home. Thou hast left home to find things different. I snorkeled in Hanoma Bay with my brother Mike and niece Amy. I swallowed a gallon of seawater, but also saw underwater scenery and dozens of vividly colored tropical fish unlike anything I'd seen in landlocked Kansas!

2. Thou shalt remember that endless waiting lines, delays, cancellations and bad food are a part of traveling, and thou shalt smile and not com-

plain. Check-in delays meant Don and I were among the last people to board the plane. We sat separately in the last two rows, but we could help ourselves to pop and peanuts from the flight attendant's cart, and I had a wonderful conversation with a new nurse who was also a new Christian.

   3. *Thou shalt not worry about things at home or at the office while thou art away, for he that worrieth hath little joy.* For the first time, I didn't call my office. And you know what? My staff capably handled every problem.

   4. *Thou shalt travel in a spirit of utter humility. The fact that people may think, speak and act differently does not make them inferior.* Simplicity and casualness characterized the islands. We worshiped with my brother's family in their plain wooden church in a service without in-strumental music or liturgy or creeds. It was a new experience, but God was present and I drew strength from the powerful words of old hymns we sang in harmony.

Lord of the universe, bless all who are on vacation. Thank You for giving us the ability to learn, grow, and refresh ourselves in new and different ways.   — Penney Schwab

9 | T U E *The race is not to the swift....*   —Ecclesiastes 9:11

Speed. Some days I move about at breakneck speed as if I were killing a snake or something.

   Yesterday, for example, I was replacing the thermostat on the car engine, and in my haste to finish I overtightened the bolts. *Crack!* The thermostat housing broke. I spent the rest of the day roaring around to auto parts stores, trying to find a scarce replacement part. It was a wasted day.

   Speed. It can slow things up.

   I have an uncle who worked in a company that makes parts for the space industry. When someone complained that he wasn't working fast enough, an efficiency expert came around and put a clock on him. Turned out he had mastered the art of wasting no motions and making no mistakes. As a result he was producing more than anyone else in the shop!

   His work style reminds me that faster is not always faster. Oh, sure, there are times when you have to hustle or you get left behind. But maybe, just maybe, I could get that paperwork done faster by working steadily, with concentration, instead of at warp speed, in a daze. The express lane might get me to work faster, but not if I get a ticket. Turning up the heat in the oven will get that pizza done quicker, but with a sacrifice of flavor and texture—and it might get burnt!

I used to have a teacher who would urge us on during tests by saying, "Hurry up and take your time," meaning, "Keep at it, but don't panic." Pretty good advice, I think. I'd like to try it today and see if I don't get more done.

Lord, teach me to respect the speed limit—my inner one. And to get the job done with grace.   —Daniel Schantz

---

10 | W E D | *By his great mercy we have...an inheritance which is imperishable, undefiled, and unfading....*
—I Peter 1:3–4 (RSV)

Old things fascinate me, and as time goes on I find myself collecting more and more dated items. My latest acquisition is a dingy, little, nondescript silver band, dulled by age, given to me recently by my mother. I like the story behind it.

When she and my dad were married during the Depression, he couldn't afford a wedding ring, so for several years Mother had none. Then she contracted pneumonia and was near death. The thought that she might die without a ring sent Dad scurrying to buy one. I don't know how he scraped together the money, even though the ring couldn't have cost more than a couple of dollars. Of course, in the 1930s that sum could buy a week's worth of groceries. All I know is that between tears and prayers for her healing, Dad slipped the ring on her finger and told her again that he loved her. Thank God, Mother recovered, and wore the ring for the rest of their thirty-year marriage. Now I have the two-dollar treasure.

Treasure? Yes, to me it represents something of great value, because it belonged to my life-givers, my nurturers, my sustainers, my encouragers, my teachers. Their faith and values helped to shape mine. And when I hold the silver ring in my hand, I sense the love it symbolizes. I feel much the same way about old churches, old hymns, old books. The words I read today from one old Book didn't have anything to say about collecting old things, but they did offer some counsel about loving collectibles too much. "Do not lay up for yourselves treasures on earth…but lay up for yourselves treasures in heaven…for where your treasure is there your heart will be also" (Matthew 6:19-21).

Good advice for an old pack rat like me.

God, make us wise enough to see
What's passing, what's for eternity.

— Fred Bauer

POINT OF LIGHT

PASS ON THE TORCH

Pass on the torch, pass on the flame;
Remember whence the Glory came;
And eyes are on you as you run,
Beyond the shining of the sun.

Lord Christ, we take the torch from Thee;
We must be true, we must be free,
And clean of heart and strong of soul,
To bear the Glory to its goal.

…

O Lord of life, to Thee we kneel;
Maker of men, our purpose seal!
We will, for honor of Thy Name,
Pass on the torch, pass on the flame.

— Allen Eastman Cross

---

11 | T H U *This woman was full of good works….* — Acts 9:36

It was 2:00 A.M. I was propped up in bed; Mother sat at the foot. We had talked since ten o'clock the night before. On my lap was a telegram offering me a teaching position in Illinois and at a salary equal to Father's. I was elated; Mother was cautious and concerned.

It was June 1941, and I was twenty-three. Only hours before, I had returned home after four years at college. Mother rose and spoke.

"You've been away. Now you're going fifteen hundred miles to a place you do not know. Supposing you fall ill? Who will care for you? I wish you'd change your mind and find work around here. But I guess you're grown now."

She left, and my thoughts clashed with my emotions. I was penniless, and Father was facing surgery (from which he would not recover). In my eagerness to travel and to teach, *Was I selfish? Was I unfair?* I agonized until dawn, and finally decided to go.

As I said good-bye the next day, Mother neither hugged nor kissed me. Instead, she handed me train fare and a large shoe box. I peeked inside. The aroma of sandwiches, pickles, boiled eggs, sponge cake and fruit rushed out to greet me. Mother was handing me all her love in that shoe box. Her heart was weeping, yet she was letting go with love.

It wasn't until July 11, 1976, that I fully understood Mother's lesson of love. My son Oscar, Jr., his wife Marie and their three-year-old son Shawn were leaving Massachusetts for Ohio. Shawn had been in our care since he was months old. His leaving was wrenching, and I felt empty. All the anguish Mother must have felt came tumbling in on me.

Then I remembered the shoe box. I could fill mine by responding with understanding. I wasn't losing Shawn. He was going to a new home where I would be welcomed. It was my turn to let go with love. Oscar, Marie and Shawn needed the same chance to grow on their own that I had received so long ago.

Lord, letting go is Your way of helping us to grow and to be free.
— Oscar Greene

12 | F R I | *But we all, with open face beholding as in a glass the glory of the Lord, are changed into the same image....*
— II Corinthians 3:18

We were hiking in the High Sierras on a crystal clear midsummer's day. In the high altitude, the sky was deep blue and the color seemed to be intensified in the thin air. My wife Carol and I took a trail bordering a fast-rushing stream lined with dusty ferns, rust-colored Indian paintbrush, purple lupine. At the top, we reached a clearing and a glacier-fed lake that was smooth as glass.

"Look," I said to Carol, "you can see the mountains twice."

Sure enough, like a mirror that reflects a face, the lake showed the image of the blue sky, the treeless mountains, the meadow and the vibrant wildflowers around it. We were reverent, hushed, as though we were in a church. The water was so placid, not a breath of wind rippling its surface, you could see all of nature reflected there.

Staring at the majestic scene, I could almost hear what a minister had once told me about prayer: "Find a place where there are few distractions. Let your body be still and your mind uncluttered with thoughts."

Now I understood why. A mind unruffled, like a lake undisturbed, can more perfectly reflect the glory of God.

Lord, empty my mind of all disturbances so that I can reflect on You.
— Rick Hamlin

13 | S A T

Judge not according to the appearance.... —John 7:24

One hot morning, I was sitting on the deck reading the newspaper when I heard this loud, irritating whirring noise. I turned the page, expecting the noise to stop eventually. By the time I finished the newspaper, the unpleasant sound still cluttered the otherwise peaceful neighborhood.

I stood up from my chair and stepped around the corner of the house. I looked up, and there it was — an attic fan in my neighbor's house whirring, clanking, making a terrible racket. My neighbor had installed it the day before.

How can anyone disturb the peace with such a machine? I asked myself. For the next few days I complained to my wife about the noise. Finally, I walked over to my neighbor's house and pressed the doorbell. My defense was prepared. My anger was controlled. I was going to ask him to disconnect the fan.

"Hi, Chris," my neighbor warmly greeted me. "Come on in."

"How are you, Jerry?" I asked as we shook hands.

"Well, better," he said. "We've had a bit of a scare the last few weeks. My daughter Anna developed a terrible breathing problem. The doctor suggested fresh air in the house, not air conditioning, so I installed an attic fan. Now she finally sleeps at night again, so all is okay."

Jerry looked at me. I looked at him. Then he asked, "What's new with you?"

"Well," I said, "I...ah...was wondering if I could borrow your hedge clippers."

When I returned to my house, I clipped the bushes, swept the driveway, drove to town, bought the newspaper and sat on my deck for the rest of the afternoon. The noisy fan has never bothered me since.

Father in heaven, remind me to walk in someone else's shoes before I cast the first stones of my anger.   —Christopher de Vinck

14 | S U N   *My fruit is better than gold....*   —Proverbs 8:19

Tired from a busy weekend away, I walked into a sweltering, humid house Sunday evening. The air conditioner had died, and four inches of water covered the basement floor. My daughter Karen had come to water the petunias in the window box and had left the hose running. Karen felt terrible, but she'd only meant to be helpful. There was really nothing I could do till morning, when I'd call someone to pump out the water and work on the air conditioner. But how in the world could I sleep in this one hundred-degree house? Inwardly, I fretted and fumed, looking for some way to change the situation.

Finally, exhausted, I remembered something I'd heard at a retreat: "When you think you have no choice, you still do have a choice. You can choose what is!"

What kind of fool would choose a miserable situation like this? I thought. But I decided to try it anyway by praying, "Lord, I accept the flooded basement, the broken air conditioner and the hot night."

Then a strange thing happened. My whole attitude shifted! The first thing I did was fix myself a tall glass of iced tea and sit in a lawn chair in the backyard. And I began to notice things—fireflies, crickets chirping, the delicate breeze tickling my cheeks, the cool moistness of the grass on my bare feet. Suddenly, I had a marvelous idea—I'd camp out in the backyard! And that's exactly what I did. I don't think I've had that kind of fun since I was a kid—or felt so much in tune with God's created world.

The next day, a cleaning company pumped out the water, and a day or two later the air conditioner was fixed. To my surprise, it was all covered by my house insurance!

Perhaps to "choose what is" is just another way of saying, "Thy will be done," so God can bring forth His unexpected fruits!

Lord of all possibilities, I now choose what I can't change, trusting You to transform it—and me.   —Marilyn Morgan Helleberg

15 | M O N   *MY GIFT TODAY...*
THE HUMMINGBIRD

"Do not work for food that spoils, but for food that endures to eternal life...."   —John 6:27 (NIV)

I was looking for a gift today when I walked up the driveway to get the mail. For weeks the papers had trumpeted the long-awaited settlement of a suit alleging airline price-fixing: "Millions of dollars in free air travel to be awarded." *What might my share be?* With fantasies of a trip around the world or a flight on the Concorde, I'd been haunting the mailbox up by the street. Maybe this would be the day!

A gift was waiting all right, but it wasn't in the mailbox. From twenty feet away I could see a blur of movement near the post where a red reflector marks our driveway. I stopped short, watching. It was a ruby-throated hummingbird—a male, glinting iridescent green in the sun.

Enthralled, I watched his miraculous aeronautics. Wings moving too fast for me to see them, he rose six inches straight up, hung there, tiny body suspended motionless in the air, then darted backward. Up, down, back and forth in front of that post. What was its strange attraction?

The reflector, of course! Red, round, alluring, promising who knows what sweetness and nourishment to a hungry hummingbird. Again and again he zoomed in to that bright plastic circle; again and again withdrew, hovered, tried once more.

In that disappointed bird I suddenly saw myself hovering about a mailbox, seeking satisfaction from a source that couldn't possibly provide it. Suppose I did win a free trip. Would it make a great difference in my life? Was it worth the energy I was putting into it each day?

There was no award in the mail that day. When it did arrive, many months later, it was three flight certificates worth fifty-nine dollars. But even before reality overtook fantasy, the hummingbird had helped me set my priorities straight. How many times God has had to remind me—even summoning a feathered messenger to my driveway—that His gifts alone are worth asking for, waiting for, watching for.

Today, Father, let me seek Your kingdom first.   —Elizabeth Sherrill

16 | T U E | *Teach a child to choose the right path, and when he is older he will remain upon it.*   —Proverbs 22:6 (TLB)

I bought a used computer for my youngest son Andrew the summer before he started high school. Before long, that machine was a source of contention between us.

"Two hours a day on the computer is enough," I told him. He would have been happier with twelve.

When I reminded Andrew that there was too much life outside the front door to spend the summer cooped up in the computer room, he thought for a minute and asked, "Mom, what did you do for fun in the summertime when you were a kid?"

I told him about the airboat my dad built and how we skimmed the backwaters of Rock River in northern Illinois, looking for carp. I explained how one summer I'd organized a whole neighborhood full of kids and we'd put on a circus in our backyard and given the money to charity. I told him about the time my mother and I lay on our bellies in the grass twenty feet away from a gopher's hole, waiting to see it pop its head up, which it did.

My list of summertime activities made Andrew laugh. It also made me remember how my folks had worked to help us create outdoor family fun. That week I started planning special things for Andrew and me to do that summer. We designed and created a new flower bed; took a trip to Wisconsin's Kettle Moraine to check out the scenery; rummaged through a huge used bookstore in downtown Milwaukee; drove to a nearby college town to explore the campus; took bike rides. And one day I took him out to a country road and gave him his first driving lesson.

It takes time, effort and organizational skills to plan family events. But the memories you give your children will last a lifetime.

Lord, help me find ways to get my children away from the TV, computer and video games, and to create their own real-life action. And thank You for such a wonderfully incredible world in which to do it.   —Patricia Lorenz

17 | W E D | *"Whenever the rainbow appears...I will see it and remember the everlasting covenant between God and all living creatures of every kind on the earth."* —Genesis 9:16 (NIV)

The summer had been a scorcher, the air extra dry. Plants drooped, and farmers feared for the survival of their crops. During one night, the rain came — not as a storm or with beating fury, but gently, tenderly. And it continued most of the next day, soaking the ground and saturating thirsty roots.

Then as quietly as it started, it ceased, and the late afternoon sun came out. I held the hand of my four-year-old granddaughter Christy as we walked out of my house and down the damp walkway. "Smell the air," I told her, drawing in a deep breath. "It's so fresh and clean. And see how tall my daylilies stand, as though they feel stronger."

"Oh, look," Christy cried out as we rounded the corner of the house, "a rainbow!" The arch of color stretched from horizon to horizon, soaring almost to the zenith.

"Isn't it wonderful?" I said. "The rain we needed so badly, then the sun. And now this beautiful rainbow. Do you know what makes a rainbow?"

I was all set to answer my own question with long-stored bits of knowledge about air currents, condensation, the breaking up of bits of sunlight on a big curve…what an opportunity for a mini-physics lesson. But before I could say anything, Christy traced the rainbow from end to end, then turned, her eyes shining to me. "Of course I know, Grandmommy," she said. "God made it all for us because He loves us so much."

Father in heaven, teach me to see You with the heart of a little child. Amen.
                                                        — Drue Duke

18 | T H U | *Let us run with patience the race that is set before us, Looking unto Jesus the author and finisher of our faith….* — Hebrews 12:1–2

For weeks I dreaded the approach of my forty-ninth birthday — the actual beginning of my fiftieth year, surely an apex of my life. So I decided to do something symbolic.

"I want to climb a tall mountain," I announced to my family, gazing out our living room window at the front range of the Rockies. As my birthday approached, I kept picturing myself sitting on top of one of the highest peaks, feeling close to God and talking to Him about the prospect of turning fifty.

So the morning of my birthday, after packing some peanut butter sandwiches, water and fruit, we started up the mountain — two almost-adult children, the dog and I. Before long, the trail grew steep and I grew warm and weary, so we stopped often to catch our breath, nibble a snack and smell the brilliant wildflowers. It was nearly noon when we finally pulled ourselves up on the peak. Just then, a blast of wind hit our faces and dark clouds swirled overhead, reminding us of a crucial rule about hiking in Colorado in the summertime: Get off the peaks by noon to avoid the dangerous afternoon lightning storms. With a quick glance at the view, we made a hasty retreat, stopping halfway down to picnic in a lovely mountain meadow.

We got home about dusk, and I went right to the window to look at my birthday mountain, but now I saw it in a whole new way—not just as a high peak, but as an entire mountain. And that has given me a new perspective on my age. The truth is, I made way too much of entering my fiftieth year, because a single apex is not the whole story. What matters most is the step-by-step journey on both sides, which is filled with God's good gifts, like brilliant wildflowers and cool mountain meadows.

Father, as I age and grow toward You, may I have the vision to see whole mountains, not just certain peaks.   —Carol Kuykendall

19 | F R I

Before a word is on my tongue you know it completely, O Lord.   —Psalm 139:4 (NIV)

The big reunion of "The Cousins" was months in the making. Since they lived in Hawaii and I lived in New York, we agreed to meet halfway—Disneyland, California!

I had grown up with my younger cousins tagging along like pesky puppies. I changed their diapers, sewed their party dresses, chewed them out for trying my lipstick. But then I married and moved away and missed their entire growing up! Now they were women with children of their own. I looked forward to our reunion, for there was so much catching up to do, so much I had to tell them.

We wandered around Disneyland, took in the scary rides with our kids, ate barbecued ribs and tacos. We talked and talked—though not about "important" stuff. About children and orthodontia and jobs. About what ride to go on next, what time to meet, who would stand in line…. I couldn't find the words to tell them how much I regretted missing their graduations, their weddings, the births of their children. How could they possibly know that I had never forgotten them, grieved at long distance when they suffered, still loved them the same as when we were kids?

On the morning when we would go our separate ways, we met for breakfast one last time. We devoured platefuls of eggs, drank cup after cup of coffee. We made silly jokes. We told "do you remember" stories. We could not bear to leave! Leaning together, talking in the kind of shorthand every family knows, we were "The Cousins" again: gossipy, goofy, loud.

I thought that words failed me. Yet they knew, without my saying so, how much I loved them from afar. They had always known!

Lord, remind us that we do not need the gift of eloquence to reveal our hearts. The most meaningful messages are encoded in the ordinary things we do and say.   —Linda Ching Sledge

20 | S A T   *Trust in the Lord with all your heart....*
                                        —Proverbs 3:5 (NIV)

I wanted to marry, but wasn't meeting anyone. "Help me, God," I prayed, "by sending along someone who's right for me." (Secretly, I added, "Hurry, please.")

When my prayer seemed to have fallen on deaf ears, I made a list of places I could go or things I could do to meet "Mr. Right." My friend Kati peered over my shoulder as I wrote, "Alumni mixers, classes on 'male' subjects (like cars), ask friends if they know anybody...."

"Isn't God working fast enough for you?" she laughed. Then seriously, "You know, Linda, God may have something in mind far beyond your list. When I needed a new apartment, I prayed for God to send me a cheaper place. Nothing happened for a year, and I thought God wasn't listening. Now I'm caretaker for an estate—and I live there rent-free."

Kati was right. God did have something else in mind. A month later, in a restaurant, I overheard someone with a beautiful British accent return an order of curried mushrooms. Three months later, at work, I went to the candy machine and a familiar voice said, "It's empty."

"Weren't you in a restaurant in Greenwich Village about three months ago?" I said. "You ordered curried mushrooms." It turned out that had been Paul's first visit to that restaurant (mine, too), and the first time he'd ever sent an order of food back. It also turned out that we'd worked for the same large company for more than a year but had never met before! Our chat led to lunch, and lunch to dinner and…. Recently, Paul and I just celebrated our thirteenth wedding anniversary.

Is there something in your life that you're trying to force to happen? Do what's within your grasp to contribute to that goal, but then pray, let go, and trust God to work.

Today, God, I want You to run the show.   —Linda Neukrug

21 | S U N   *The earth is the Lord's and all that is in it….*
                                          —Psalm 24:1 (NRSV)

When we built our cottage in the foothills of the Adirondacks, we luxuriated in the privacy of the woods, the stream and our view of Lake George from the windows. But a few summers later, the lots surrounding our cottage were bought, and suddenly we became very conscious of boundaries and property rights. When the land directly south of us was sold, we decided to locate the line between us and the new owners. Was the old apple tree on our land or theirs? How much of the stream belonged to us?

My husband found a stake with an orange flag down by the road while I went up in the woods to locate another. Under the dark trees I spied a splotch of brilliant color. "I've found it!" I called out. My cry startled a scarlet tanager who rocketed up from its low branch, its bright red-orange wings piercing the blue of the summer sky.

As I watched my boundary marker fly away, I could almost hear the gentle laughter of the Creator and Owner of all things.

Lord, don't let me ever forget that the earth and all that is in it belongs to You.   —Katherine Paterson

22 | M O N   *Making the most of the time.*   —Colossians 4:5 (RSV)

"You know, Drew's been acting up lately," my wife Beth commented as I helped her clear the table one evening. Drew was at that awkward point in life when he was no longer a little boy and not yet a young man. "He needs time with you. Don't you think you should take your annual trip together?"

So the next day, my twelve-year-old son and I started on a drive through some of my old stomping grounds in Georgia. One thing I know Drew enjoys is stories about my childhood. So I showed him my high school, now a deserted building. We walked on the football field, up to our knees in weeds. I recounted the horrors of summer football practice and the glories of games we had won. We looked at the cracked tennis courts, the dilapidated gym and the old cinder track. We drove to the water tower. "My buddies and I climbed this to paint the 'Class of '69' on its side." Drew laughed. We saw the church I attended, the house where I lived, the peach sheds where I worked in the summertime. Finally, we prepared to leave.

On the way out of town, we passed the cemetery. On impulse, I said, "It's time you met your family, son."

I showed him where his Civil War ancestor was buried. Slowly, we walked through the generations until we came to my father's grave. He had been dead now for thirty years. As I stood there with my son, the years came together. I placed my hand on his shoulder and said, "We didn't bring any flowers, but let's say a prayer before we leave." Drew nodded.

As I bowed my head, I noticed his hand reach up and take his baseball cap from his head and hold it by his side. And when I finished thanking God for our family, I heard his quiet voice say, "Amen."

Tears filled my eyes. A boy was coming of age in the midst of the ages.

Father, help me to take the time to create stories with my children. May good memories hold the generations together. Amen.

— Scott Walker

23 | T U E   *For every creature of God is good....*   —I Timothy 4:4

Last summer, during a dry spell, I decided to water some newly planted shrubs. As I approached one nestled in a corner, I heard a rustling sound and, suddenly, out came one, two, three, four baby rabbits! The terrified bunnies darted under some big older bushes and were still. I saw no sign of an adult rabbit anywhere. *What would happen to the babies?* I wondered. I wanted to help them, but didn't know how.

Then I remembered my friend Mary Jane Stretch. She's a wildlife rehabilitator who knows how to help orphaned animals. Surely, she could tell me how to feed the baby rabbits.

"Leave them alone," Mary Jane told me. "Just because you don't see the mother, that doesn't mean she isn't there."

"But won't they starve?" I asked.

"Watch them," Mary Jane said, "but from a distance. Let the mother find out it's safe to come and get them."

"And if she doesn't?" I wanted to know.

"Then I'll tell you how to feed them."

From my garage window I could see the bushes where the bunnies had taken shelter, and I looked out every few minutes. Sure enough, after about two hours, the mother rabbit cautiously made her way to one of the bushes and scurried under it. The babies quickly joined her.

I was so glad I had waited. The mother rabbit could do more for her babies than I ever could. And while I will continue to welcome every opportunity to help an animal in distress, I'm learning that sometimes the first thing to do is to find out what it needs. Otherwise, I may do more harm than good.

Almighty Father, help us to become more aware of the needs of Your wild creatures.
                                                        —Phyllis Hobe

24 | W E D   *To Timothy, my dear son: Grace, mercy and peace from God the Father and Christ Jesus our Lord.*
                                          —II Timothy 1:2 (NIV)

"Mr. Weary, can I talk to you?"

It was John, the coordinator of our Mendenhall Ministries recreation activities. He and his wife have been living here and volunteering their services for a couple of years now.

"How are things going?" I asked.

"You know," he replied, "I've been thinking about who would take my place after I leave. I want so much for the leaders to come from here in Simpson County." He was working with several young men, he said, and one high school student in particular. "Richard has great potential," he told me, "and I am committed to working with him. We've been having Bible studies together."

As he talked, my mind went back thirty years to the time I was a high school student from a poor family, with little hope of anything like a college education. A local barber, Leonard Stapleton, took an interest in me. He introduced me to John Perkins, the man who started Mendenhall Ministries, who introduced me to Jesus Christ. Leonard and John helped me go to college, and then John brought me back here to Mendenhall.

"The other day," our coordinator went on, "I asked Richard to open the gym and be responsible for the evening activities while I was out of town, and he did a wonderful job."

"What you are doing with Richard is just what the Apostle Paul did with Timothy," I told John. "Paul called Timothy his dear son, because he walked with him in his development. Now you're willing to walk with Richard and challenge him to grow in Christ and 'fan into flame the gift of God' in him" (II Timothy 1:6, NIV).

John left my office on a super high, encouraged and energized to be the best "Paul" he could be. And I was reminded that I, too, needed to be conscientious about the Timothys in my life, those who might be following my example with or without my awareness. And then it hit me — maybe John is my Timothy!

Lord, thank You for the opportunity for us to be "Pauls" to "Timothys." May we be faithful encouragers. — Dolphus Weary

---

25 | T H U *His name shall be called Wonderful....* — Isaiah 9:6

I have what my husband David calls a love affair with words. There are only twenty-six letters in our alphabet, and it seems pretty amazing to me that lined up in a particular way, those letters form the words that offer unimaginable power.

Sometimes when I need a bit of help in saying just what I want to say, I turn to my well-worn thesaurus. If, for instance, I want to talk about *happiness* but feel the word suffers from overuse, the thesaurus offers *joy*, *delight*, *bliss* and *elation* as handy alternatives. My thesaurus extends my comprehension of happiness and stretches the horizons of its meaning.

Over morning coffee, David and I talk about new sermon ideas for him. "I don't suppose we'd find words like *Jesus*," he says as he leafs through the thesaurus. "Why, here it is." He reads silently, then hands it to me.

I read out loud, "Jesus, Jesu, the Redeemer, the Savior, Emmanuel, the Messiah, the Star of David, the Expected One, the King of Kings, the Prince of Peace…." In all, there are no less than twenty-five lines offering synonyms for Jesus, including *the Morning Star, the Good Shepherd, the Healer*, and finally ending with *the Way, the Door, the Truth, the Life*.

The sunlight filters through the window and brings a reverence to our morning. David and I sit in awe, unable, really, to understand the unending list of titles that have evolved since "the Word was made flesh, and dwelt among us" (John 1:14). Just considering the scope of meaning behind all the names attributed to this one lone man fills me with, well, bliss…elation…joy!

Everlasting Father, You are our Word of words. We praise Your name.   —Pam Kidd

26 | F
R
I | *God…richly provides us with everything for our enjoyment.*   —I Timothy 6:17 (NIV)

"Why do I get so much junk mail?" I complained to my friend Desila recently. My entire dining room table was covered with mail-order catalogs. Again. An avalanche of colorful pages offered hiking clothes, athletic shoes, kitchen doodads, electronics, even greeting cards and seasonal decorations.

Desila laughed. "It's because you keep ordering out of them!" She was right. Time and again I had found just the item I'd been wanting and placed an order.

After Desila left, I began to paw my way through the mess, tossing out some catalogs, saving others. That's when I noticed it. Buried beneath the barrage of solicitations was my Bible.

Embarrassed, I pulled it out and began flipping through its pages. And, suddenly, I realized that the Bible, too, is a "catalog" of sorts. It tells me how to get peace and contentment (Romans 8:6). It encourages me to ask for joy (John 16:24). It even lets me order laughter (Job 8:21)!

So I've decided to keep the Bible on top of my catalogs. It will remind me that it's not the mail that delivers the things that bring true enjoyment. It's God! And He always gets the order right.

Dear God, You know what I need before I ask. Remind me to store up spiritual treasures and not mail-order ones.   —Mary Lou Carney

27 | S A T | *Better is a neighbor who is near than a brother who is far away.* —Proverbs 27:10 (RSV)

I was looking forward to a quiet vacation in the woods. My husband Terry set up our tiny travel trailer for me in a grassy clearing beside Willow Creek and left me to my solitude. Suddenly, the quiet was broken by a huge motor home moving in and parking fifty feet away.

When an amiable-looking, white-haired man appeared outdoors, I grudgingly walked over to introduce myself. Jack and Darlene were from Missouri and had come to Alaska to do some gold prospecting along the creeks. "How long are you planning to stay?" I asked.

"Oh, thought we'd stick around a couple of weeks," Jack replied matter-of-factly.

Two weeks! There goes my quiet vacation! I went back to my trailer to sulk. But by the end of the two weeks, I had a stack of reasons for needing my neighbors from Missouri. My car had a flat—Jack changed it. The battery went dead—Jack recharged it. I ran out of ice—Darlene shared hers. I needed to make a call—Jack lent me his cellular phone. I left overnight to restock supplies and accidentally forgot to feed my dog—Darlene fed her scraps from her own table. And in between all that, I still had plenty of time for uninterrupted reflection while Jack and Darlene were off prospecting.

The day Terry returned to haul the trailer home, the retirees were away. He and I found the summer's first blueberries along a hiking trail. I picked a hat full and left them on Jack and Darlene's doorstep. It seemed the perfect farewell gift for the perfect neighbors.

Lord, may there always be room at my campfire for a neighbor.
—Carol Knapp

28 | S U N | *Whatever you do, do all to the glory of God.* —I Corinthians 10:31 (NAS)

"We've had a sudden change in plans and I'm wondering if you can help out." It was our pastor on the phone, on a busy Saturday afternoon in gardening season. "Can you host the guest soloist and her husband for lunch after church tomorrow?"

I gasped inwardly as I looked around the kitchen. We'd been tending to an abundant crop of vegetables from our garden, and our four kids had all been "helping," as evidenced by a trail of empty pea pods leading to the TV and wilted carrot tops strewn about on the counter. I was stirring a big kettle of brine to pickle the bushel basket of muddy cucumbers sitting on the table. The entire family had tracked in so many grass clippings I could have mowed the kitchen floor instead of mopping it. Having company tomorrow would necessitate a major cleanup campaign *today*.

I was about to say no when I remembered the sermon from last Sunday about showing hospitality to strangers. "Yes, Pastor, I think we can manage it," I responded, though with a grimace and a sigh.

Hastily, I finished the pickling, then mopped, tidied, dusted and vacuumed the entire house. *What a lot of trouble that was just for them,* I thought as I collapsed, exhausted, into bed. *I hope it's worth it.*

The next morning at church I found that our guests were not strangers at all. They were good friends, Gail and Gary Varty. And they are both *blind!*

I needn't have gone to all that trouble! I told myself during church. Later, as we ate lunch, we all had a good chuckle about the futility of my cleanup efforts when they couldn't be seen anyway.

"Oh, but I can *smell* the difference," Gail declared.

Her comment has never left me. It reminds me that though much of my work may be behind the scenes, like typing the church bulletin or folding the laundry, the results are almost always proportionate to the time and effort I expend. And perceptive people can "smell" the difference.

Father, thank You that You see and appreciate whatever I do for You, however small. Help me always to do it to the best of my abilities.
—Alma Barkman

---

29 | M O N | *What is man that thou art mindful of him, and the son of man that thou dost care for him?* —Psalm 8:4 (RSV)

A girlfriend once sent me a cartoon. The first little guy said, "Life is unfair." The second little guy said, "Yeah, but I wish it was unfair my way for a change!" She'd sent it because I was feeling sorry for myself because of a job I didn't get.

Interestingly enough, a few days later, an insurance salesman came by to see if he could provide me with a better medical plan. He was astounded that I paid fifty dollars a month for premium coverage. "The cheapest I can do is two hundred forty-five dollars!" he said.

From my perspective, fifty was steep. But two hundred forty-five?

"I've never even heard of that company," he went on. "You sure they're legit? Do they ever pay out?"

I told him how much, and he nearly fell off his chair. "How you lucked out, I'll never know."

Yes, sometimes life is unfair. Yet, occasionally, life is unfair *my way.* Like when I put my hand in my pocket and found fifty dollars I'd forgotten about. Or when I fell behind in a class in graduate school and my professor, who knew my circumstances, excused me from the work and gave me an A anyway. I definitely was on the receiving end more than I had realized.

So now when I get bogged down in feeling sorry for myself, I take three minutes for self-pity, then start recalling how many times life has been "unfair my way." And I thank God.

Heavenly Father, thank You for Your many interventions on my behalf. Help me to remember these acts of grace when I am tempted to feel sorry for myself.   — Brenda Wilbee

30 | T U E   *A man of understanding shall attain unto wise counsels.*
                                          — Proverbs 1:5

Years ago, when I was applying for admission to graduate school, I was petrified at the thought of the preliminary exam I'd have to take — five hours on five essay questions. I had never felt good about tests, especially essay exams. "What if I read the questions and don't understand them?" I asked my friend who was an assistant in the department. "What if I have a mental block and can't remember the things I've studied?"

His smile let me know that while he understood my anxiety, he didn't think I should worry. "When you open the envelope, take a minute to read the questions carefully," he counseled. "There will probably be at least one question that leaves you cold, but there will also be one you know so well that you can answer it with ease. Ignore the one that frightens you and answer the one you know well."

He was right. By the time I had written a couple of hours on the easier questions, I was more relaxed and could remember the things

I'd studied. I even did a good job with the question that had originally frightened me.

Even today, I sometimes find myself daunted by a list of things I
must accomplish in a day or a week. The more difficult items intimidate me, and I'm tempted to tear up the list and go fishing! But then
I remember my friend's advice. I say a prayer, pick out several of the
easier tasks and start on them. When they're finished, it seems easy
to go on to the ones I dreaded. And almost before I know it, the harder
ones are finished. Then I thank God for His help and for the wisdom
that came to me through a friend.

Father, help me to do what I can, and in the doing to find new
confidence for larger responsibilities.   —Kenneth Chafin

31 | W E D *"Thy friends be like the sun...."*   —Judges 5:31 (RSV)

Maybe I was too cocky. Maybe it had been too easy.

I had graduated from college on time. I had taken a once-in-a-lifetime trip to Europe with the money I had been investing since high
school. And now I was home and ready to begin my dream job. Only
the man at the bank who had said, "We'll have your job waiting when
you return," was now telling me, "I'm so sorry, Brock, but while you
were gone the board instituted a hiring freeze." I was in shock, and I
felt so alone. I was embarrassed to face my family with the news,
much less anyone else.

Almost immediately, I pounded the pavement, résumé in hand.
The next week was filled with, "Sorry, twenty-two is just too young."
"Come back when you have experience." "Actually, we're not hiring
right now, but if you'll leave your name...."

The second week was no better than the first. The third week was
worse. I prayed, "God, please give me the job I want before everyone
finds out that I'm unemployed." But, eventually, the news leaked out
to my church.

Sam Oakley, a young mentor of mine, telephoned. "Brock," he said,
"the same thing happened to me when I got out of school. Believe me,
things will turn around." A young businessman, Sherman Mohr, offered his office facilities as a home base for incoming calls. M.R.
Bracy dragged a banker friend to church for the express purpose of

introducing him to me. And Kate Wells, Frances Faulkner and John Upham called to say they were praying for me.

"No man is an island," I've always heard. And as the love and support of family and friends warmed me and gave me new hope, I began to understand just what that saying really meant. My prayers changed from "give me" to "forgive me"—for my foolish pride.

Thank You for the strength I receive from my many friends—and from You, dear God.   —Brock Kidd

GIFTS OF LIGHT

1 _____

2 _____

3 _____

4 _____

5 _____

6 _____

7 _____

8 _____

9 _____

10 _____

11 _____

12 _____

13 _____

14 _____

15 _____

16 _____

17 _____

18 _____

19 _____

JULY 1996

20 _____

21 _____

22 _____

23 _____

24 _____

25 _____

26 _____

27 _____

28 _____

29 _____

30 _____

31 _____

O send out thy light and thy truth: let them lead me....

—PSALM 43:3

AUGUST

S	M	T	W	T	F	S
				1	2	3
4	5	6	7	8	9	10
11	12	13	14	15	16	17
18	19	20	21	22	23	24
25	26	27	28	29	30	31

1 | T
  | H   *Let the heavens rejoice, and let the earth be glad....*
  | U   —Psalm 96:11

When we were traveling in England and Ireland last summer, wherever we went it rained. And rained. And *rained.* Our coach driver in Ireland took a positive view. "Sure," he said, "it's only rained twice this week. The first time for four days, the second time for three!"

So we had to content ourselves with glumly scanning the weather reports. Usually, they promised fog, mist and clouds. But sometimes there was a hopeful line: "Possible bright intervals." So if even a flicker of sunshine came through, someone was sure to shout, "Look! Look! A bright interval!"

"It's like life, isn't it?" said one of the youngest members of our group. "You just have to keep looking for bright intervals."

"Not at all," said our oldest member. "Life is mostly sunshine for most of us. You just have to be prepared for a few rainy days now and then. And not complain too much. After all, God made them, too."

God made them, too. I thought of that ringing phrase from Psalm 118:24: *This is the day which the Lord hath made; we will rejoice and be glad in it.* The psalmist didn't distinguish between rainy days or sunny days, cold ones or hot ones. We were supposed to rejoice and be glad. For what? For the gift of life itself, regardless of the circumstances. When I kept that thought in mind, the rain seemed silvery, not gloomy.

Amazing what the Bible will teach you. If you just give it a chance.

Thank You, Lord, for the marvelous diversity that surrounds us, today and every day.   —Arthur Gordon

2 | F
  | R   *Unless the Lord builds the house, its builders labor in*
  | I   *vain....*   —Psalm 127:1 (NIV)

"What's troubling you, Harry?" I asked, awakened by my husband's restlessness.

"I'm worrying about the hole we excavated for the foundation today. I think we put too much gravel in there—it's going to make the house too high out of the ground. I got distracted by the work and didn't pay enough attention to the plans. If only I had watched it more carefully."

It was obvious that neither of us would sleep for a while, so we lay in bed talking it over. For months, we had carefully considered the placement of the house on the sloping site. We had already moved it up or down by a foot or two several times — but always on paper. This time was for real.

Yesterday, before the excavating equipment arrived on the scene, we had stood on the site and prayed for this place. "Lord, we want this to be Your house. A place of beauty and peace, a place that will welcome others and will nurture us. Help us to be good stewards of what You have given us."

The next morning we went out to look it over. We measured and marked and debated, and when the contractor arrived we discussed it with him. Over the next few days, as work progressed, it became evident that the higher floor would actually give us a much better view, plus a more usable, walkout basement instead of a windowless storage area.

We still find ourselves worrying about things we can't control. *What if it rains just after we pour the concrete? What if winter arrives before we get the house weathered in? What if…?* But now we have an agreement: Whenever we catch ourselves worrying, our automatic response is, "Whose house is this anyway?"

Heavenly Father, help us to do our very best with this project, while always remembering that You are ultimately in charge.
— Mary Jane Clark

3 | S A T   *Whither shall I go from thy Spirit?…*   — Psalm 139:7

The Summer Olympics end in Atlanta tomorrow. For the past two weeks I have played a spectator's game that is all my own. It's a search to find the picture that visually sums up my choice for the Games' most inspirational story. I will then add it to a memory file that I can turn to when I need visual reminders of God's care for His children.

In 1992, the picture I found at the Summer Olympics was of runner Derek Redmond. Redmond was the British record holder for the 400-meter race. He missed the 1988 Summer Olympics because of injuries. After five operations on his Achilles tendon and working hard to get back into top shape, he made the 1992 British Olympic team and had all his hopes pinned on the 400-meter race. But halfway through the semifinal heat, something popped in his right leg and he fell to the ground, writhing in pain while the others finished the race. For a moment, he knelt on the track as if in prayer, and then struggled to his feet, looking toward the finish line. With his face contorted in pain, he slowly began hopping, dragging his useless leg behind him.

Soon everyone in the stadium stood up and began cheering his courageous effort. A man began moving down through the stands, brushing by the officials who tried to stop him. "That's my son," he said simply as he made his way across the track to the runner's side. The two spoke briefly, and then the father put his arm around his son and the pair slowly made their way toward the finish line.

This picture powerfully portrays a father's love and reminds me that our Father is always with us.

Father, thank You for every reminder that You always walk alongside us.
— Carol Kuykendall

4 | S U N | *So we, being many, are one body in Christ....Having then gifts differing according to the grace that is given to us....*
— Romans 12:5–6

Last Sunday, the choir director came up to my daughter Karen who, like her mother, doesn't carry a tune very well. "I've noticed that you don't sing the hymns," he told her.

"I can't sing!" she said.

"It doesn't matter," he replied. "Really! Some voices are right on pitch, and we need those people. But in the congregation, we also need the voices that aren't perfectly pitched in order to round out the sound. All of them blend together *and God hears it whole!* So please, go ahead and sing!" Karen decided to do just that the next Sunday... and her mom might even get up the courage to do it, too.

Maybe it's the same with any other ability. The world surely needs the very talented ones, those who truly excel. But perhaps, just as in the singing of hymns, those with average talent still have a contribution to make. So, with my writing and teaching, I will quit comparing myself to others. Instead, I'll work hard at what I do. I'll sing my own part of the song, knowing that "God hears it whole!"

Thank You, Lord, for giving each of us valued parts in Your inclusive song.
— Marilyn Morgan Helleberg

5 | M O N   *"For we have heard for ourselves, and we know that this is indeed the Savior of the world."*   —John 4:42 (RSV)

Returning from a visit with our exchange student's family in Japan, my sixteen-year-old daughter Brenda and her friend Kirsten stopped in Seoul, South Korea—the second largest city in the world, with a population of ten million. Brenda telephoned in the evening to say she had only forty dollars, the airport was closing, and they had no place to spend the night. "Gotta go. Bye, Mom." *Click.*

There I was, far away at home in Alaska, worried, powerless to help. "Jesus," I prayed, "be a shield of protection around the girls." Later, I learned what happened next.

The girls were loaded down with luggage, waiting outside the airport for a ninety-minute bus ride to a cheap hotel. At the bus stop, they met a Korean gentleman on business from Sydney, Australia. He offered them sanctuary in his brother's medical clinic, which wasn't far—and it was free. A profound peace enfolded Brenda, and she was certain it was okay to go with this man.

The next day he suggested they store their luggage at the clinic, and he guided them safely to the marketplace to begin their sightseeing. While there, Kirsten left her wallet with her passport in one of the crowded shops. An hour later, they relocated the store and an employee had the wallet. After that, they met two young Koreans in a public park who offered to give them a walking tour of the city, and even paid their admission to the Changdok Palace. Then they helped the girls find their way back to the clinic to retrieve their luggage before their flight home.

"Powerless" did I say I'd been after receiving Brenda's phone call? That's not true. I may have been worried, but I had the power of prayer. There are times when prayer is the only thing you can do—and the best.

Dear Lord, prayer protects, prayer produces effects, and prayer is too critical to neglect ... for You are the undeniable power in prayer.
                                                        —Carol Knapp

6 | T U E   *A time to heal....*   —Ecclesiastes 3:3

Jamie, my eleven-year-old granddaughter, phoned today and didn't seem to have much to say. Her silence told me that something was wrong. Usually, she talks nonstop, laughs often and asks enthusiastically, "Guess what, Nanny?" Finally, she blurted out, "Nanny, I miss Robbie so much today. I know it's stupid. He's been dead for nearly three years. But I can't stop thinking about him — what he would have looked like."

Robbie was her little brother. He'd lived only twenty-five minutes. He was a beautiful baby. She continued, "I mean, why am I so sad *today?*" Her voice broke, and she released her tears into the phone.

How do you explain to a child that grief is a sneaky thing? That you think it's all over and, suddenly, it reappears. That grief doesn't play fair. "I miss him, too, Jamie."

"I do something pretty dumb, but it helps," she sniffed.

"What, Jamie?"

"You won't laugh? Promise?"

"Promise."

"Well, I've discovered that if I write his name, that it helps somehow. I don't know how, but I've been writing it a lot today."

We hung up after a bit, and I sat at the phone and began to print, "Robbie — Robert Clifford Garmon — Robbie, Robbie, Robbie...."

Dear Lord, I had forgotten that steps to healing are sometimes very simple. Amen.   — Marion Bond West

7 | W E D   *A man's enemies are the members of his own family.*
                                      — Micah 7:6 (GNB)

I seldom go to New York City because I've always considered New Yorkers rude. Then, on one of my rare trips, I was on an upper floor of the World Trade Center in a cafeteria line, hoping to spear my lunch from the midst of the ravenous hordes. I was in doubt that I, a gentle Minnesotan, would be allowed my place in line as pushy New Yorkers struggled for their food.

I was next up to tell the cook what hamburger I wanted when, just as I expected, two gray-haired ladies attempted to slip in ahead of me. I was having none of it. I moved my bulk between them and the cook, feigned ignorance of their fluttering behind my back, placed my order, received my hamburger, stalked to my table victoriously, and left them to cut off the next person in line — who happened to be a friend and colleague of mine.

When that friend sat down, she asked me, "Why did you block the two ladies from their meal?"

"I am tired of pushy New Yorkers," I said. "They tried to shove in ahead of me. I'm not taking it."

Very gently she replied, "They are not New Yorkers. I heard them earlier. They are visitors. They were ten places ahead of us in line and the cook asked them to be seated while he prepared their salads. He had just called them back to the counter when you blocked their way."

Well, so much for "rude New Yorkers." How in the world did I become as nasty as I imagined those around me to be?

Dear Lord, prevent me from turning other people into ferocious enemies out of the whole cloth of my fears.   —John Cowan

8 | T H U *I tried to find fulfillment by inaugurating a great public works program: homes, vineyards, gardens, parks…. But as I looked at everything I had tried, it was all so useless….*
—Ecclesiastes 2:4–5, 11 (TLB)

An old teacher friend of mine, Norval Campbell, once advised me, "Don't make your garden so large that you can't tend it." I didn't understand his advice at the time, but I do now—after the Great Missouri Flood of '93.

The heavy rains that started in the spring and never let up discouraged me from having my usual large garden out behind the college where I teach. Instead, I just set out a few things around the house: four tomato plants, a dozen okra plants, a few flowers and some asparagus.

I was amazed to discover that this little planting gave me more pleasure than my large garden, and plenty of produce. The reason? The small garden was more manageable. The bigger garden was always ahead of me with weeds and bugs and the need for cultivation. But four tomato plants? I could weed, water and fertilize them, stake them, and check them for worms in only a few minutes a week. And those four produced more tomatoes than the fifteen plants I had last year, and I had enough okra to feed the neighbors, too.

Overextending is an easy mistake to make. Next time I'm tempted to do too much, I'll remember my garden.

Lord, sometimes bigger isn't better. Help me to live a manageable life.   —Daniel Schantz

9 | F R I

The eternal God is thy refuge, and underneath are the everlasting arms....   —Deuteronomy 33:27

For weeks I'd been putting off a phone call to schedule some rather unpleasant intestinal tests. I dreaded both the tests and the possible results. I'd tell myself, *I'll do it today*, but when evening came, the call was still unmade. Then at a picnic in the park one day, God met me at my point of fear.

Seated on our picnic blanket, my husband John and I watched the family next to us. The children, four of them, were playing a game our own two children had loved. They spun themselves about, then took turns falling backward into their father's arms. One little tot was apprehensive. He giggled and laughed as his brothers spun him, but when it came to falling backward, he was afraid and wouldn't do it. We watched as the whole family urged the little fellow on. When finally he got up the gumption to trust his dad and fell into his arms, we all clapped our hands and yelled, "Yeah!" Suddenly, there was no stopping him—he did it again and again until the other children insisted on their turns.

"Dear Lord," I prayed that night, "I'm afraid to take these tests, but I will put my trust in Your everlasting arms. I know You will catch me and set me on my feet again." I could almost hear God's voice shouting, "Yeah!"

The next morning I made the appointment, and a few days later I took the tests. They were not easy, but I was not afraid as I took the plunge. My Father's arms were there. And the results of the tests showed no problems.

Dear Father God, I put my trust in You to meet me at my point of fear.   —Fay Angus

10 | S A T

...To be a joyful mother of children....   —Psalm 113:9

It's a late summer afternoon. My daughter Keri, seventeen, and I are out running together. As we jog along, I can't help but think ahead to the weekend when my husband David and I will be driving Keri to Alabama for her first semester at Birmingham Southern College.

Her first day of kindergarten replays in my mind. She lets go of David's and my hands and walks straight into the classroom without ever glancing back. I stand out in the hall, weeping. Yet don't misunderstand those long-ago tears. When Keri stepped into kindergarten with confidence, it was akin to winning a motherhood award. Temporary sadness quickly gave way to a greater joy.

There were other triumphs mixed with tears. During Keri's mid-teens I wasn't sure I was up to the challenge of motherhood, but we both hung in for the long haul. Now here we are running through the neighborhood together, except I am getting winded. I fall back; Keri keeps running. Up ahead, a burst of sunshine tangles in her long blonde ponytail as she makes a turn in the road and disappears from my sight. She never looks back. I know I'll miss her. But she's going into the future with confidence, and I feel like I have won one of those six-foot-high trophies.

I retrace my steps toward home, alone. How beautiful life seems as the evening settles in around me with a clear message: *There are no endings in motherhood.* And I find myself anticipating all the news Keri will be bringing back from a future I cannot know. For now, "being there" for her is my greatest privilege. And I feel proud and look forward to whatever lies ahead in my next stretch of motherhood, knowing full well that joy comes with the journey.

God, to be a mother is to know great joy, and I thank You for this best blessing.
                                                        — Pam Kidd

11 | S U N | *I can do all things through Christ which strengtheneth me.*
                                                        — Philippians 4:13

To walk on a beach is, for me, a time of meditation. I agree with the psalmist who wrote, "Deep calls to deep at the sound of Thy water-falls" (Psalm 42:7, NAS). To stroll beside the waves is to listen to the voice of my soul.

Yesterday, I spent such a day at the beach. It was a time of evaluating my forty-three years, my past with its victories and failures, weaknesses and strengths, as well as wondering about the future and my ability to cope with all the responsibilities that I could see ahead of me.

I was deep in thought as I walked along when I saw a sight that amazed me. A balding man, middle-aged and athletic, was standing in the pounding surf. Facing the breakers, he braced as each wave hit him, a broad smile of joy on his face. But he had only one leg! Hopping around like a wounded flamingo as he battled each wave, he managed to keep his balance. His crutches lay behind him on the sand. Then a wave knocked him flat. As he struggled to stand, he laughed joyously, delighting in the battle.

The sight of this one-legged man in the surf spoke volumes to me. No matter how I might see myself injured by life — and we all are — no matter my weaknesses and failures, I have a choice. I can sit safely on the beach with my crutches, or I can boldly confront life's challenges.

Today, I have returned to my many responsibilities and tasks with joy, exulting in the demands of the day.

Lord, help me to rejoice in challenge and learn from adversity.
— Scott Walker

12 | M O N *I will therefore now make preparation for it....*
— I Chronicles 22:5

I was a college sophomore when I was called into the U.S. Army to fight in World War II. I was sent to Camp Wolters, Texas, where on the very first day, in 110-degree heat, we were marched to the parade ground to learn close-order drill.

Sergeant McElwain, heavyset and red of face, barked out orders. "Ri-i-i-ight, face!" After being chewed out a few times, we learned never to move on the word *Ri-i-i-ight*, but only on the word *face*.

I soon discovered that Sergeant McElwain was following a time-tested pattern for giving an order. First comes the slow, drawn out "preparation command" after which the officer snaps the "command of execution."

I have since found this same sequence often applies to my ongoing walk with God: A long period when nothing seems to happen is followed by a sudden rush of activity. I remember how, years ago, my wife Tib and I had run out of living space in our small starter home. The baby slept next to the laundry machine; the garage was full of bikes and boxes; our bedroom doubled as an office. Clearly, it was time to move. We began looking for a new home, but in spite of our continuing prayers nothing showed up. An entire year passed. Two. And still we saw nothing we liked or could afford.

Then one day a neighbor told us about a house that had just come on the market. It had exactly the number of rooms we needed; it had woods, a brook, two fireplaces. Tib walked around the house in one direction, I walked around it the other way. We met in the front yard, nodded and threw our arms around each other.

The long preparation command had been followed by an abrupt command of execution. Now we acted in a hurry. Within one week we agreed on terms, and we have been happy in our home for more than thirty-seven years.

Lord, how I appreciate Your preparing my heart and mind for the things You have in store for me to do. —John Sherrill

13 | T U E *We do not know how to pray as we ought, but the Spirit himself intercedes for us....* —Romans 8:26 (RSV)

Sometimes as I hurry from home, to the train, to work, to the health club, to home again, I feel like the White Rabbit in *Alice in Wonderland* who rushed about looking anxiously at his pocket watch and muttering, "Oh, dear! Oh, dear! I shall be too late."

So when I read the other day in *Life* magazine (March 1994) that twenty-eight percent of Americans who pray (and nine out of ten of us do) pray for more than one hour a day, I felt guilty. *How could anyone find an hour a day to pray?* I asked myself. I couldn't even find five minutes except to mutter, "Please God, let me not miss the train." What was wrong with me?

This whole dilemma was on my mind as I changed into my gym clothes to do my daily exercise routine. I'm pretty good about exercising because I feel that sitting all day is bad not only for the figure but also for the temper. I began my customary twenty-five-minute brisk walk on the treadmill, looking idly out of the window. *I wonder if we're out of milk*, I thought. *No, there's half a carton left. Charlotte [my daughter] might call tonight....*

Then a story I had read flashed into my mind. It was about a woman who learned to pray while waiting in line at the supermarket. She had realized that fretting and irritation didn't make the time pass any quicker. So she got into the habit of giving thanks for family and friends as she waited.

If she could pray in the checkout line, why couldn't I pray walking on a treadmill? Twenty-five minutes may not be an hour, and a busy fitness club may not have the quiet reverence of a church, but I was alone and my mind was free. Then and there, I dedicated my daily walking to prayer, beginning with the most familiar words I knew:

"Our Father, Which art in heaven, Hallowed be Thy name. Thy kingdom come. Thy will be done...." —Brigitte Weeks

14 $\begin{smallmatrix} W \\ E \\ D \end{smallmatrix}$ *If it is encouraging, let him encourage....*
                                    —Romans 12:8 (NIV)

I have a confession to make. I pray about fishing. It may not be fair to
the fish, but I need all the help I can get. I admit, however, that in
thirty-five years of the sport, prayer has never worked...except once.

During our houseboat trip last summer, my son Jon and I were
teaching my cousin Gary and his son Caleb how to fish. After discussing baits, locations and weather, we settled down to an afternoon
of limited success. Which caused Gary to comment, "So, fishing is
like life. You work and work at it, and every once in awhile you have a
little success to keep you going."

We all laughed, but I noticed a look of determination settle on Jon.
Being the youngest, he'd had a tough summer with his brothers who
constantly reminded him he wasn't big enough, old enough or smart
enough to do all the fun things they did. I could tell he needed a little success, so I prayed, "Lord, it has never worked before for me, but
how about letting Jon catch a fish today?"

A few minutes later I guided the boat into a remote bay where
grassy weeds and lily pads rimmed the rocky shore. "Perfect water for
northern pike," I announced, switching to the hum of the trolling
motor. Jon stood and flicked a cast just to the edge of the weeds. As
he cranked it back, something grabbed it hard. Sure enough, after
skillfully fighting the fish for about ten minutes, Jon boated a nice
northern pike. In the middle of all the excitement, he looked up at
me and asked, "Dad, Jason and Nathan never caught one that big,
did they?"

Did God send that fish? You decide. All I know is that praying for
fishing never worked until I wasn't praying for myself, but for the
need of a little success in the life of someone else.

*Thanks, Lord, that You care about everything, even fishing, but
especially our need for a little encouragement once in awhile.*
                                    —Eric Fellman

15 $\begin{smallmatrix} T \\ H \\ U \end{smallmatrix}$ *"What do those stones mean...?"*   —Joshua 4:6 (RSV)

At the end of World War II in August 1945, when the first American
military personnel came to take control of Shanghai from the Japanese,
a number of American sailors visited the camp where my family and
I had been interned for two and a half years. They brought with them

AUGUST 1996   215

candy, chewing gum and the newest American movies, including *Meet Me in St. Louis*! We were anxious to find someone from Arizona, my mother's home—perhaps one of my Navy cousins. But every sailor we asked turned out to be from New Jersey! All I knew about New Jersey at age thirteen was that it was so small, its name on the map was usually written in the Atlantic Ocean. How could such a small state have so many sailors on one ship?

Now, more than fifty years later, I am living in that "small" state, which I now know is densely populated. But I hadn't thought of those New Jersey sailors until the day I walked through a small park near my home in Jersey City to read the markers that stood in front of a row of trees. Instead of the names of trees, I read the names of New Jersey veterans who served their country in the wars of this century, including some who had served in the Pacific in World War II. *Were any of them on that first ship to get to Shanghai?* I wondered.

So now, each year, August 15 is a personal reminder not only to mark the day the war ended for me, but also to pray for all servicemen and servicewomen and to remember with gratitude all veterans — in particular, those from this "little" state who brought us such a large taste of freedom.

Lord, thank You for all who have given their lives for their country.
— Mary Ruth Howes

16 | F R I *MY GIFT TODAY...*
THE RECEIPT

He calleth his own sheep by name....   —John 10:3

I found my gift today in a grocery sack. I was putting away the food I'd brought in from the car, checking the items against the cash register receipt. Skim milk, orange juice, Earl Grey tea, carrots.... How could three bags of groceries come to sixty-two dollars and seven cents?

That's when I came to my gift — on that white strip of figures from the register. At the bottom of the long column, just below the dismaying total, I read: "Valued Customer 43220884464."

I gaped at the eleven-digit figure. Was I really valued customer forty-three billion, two hundred twenty million, eight hundred eighty-four thousand, four hundred sixty-four? Truly valued, as the receipt claimed, among so many?

It's a question I remember asking, many years ago, of God. In a universe with billions of galaxies, on a planet with billions of people, could He possibly care about me?

Staring at the register receipt, I recalled His answer. *I do not count My children,* He seemed to say, *I name them.* It was a new thought to me — the importance of names, all through the Bible. How genuinely valued a name makes us! To my heavenly Father I am not a number, but an individual. Not Valued Child 873972491, but Elizabeth. Known by name, called by name, written by His own hand in the Book of Life.

I'm so grateful, Father, that You count not in billions, but one by one.
                                                    — Elizabeth Sherrill

17 | S A T | *How good and how pleasant it is for brethren to dwell together in unity!* — Psalm 133:1

"Amy wants you to come for her graduation," my brother Mike said when he called us from Hilo, Hawaii, where he has retired from the U.S. Marine Corps. "Besides, you've *never* visited us."

So my husband Don and I went. Mike was better than a professional tour guide at showing us the sights. His wife Connie and I made leis to drape around Amy's neck when she graduated (summa cum laude!) from Kalaheo High School. We walked on the beach with my nephew John and his girlfriend. We shared memories and tears — of Daddy, who died when Mike was only twelve. Of Mother, whose death in 1993 left us as the family elders. Mike talked about his time as a U.S. Marine in Saudi Arabia, and I admitted I still had every single letter he'd written to me.

We laughed a lot, too! I laughed more than Mike when ladies from his church thought I was the youngest. (My hair still isn't as gray as his!) He laughed hardest when I swallowed half the Pacific trying to snorkel. Everyone else laughed at us when we played with the cat. "I bet you're the only two people in the world who ask cats questions and then answer in cat voices," Amy said.

What a precious gift the trip gave Mike and me: the opportunity to rediscover what it means to be family. I hope our experience will encourage you to make plans to reconnect with your family today if time and distance have kept you apart. Being family is too valuable to lose.

Father, thank You for the tears and laughter and memories and love that unite us.
                                                    — Penney Schwab

18 | S U N | *For unto every one that hath shall be given, and he shall have abundance....* — Matthew 25:29

Recently, we had occasion to get rid of a large double stroller. It was almost new and we figured we could put up a sign at our son Timothy's nursery school and sell it, pocketing whatever sum it brought. On the other hand, there was a good church thrift store near my office that could probably use a donation like this.

As I was debating the options, I happened to read the parable of the talents and how God's wrath was reserved for the servant who did nothing with the money left him. I wondered about our slightly used double stroller. *What was the best way to multiply our unexpected bounty?* As always, my wife Carol had the last word: "Give it away."

A week later we were at church, when a good friend who'd just had a second child rolled in with the nicest looking, turquoise double stroller. Suspicious of its origins, Carol asked her where she'd gotten it. "You'll never guess," our friend said. "I'd just given up hope of buying one when Mom found this at a thrift shop."

Not bad for multiplication of talents, I thought. *A charitable gift from us, a bargain for a grandmother, a modest sum for the thrift shop and the perfect double stroller for a good friend.*

Dear Lord, I know I can never go wrong with the talents You've left me if I give them away. — Rick Hamlin

19 | M O N | *I do not cease to give thanks for you, remembering you in my prayers.* — Ephesians 1:16 (RSV)

"We just can't decide where to send Elizabeth to school in the fall," I told my friend Deborah. "There are so many possibilities."

"Well," Deborah said, "Tom and I have been asking God to give you and Alex knowledge of His will, with wisdom and understanding."

"That's exactly what we need!" I said. "What a wonderful prayer!"

Deborah laughed. "We didn't think of it ourselves. It's one of the Apostle Paul's prayers [from Colossians 1:9]. We use his prayers often, especially when we're not sure how to pray."

When I told her I had been struggling to pray for other situations, Deborah gave me a list of Paul's prayers. Here's how I've paraphrased some of them:

For a discouraged friend: "God of hope, please fill her with all joy and peace in believing. By the power of the Holy Spirit may she abound in hope" (Romans 15:13, RSV).

For our church, struggling with disagreements: "God of steadfast-ness and encouragement, help us live in harmony with one another, in accord with Christ Jesus. May we together with one voice glorify You" (Romans 15:5–6, RSV).

When my husband's friend Ernie was dying of cancer and confided that he longed to believe in God and in a new life to come, Ephesians 1:17–18 and 3:16–17 (RSV) became our prayer: "Father of glory, give Ernie a spirit of wisdom and revelation in knowing You. Enlighten the eyes of his heart. May he know the riches of Your glorious inheritance for him. Strengthen him through Your Spirit. May Christ dwell in his heart through faith."

And for Deborah, who launched us on this prayer adventure, and for each of us:

May God make us worthy of His call, and may He fulfill every good resolve and work of faith by His power, so that the name of our Lord Jesus may be glorified in us (II Thessalonians 1:11–12, RSV).

— Mary Brown

20 | T U E | *If we walk in the light, as he is in the light, we have fellowship one with another....* — I John 1:7

When people who don't know me see me walking my dog Suzy, they often go the other way. Suzy is a rottweiler, weighs more than one hundred pounds and, as a friend put it, "looks very intimidating." Actually, she's a giant puppy with a loving disposition, but not many people want to get close enough to find that out.

Not long after I got Suzy, on our morning walks we began to meet a woman walking her golden retriever. We both pulled our dogs in close to our sides, and as they passed each other, the fur on their backs went up. That bothered me because that wasn't like the Suzy I knew. So I decided to take a bit of a risk. The next morning, as my neighbor and her dog approached, I stopped, put Suzy on a "sit" command and asked, "Do you think it might be a good idea for our dogs to get to know each other?"

The woman smiled and said, "I certainly do."

The dogs got along wonderfully, and so did their two owners. Now all four of us look forward to our morning meetings.

Every now and then I come across people who intimidate me be-cause they seem to be more confident and capable than I am, so I make no attempt to know them better. I stick to my own side of the road. But the next time I feel intimidated, I'm going to take a risk. I'm going to say hello and hold out my hand. I might discover some-one who's just like me — a person. And instead of making a fool of myself, I might make a friend.

Father, help me not to let fear and imagination keep me from seeing people as they really are.   —Phyllis Hobe

21 | W E D   *This is the gift of God.*   —Ecclesiastes 5:19

Unusual amounts of rainfall had turned our garden into a quagmire, so my husband and I were picking the vegetables before they spoiled. As we trudged back and forth, our rubber boots sank into the squishy clay, creating a suction we had to break with every step. Exasperated, exhausted, Leo suggested, "Let's wear bare feet!"

I couldn't think of any reason not to, so we pulled off our rubber boots, peeled off our socks and rolled up our pant legs. It had been close to fifty years since I'd experienced cool, wet mud pressed against the soles of my feet, packed against my insteps, squished up between my toes. Since I was no longer bogged down by those heavy big boots, it was much easier to pick the vegetables. We searched for cucumbers, stepping gingerly among the wet, prickly vines. Leo gathered the rain-washed sprigs of fresh dill; I found plump tomatoes hiding under foliage. We were having more fun than a couple of kids.

It was one of those small moments in life when joy filled us. I was reminded of Psalm 126:2: "Our mouth filled with laughter, and our tongue with singing." The blessings of God were upon us.

Dear God, today let me find a moment to bask in the glory that is You.   —Alma Barkman

22 | T H U   *"In quietness and in trust shall be your strength...."*
                                                  —Isaiah 30:15 (RSV)

Two long months passed without a job offer. One day, I took some time off from interviewing and went to my favorite fly-fishing stream. As I made my way through the lush green woods, soft moss quieted my footsteps. The deeper I walked into the forest, the calmer I be-came. "God," I found myself praying, "I've been asking that You send me the perfect job. Send me a job—any job—and I'll trust You, whatever Your plan."

For the first time since my job search began, I felt content. At last, I'd given it to God. Casting my line out into the clear water, I knew everything would be all right.

And it was. First, a bank offered me a position—not in the investment department, but in sales. *Okay, God, I'll follow Your will.* But two days before I was to start, a call came from George Allen, a friend from my church, who had told the president of his bank about me. The bank president granted me an interview, then offered me a dream position as a sales assistant—in the *investment* department!

What is amazing to me is the intricacy of God's plan, which held me back until I was ready to trust Him. And recognizing this, I can work hard but rest easy. Because no matter what lies ahead, my future is truly secure.

God, it is good to stop and listen for a change, and to trust in You.
—Brock Kidd

23 | F R I　　*"Fear not, I will help you."*　　—Isaiah 41:13 (RSV)

I've always wanted to see Loch Ness. So a few years ago, on a trip to Scotland, I found a bus in Inverness that would take me there. On the way, I got to talking to the driver, who explained which returning bus I should catch at Loch Ness. "I'm sorry I cannot be your driver then," he said with a grin. "We trade off. But the chap who'll take you back is a fine bloke indeed."

Two minutes after disembarking, I discovered I'd left my camera on the bus! And my American immigrant card, which I needed to return to my U.S. home, was in the case! "Oh, God," I prayed, "I need to get my camera back!" But even as I prayed, I doubted. The chances of getting it back were almost nil.

When I called the station back in Inverness, I was told that that particular bus was starting its return trip and would be coming past the very phone booth I was calling from in about two minutes. I'd no sooner hung up than the bus rumbled to a stop five yards away. I couldn't believe it, but it was my bus driver who opened the doors and held out my camera!

"I thought you were trading buses," I said, running to thank him.

"Aye! But I saw your camera, and I had a wee think. Your heart would be broken, I knew, if I didn't take care of you and bring it back. So I traded to keep my own bus. And what's more, lass, I'll be around to pick you up when you're done. 'Tis plain you need a better bloke to watch out for you, aye?"

What an answer for my doubts! 'Tis plain I have a better Bloke that watches out for me. As He does for us all.

Father, thank You for answering my doubts as well as my prayers. And thank You, too, for the special people You send to watch over me.   — Brenda Wilbee

24 | S A T *Forgive, and ye shall be forgiven.*   —Luke 6:37

When we planned our fifteen hundred-mile drive to visit relatives in Illinois, we had little money but plenty of enthusiasm. Five of us, including nine-year-old Oscar, Jr., were ready to hit the road.

It was July 1954, and we depended on our copy of *Recreation Without Humiliation*. This booklet listed accommodations and eating places available to African Americans.

After driving all night, we were weary and hungry. But the booklet didn't list any places nearby. We chanced it and entered several eating places, only to be turned away each time. The women looked at me, the only man in our group. I looked at my son. His eyes showed disbelief. Daddy was helpless! My humiliation was deep, and I whispered, "I will never travel our nation again!"

Years passed, and I created excuses when others suggested cross-country vacations. I was still hurt. Then, in 1969, our relatives in Illinois begged us to motor out to see them. "We're getting older," they warned. "You'd better travel while you can carry your own bags!"

Reluctantly, I consented. *Recreation Without Humiliation* was no longer available. Cautiously, I entered a restaurant in the same town where we had stopped years ago. The owner greeted me with, "It's good seeing you. Where you from?"

His words helped me to see that the people who rejected me were influenced by the segregation, the traditions, the customs of forty years ago. But people can change and can learn understanding. I, too, had been influenced by tradition. Over the years, I had allowed this incident to discolor and obstruct my thinking. I had lumped people together and rejected them.

There in that restaurant, I bowed my head, said the blessing and asked God for forgiveness. The owner stared, then turned away. How was he to know he had freed me of my burden and given me a chance to grow?

Forgiving Father, I was blind and You helped me to see. I thank You.
—Oscar Greene

POINT OF LIGHT

Lamps do not talk, but they do shine. A lighthouse sounds no drum, it beats no gong; and yet far over the waters its friendly spark is seen by the mariner. So let your actions shine out your religion. Let the main sermon of your life be illustrated by all your conduct.

—Charles Spurgeon

---

25 | S U N *He brought me out into a spacious place; he rescued me because he delighted in me.*   —Psalm 18:19 (NIV)

Dear Chris,

Could you hit the "pause" button for a moment? Something strange is going on here, and I'm confused. Was that really us in Charleston last week for your college registration? Just last fall you were teasing me about being left behind in Miss Tullen's sixth grade while you ventured on to junior high. It was last fall, wasn't it, Chris? Our kites are soaring too high; too much string is being let out too fast. I don't feel in control anymore.

I thought I'd wait for a more private moment like this, safe in the quiet of my room, to let you know that you didn't fool me a bit last week. Beneath your layered "preppy" look and eager smiles, I know you were a little frightened by it all. You can't keep things like that from an old friend who's kind of scared herself.

Remember when I was eight and you were nine, and we camped overnight in Winkler's lot? Night came, and I cried. You were kind and didn't tease. Instead, you matter-of-factly mentioned that while you were out checking our tent ropes, you thought you saw our old friend Jesus just on the other side of the clearing, pitching a wild-looking orange poplin tent under the "hawk tree." You told me you guessed He was planning to camp the night there Himself. I wasn't sure if I believed you, but still, I kept peeking through the flap looking for a patch of orange somewhere in the dark. I never saw His tent, but somehow, the thought of His being near made me feel better, and I slept well that night.

By the way, guess whom I ran into while you were taking your math placement test last Thursday? He was on the quad lacing up flashy new sneakers with wild orange laces! You guessed it, our old camp-out neighbor Jesus. He told me He was getting ready to run with "My old pal Chris" because He knew you had a long, fast run ahead of you and might need some company along the way. Feels good to know old friends are close when you need them most, doesn't it?

Love ya,
Jen

Lord, as the pace of my life quickens, run with me and stay by my side.
— Jenny Mutzbauer

26 | M O N *In everything you have put your hand....*
— Deuteronomy 12:7 (NIV)

There is a swimming pool in the complex where my husband Paul and I live. One day he rushed into the house saying, "There's a tiny field mouse treading water in the pool! It's almost dead!" We grabbed a large piece of cardboard and raced outside. We tried to entice the mouse onto the board, and when it climbed on, we swooped the cardboard up and out of the water and deposited the mouse safely at the side of the pool. As we watched, enthralled, the mouse shook itself off, then scampered away.

Afterward, Paul and I couldn't believe what had just happened. "We saved that mouse's life!" I marveled.

"And we didn't have to give it 'mouth-to-mouse' resuscitation," Paul joked.

Still in a silly mood, we speculated what that mouse would tell its buddies when it returned to the field: "And there I was, nearly drowning in a huge body of water, when out of the sky a huge hand came down and rescued me."

Later, though, I considered more soberly several near misses in my life: I had been in a car accident and, fortunately, had not sustained any serious injuries. Another time I was the victim of a mugging, but was not injured. And when I started college, a routine X ray detected a heart problem that could have been fatal if it hadn't been treated immediately. Perhaps what I thought had been happenstance or a "lucky break" was really "the hand of God."

Today as I meditate, God, I want to be aware that at this moment I am safe. And I want to thank You for leading me safely through dangerous situations.
— Linda Neukrug

27 | T U E *Go, eat your food with gladness, and drink your wine with a joyful heart, for it is now that God favors what you do.*
— Ecclesiastes 9:7 (NIV)

In the last days of August, the beauty of God's earth shines through with special purity. The sun falls like gold through the trees in my small suburban village of Pleasantville, New York. The air is heavy, hot, still. There is a sense of hushed expectancy before the frenzy of the new school year bursts forth in the fall.

I move in slow motion with the rest of my town. Even those neighbors not on vacation saunter languidly in the shops and streets through the heat of each lazy day. How tempting for all of us to let the glory of summer slip by unnoticed. The opposite is no less appealing: to fill each day with such frenetic activity that August becomes as harried as the rest of the year.

So here's how to make this slow-moving month worth celebrating. Bless each day by permitting yourself one pertinent pleasure — just one — every day. It can be as simple as two scoops of peppermint ice cream in a waffle cone. Or browsing the racks of the local bookstore for one favorite title to savor over a quiet office lunch. Or listening for God in the stillness of a sleeping house as you sip your early morning cup of coffee.

I feel You beside me, Lord, in this special moment of lazy, late-summer joy.
— Linda Ching Sledge

28 | W E D *Ye have not, because ye ask not.*
— James 4:2

Last year, I planted bachelor's buttons. How wonderfully tall they grew, their fuzzy pink and periwinkle heads waving above the other flowers! Then one day I noticed they had drooped, their leaves sagging on the ground. But after a long, gentle watering they perked right back up again. Those bachelor's buttons were certainly not shy about showing their needs. When they wanted water, they made it abundantly plain!

I'm trying to be more like those lovely, candid plants by learning to ask for what I need. If I need my husband Gary to slow down and give me a hug, I'll say so. If I want my son Brett to turn off the TV and make conversation with me, I'll ask him. If I want my secretary to give me a few uninterrupted hours, I'll let her know. And when I need extra help from the Giver of Living Water, I won't be shy to talk to Him about my shortcomings and my needs.

Like those bachelor's buttons, I want to be healthy and well-watered — able to hold my head up high.

Great Giver of all good gifts, give me wisdom to discern my needs and courage to seek their fulfillment.   — Mary Lou Carney

29 | T H U   *Become as little children....*   — Matthew 18:3

What a pleasure it is to watch my granddaughter Saralisa (eight months old at this writing) discovering the world! Wherever she is — home, Grandma's house, the park, the doctor's office—there's something fascinating to "check out." She's crawling now, so she picks up little bits of things, such as a piece of thread on the carpet or a leaf in the grass or a measuring cup her mommy has dropped on the kitchen floor. Then she explores them with all of her senses, turning them over to see all sides, shaking them to see if they rattle, sniffing and blowing on them, banging them on the floor and, of course, tasting them, if Mommy decides it's okay. She even talks to them sometimes, saying, "*Ah, te da ta,*" or some other expression in her private language. Then, almost without fail, she looks at the adults and grins with satisfaction.

Her delighted exploration has made me aware of how mindlessly I often go through my days, taking the wonders of God's world for granted. So I've been making it a point to spend a few minutes each evening at the beginning of my prayer time just looking at something in the room or outside the window, trying to see it as if for the first time. Then I close my eyes and in the silence, I try to hear and listen to whatever sounds there are. Last night, for the first time in ages, I saw the painting that hangs above the TV and let its beauty soak into me. Then I really heard the sound of the cicadas in their nightly serenade. How lovely! With a thankful heart, I came to prayer.

Loving Creator, help me reawaken my childlike sense of wonder at the delights of Your world!   — Marilyn Morgan Helleberg

30 | F R I   *A man's mind plans his way, but the Lord directs his steps.*   —Proverbs 16:9 (RSV)

Our kids had done it, and described the entire experience with an exclamation point. True, they were teenagers and we were "fortysomething"— but certainly we could manage a thirty-eight-mile, four-day backpack trip. Or so Terry and I thought when we joined Dave and Anita Bacon at the start of Alaska's Resurrection Trail last August.

After the first two miles, our "fortysomething" body parts began sending out alarming signals. Anita's old, too-tight boots cramped her toes so badly, she barely hobbled to our first camp. There, Terry ingeniously created an "open air" hiking shoe by slicing off the upper toes of both boots! By the second day my shoulders were screaming from carrying a forty-pound pack. Dave cut up part of his foam sleeping pad to use as extra cushioning under my shoulder straps. The soles of his feet were beginning to feel like "raw hamburger," he said, so more cushioning foam disappeared inside his shoes. The poor guy ultimately ended up with a sleeping pad the size of a place mat!

We attained Resurrection Summit on the third day, and we laughed ourselves senseless over another hiker's entry in the trail log book: "Came in pain, slept in pain, left in pain!"

What's hard to figure is that even as we doggedly approached the end of the hike, we were actually sorry it was over. We had traversed some fantastic country, the memory of which was ours to keep. We'd shared our campfire with a fellow traveler and talked about how Jesus walks with us along our personal trails. We had looked back across the valley and taken courage at how far we'd come... together. And we discovered that the things that got us up the Resurrection Trail were the same things that have brought us this far along in life. And, you know, I think we "fortysomethings" are going to keep on making our way just fine.

Lord, thank You for giving us what it takes to challenge life's trails — Your secure presence, a little team spirit, a lot of determination and maybe, for some of us, a new pair of hiking boots! — Carol Knapp

31 | S A T   *I urge that supplications, prayers, intercessions, and thanks-givings be made for... all who are in high positions....*
—I Timothy 2:1–2 (RSV)

I had no intentions of liking Washington, D.C. I prefer small towns, country roads, two-lane traffic and tiny shops. Besides, I'd heard too many negative comments about the city and about the federal government. But the workshop I was attending would be held there, so I went.

The heat in the taxi was overwhelming. Traffic was stop-and-go. We came to a quick standstill, and I suddenly realized that we were right in front of the White House! I hadn't expected to get even a glimpse of it because of the workshop's tight schedule. I leaned out the open car window in fascination. To my surprise, my heart began to pound, powerful emotions of gratitude and patriotism overwhelmed me, and tears came to my eyes.

Peering from the taxi, I seemed to see all the presidents down through the ages, men of faith, courage and valor, alive again there at the White House. I had the strange sensation that I was being permitted to view the actual beating heart of a living being — the very center, the innermost part of our country. How could I have come to the nation's capital with a critical, even cynical attitude? Why hadn't I known that Washington would be magnificent as well as humbling? Suddenly, I wanted to lift up in prayer all those going about their daily duties and responsibilities inside the White House and on Capitol Hill.

The taxi moved again through the traffic and the heat. Never again would I say I disliked Washington, and I bowed my head to pray for those in authority whom I had been criticizing.

I offer up my prayers, Father God, for all of our nation's leaders. Amen.   — Marion Bond West

GIFTS OF LIGHT

1 _____

2 _____

3 _____

4 _____

5 _____

6 _____

7 _____

8 _____

9 _____

10 _____

11 _____

12 _____

13 _____

14 _____

15 _____

16 _____

17 _____

18 _____

19 _____

20 _____

21 _____

22 _____

23 _____

24 _____

25 _____

26 _____

27 _____

28 _____

29 _____

30 _____

31 _____

"Men put an end to darkness, and search out to the farthest bound the ore in gloom and deep darkness.... Man puts his hand to the flinty rock.... and the thing that is hid he brings forth to light."

—JOB 28:3, 9, 11 (RSV)

S E P T E M B E R

S	M	T	W	T	F	S
1	2	3	4	5	6	7
8	9	10	11	12	13	14
15	16	17	18	19	20	21
22	23	24	25	26	27	28
29	30					

1 | S U N | *"I am sending you to open their eyes so that they may turn from darkness to light...."* —Acts 26:18 (NRSV)

I sat in the sun-room of a palliative care ward, part of the hospital in Switzerland where cancer patients come for terminal care and pain control. From my window seat, I watched a woman, whose red-dyed hair fibbed about her age, lovingly fingering the blossoms on a Christmas cactus. She was talking to another patient in a mixture of Italian and Swiss German, her native language mixed unapologetically with that of her adopted land. It was obvious that this woman seemed to fill the room — and the other patients — with light.

The doctor in charge of the ward came to fetch me, and I left with her, reluctant to give up this moment. "That Italian woman," I commented, "she seems to minister to the other patients." I wondered what sort of cancer she had, how long she had to live.

"Oh, yes," the doctor answered, "I know who you mean. She doesn't have cancer at all. She's in the ward only because there were no other beds in the hospital. Yes, she's wonderful with the other patients."

How remarkable, I thought. *She's not afraid to be there. She's not afraid of those others who will surely die. Instead, she walks with them and gives them courage.*

I thought about the times I've been caught off-guard in a frightening place where I don't belong. When I looked at this woman, I saw that the way to deal with dark fear is to face it and turn it into light.

Lord Jesus, thank You for the people I meet who remind me of Your holy presence.
— Diane Komp

POINT OF LIGHT

LIGHT FOR DARKNESS

The hero is one who kindles a great light in the world, who sets up blazing torches in the dark streets of life for men to see by. The saint is the man who walks through the dark paths of the world, himself a light.

—Felix Adler

2 | M
  | O
  | N

As each has received a gift, employ it for one another, as good stewards of God's varied grace.

—I Peter 4:10 (RSV)

For loving parents, every day is Labor Day. And the rewards are great. Take the other day, for example. After a busy day at work, I came home to find a lot of errands that needed to be run for my wife Roe and the children.

When it was the children's bedtime, I went upstairs and read to Karen, tucked her in, brought her a glass of water, prayed with her, chased the ghosts from her closet, pulled down the blinds and kissed her good night.

Then I read to Michael, tucked him in, brought him a glass of water, prayed with him, chased the pirates out of his closet, pulled down the blinds and kissed him good night. I was five seconds away from my bed, when Michael said in a quiet voice, "Daddy, could you get my blanket? Karen hid it on me."

The blanket that Michael won't go to bed without was in the basement, in a closet, under a basket. All I wanted was sleep, but I made it down the two flights of stairs, found the blanket and climbed back up as if my legs were made of cement. I placed the blanket beside him and kissed him good night. Just as I got to the door, he whispered, "Daddy, thank you for going all the way down in the basement for my blanket."

"Thank you, Michael," I whispered back, feeling as though I'd won a medal or been given a raise. "I love you, too."

God, help us to do our work with faithfulness and grateful hearts.
— Christopher de Vinck

3 | T
  | U
  | E

As the Lord has forgiven you, so you also must forgive.
— Colossians 3:13 (RSV)

It's the day after Labor Day and my second time to pick up my five-year-old Elizabeth after school, along with our neighbors' two girls Elise and Annie. As I walk into the building, the kindergarten door swings open, and Elizabeth and Elise fly out to me. "We had a sing-along with the big kids!" Elizabeth exclaims.

"In the cafeteria!" Elise adds, and the two of them rush out to the sidewalk for the ten-block walk home.

Halfway there, a car drives up and stops beside us. It's my neighbor Julie, Elise's mom. "Annie called from the principal's office crying," she tells us. "She couldn't find you anywhere and was really scared."

Annie! I completely forgot to wait for Julie's third-grader! "I'm so sorry."

"That's okay," Julie soothes. "Annie had the sense to call home. I'll get her." She zooms off, and I stand there feeling utterly terrible. *How could I have forgotten Annie?*

We're almost home when Julie and Annie pass us. When we reach their driveway, Annie is heading into the house. "Annie, please," I say, "I'd like to talk to you." She slowly comes down the steps. "I'm so sorry, Annie," I tell her. "Please forgive me. I promise I won't forget you again."

She reluctantly returns my hug. Then, as we're halfway down the drive, she picks a yellow chrysanthemum from a pot and runs to me. "Here, Mrs. Brown. It's okay."

"Oh, Annie, thank you! It's beautiful!"

Later, telling my husband Alex about the mistake, I continue to berate myself. "It sounds like you two worked it out okay," he says. "She's probably forgotten all about it."

We look at the chrysanthemum in a little vase by the sink. "Now," Alex continues, "if you can forgive yourself, you can put it behind you, too."

Father, thank You for the gracious forgiveness of a child, and for giving Your Son on the cross to wash away my guilt. — Mary Brown

4 | W E D | *And the Lord caused the sea to go back by a strong east wind all that night... and the waters were divided.*
— Exodus 14:21

On that first early autumn morning, I slowed my minivan to a crawl at the end of the freeway on-ramp as a steady stream of cars zoomed past me. Finally, I held my breath, gunned the accelerator and squeezed into the merging traffic. With a sigh of relief, I relaxed a bit, then glanced into my rearview mirror. *Egad!* It looked like a zillion cars were all chasing after me.

Get a grip, I told myself. It was the first week of my new job in Denver, which meant commuting fifty miles round-trip on the freeway. I needed to get over this silly case of "Freeway Phobia."

So the next morning, as I drove down the on-ramp, I tried a visual prayer. I asked God to go before me on this journey and part a safe path through the traffic. All the way to Denver, as I maneuvered through the cars, I held on to that image, and it worked! Every time I had to switch lanes or move toward an exit, I felt protected and my fear disappeared.

I've been commuting to Denver for several months now, and I still ask God to "part the way" as I enter the freeway. And this morning, I realized I hardly ever feel afraid anymore. Why the change of attitude? It's an old solution that I've learned in a whole new way: Doing the thing you fear the most helps you overcome that fear, especially when you wrap it in a visual prayer.

Father, I'm so thankful that You meet me at the edge of my fears and go before me to provide protection, even as You went before the Israelites at the edge of the Red Sea.   — Carol Kuykendall

---

5 | THU   *He was lost, and is found....*   Luke 15:24

In 1946, my spiritual life crumbled. The downside began during a fifteen-day downpour in poverty-stricken, war-torn Korea. Everything seemed in conflict with the Ten Commandments, the Sermon on the Mount and the Golden Rule. People were suffering, and the children were ill-clad and underfed. Then, my possessions were stolen, along with my *Book of Common Prayer* received at Confirmation in 1932. My faith vanished. I no longer believed in God.

After leaving the Army, I avoided church. My working hours were three until eleven, six evenings a week. Sunday was *my* day, and I pretended not to hear the tears in my wife Ruby's voice as she begged me to go to church. Even though the church bells left me feeling isolated, I held firm. I clung to wartime memories, and I struggled with disruptive dreams.

In September 1954, nine-year-old Oscar, Jr., pleaded with me to attend church. "All the daddies will be there," he said. I shook my head. Why should I pretend?

That evening another nightmare struck: I was back in Korea trudging that mud-filled path. A child was there, huddled, shivering and crying. As I knelt, the child looked up. It was our son! I awakened shaken and weeping.

War had deprived those children, but wasn't I waging a war of my own? Weren't Ruby and Oscar, Jr., victims seeking my understanding, cooperation and love? Wasn't I using the war, my working hours and twisted reason to get my own way?

Hesitantly, I entered church the next Sunday. Ruby smiled from the choir loft, and our son clapped. I returned the following Sunday and the next. Gradually, I learned there was a spiritual family waiting to welcome me and to lessen the trauma I had suffered in Korea. My nightmares melted into dreams.

Risen Lord, I lost my way. Thank You for using loved ones to help me return to You.
                                                         — Oscar Greene

6 | F R I | *Neither can they die any more…being the children of the resurrection.*
                                                         — Luke 20:36

I was still waving to our daughter as she left for college after the holidays, when her little sister asked, "Why do people wave at people? Why do we wave when we say good-bye?"

And turning back with that sense of puzzled loss that so often follows when someone leaves, I, too, wondered, *Yes, why? Why do we teach even babies this first, and perhaps last, of life's gestures?*

"Wave at Daddy," we urge. "Blow him a kiss. Tell Daddy good-bye." And we are absurdly pleased when the little hand flies up in that spontaneous signal that announces long before words, "Look, look! I'm here!"

And all our lives, at parting, we are likewise impelled to hoist these mute flags after the futile farewells: "Do you have everything? We'll miss you. Give my love to everybody. Don't forget to write."

Now the dear figure that filled the house only moments ago is disappearing into a bus, or plane, or train, or car. Sometimes we glimpse a face at a window. And there's nothing left us but to stand waving, hoping until the very last second to be noticed, to communicate. It's as if these hands that so recently touched the child, the husband, the wife or the friend were striving yet to reach across the onrushing silence, the distance bearing down upon us, and signaling one more time: "Take care. I love you. I'll always be here. Come back as soon as you can. Good-bye!"

It always hurts to part from the ones we love, even for a little while. And we all dread the final parting. But, surely, the richest reward we have is Jesus' promise of eternal life. To know that for those who believe in Him and do our best to follow Him, there will be no final partings. We will be together forever in paradise.

Dear Lord, please stay close to all those who are so dear to us. Bring them into the kingdom with us. — Marjorie Holmes

7 | S A T | *I am reminded of your sincere faith, a faith that dwelt first in your grandmother....* — II Timothy 1:5 (RSV)

Outside my grandparents' home one day, a neighbor's child suddenly announced, "I don't like you."

Well, I ran crying to Grandma, who wrapped her arms around me and kissed me. "Let's see if a cookie will help," she said. Grandma was right. A cookie, plus a glass of cold milk, did help. But soon anger replaced the tears.

"I'm going back out there and tell that Emily I don't like her either!" I announced.

"Tell you what," Grandma answered. "Why don't you ask her to come inside and have some cookies, too. Remember, the Bible says we should return good for evil." I glowered in skepticism, but finally gave in.

Grandma was right again. The promise of another cookie did it. Soon Emily and I were cutting out paper dolls in the front room, then playing jacks on the sidewalk. That was the beginning of our being "best friends."

Now here I am a grandmother, nearly seventy years later, and not much has changed. I still believe that returning good for evil is the best way to treat others. I'm thankful that I learned that early in life from my dear grandmother. It is the seed I want to plant in the tender hearts of my growing grandchildren.

Father, thank You for the lesson my grandmother taught me — and for her faith. Help me to pass my faith on to my grandchildren today and every day. Amen. — Isabel Wolseley

8 | S U N | *In her tongue is the law of kindness. She looketh well to the ways of her household....* — Proverbs 31:26–27

For me, the ultimate symbol of kindness is a bottle of red soda pop.

My Grandmother Schantz lived in Springfield, Ohio, when I was a boy, and she was known for her kindness. It was visible in the softness of her deep-set French eyes and audible in her easy, musical laugh.

Grandma was not well-set financially. Because Grandpa was disabled, she worked long hours in the electric motor plant. Yet in spite of her fatigue and poverty, she found ways to make us kids feel special. For example, she saved small coils of bright copper wire, leftovers from her motor rewinding work. With this wire we boys made crystal radios and toy telegraphs. She saved postage stamps whenever she was sorting out old letters, and they went into our stamp collections. She hoarded cigar boxes, which we used to file our collections of baseball cards.

Best of all, she kept the refrigerator stocked with Barq's red soda pop, which she let us drink freely, even for breakfast! I drool every time I recall sitting in her living room, watching *Highway Patrol* on her black-and-white television. Just as the program started, she would stroll into the room with a large tray loaded with bowls of Seifert's potato chips and Barq's red pop. It doesn't get any better than that!

Today, on this Grandparents Day, Grandma's style of kindness reminds me often that it doesn't take riches or extravagance to express love — just a little thought and interest. It's a technique to remember when we're shopping for gifts or seeking to express thanks to a friend. Look for little things that say, "I know you and the things you love."

God, bless all the grandparents who know best how to give good gifts.
                                                    —Daniel Schantz

9 | M O N   *The one thing I do … is to forget what is behind me….*
                                        —Philippians 3:13 (GNB)

I recently started a job as a supervisor in a research library. Although it seemed ideal in the beginning, it wasn't long before things began to fall apart. I found the office politics distasteful and, finally, I ended up resigning. But I could not easily let go of the disappointment. *Had I been overbearing with the staff?* I kept asking myself. *Had I been unprofessional?* Again and again the answer was no. I had handled myself in a professional, forthright manner.

About that time, I bought my five-year-old son David a fishing game. It came complete with a cardboard fishing tank, rods, sea creatures—a colorful sunfish, a sawfish, a dolphin and a squid—plus other underwater objects like a tin can, an old boot, a bottle, and even a treasure chest.

You know, it's surprising what an adult can learn from a child's game. One day, when David was "fishing," he said, "Mommy, look!" He had snagged an old boot on his fishing line. "Another bad catch." He took the boot and threw it back into the tank. "I'll try again—for the sunfish this time." And he tossed his line in.

Then I saw it clearly: This job had simply been a "bad catch." In time I would find the right job. And, for now, I needed to let go of my tin cans of disappointment, my old boots of bitterness and, instead, trust God to help me with my next "catch." Which, with His help, just may be a treasure of a job!

Father, help me to let go of the sting of disappointment, and to hold on to hope in You. — Robin White Goode

10 | T U E *"Behold, I will create new heavens and a new earth....The wolf and the lamb will feed together, and the lion will eat straw like the ox...."* — Isaiah 65:17, 25 (NIV)

I'd never thought much about patron saints until it was time for my beloved dog Josie to be put to sleep. She was old, crippled; her eyes faded and weary. This mutt friend had shepherded my four children from preschool to young adulthood. She'd spent endless hours guarding at bus stops, running behind bikes and ponies, playing ball in the yard. She'd lent her floppy ears to my confidences, some that I could never tell another human. Only God and Josie. How could I find the courage to take her to the vet? To let her go?

"Dear God, help me," I prayed, petting her, as she lay on her warm bed, her white-tipped tail wagging listlessly.

Hours later, in a conversation with a friend, I learned that her faith had assigned a patron saint to dogs. St. Hubert lived during the Middle Ages and was a friend to dogs. He is believed to stand at a special garden gate in heaven, just for dogs, welcoming each one royally.

"Of course, it's not in the Bible," I said warily to my husband that night. Then added wistfully, "But, still, I feel it's a gift."

"Then take it," said my ever-practical husband.

The appointment was made. And when the time came, I led Josie, frail and tottering, to our car, opening the backyard gate for the last time to let her through. Tears ran down my cheeks. I clicked our gate closed, then paused. And in that brief moment I could almost hear St. Hubert's loving hand unclick the heavenly latch.

Lord God, our Creator, thank You for Your gift of faith that lets us see how close and real heaven is. —Shari Smyth

11 | W E D
Blessed is the man who perseveres under trial....
—James 1:12 (NAS)

A neighbor was telling me about her friend who had recently been diagnosed with multiple sclerosis. "She's having a difficult time accepting it," she said. "She's having such acute bouts with depression."

"Yes," I said, "she'll do that for a while, but then she'll adjust and be able to cope with it."

My mind went back to one year ago when I had come home from heart surgery and a lengthy stay at the hospital. The worst thing was that I had only twenty-five percent of normal heart function. *A fourth of a heart!* I was told that my prognosis for any kind of real cure was zero. I was living on borrowed time, but with great care I might have from one to four years more to live. "We'll try to keep you going for as long as we can," my doctor said.

Every night after that when I went to bed I'd think, *Will this be the night?* Then next morning it was, *Will this be the day?* But one sleepless night, after many, I thought, *This is ridiculous! I must stop thinking this way.* And I prayed to God to give me peace.

Time and acceptance have made it easier. Now, as I pray for that lady with MS, I feel certain that she will find her answers also. It just takes awhile to adjust to whatever must be...with God's help. And it's amazing how much love, concern and dedication just one-fourth of a heart can hold.

Lord, let me not waste a single day that You give to me. Let me not groan about the things I cannot do, but take joy in the things I am still capable of doing. —Dorothy Nicholas

12 | T H U
He is like a tree planted by streams of water, that yields its fruit in its season, and its leaf does not wither. In all that he does, he prospers.
—Psalm 1:3 (RSV)

Last year was a bad year for tomatoes in Bellingham, Washington—

worse than usual in this area where growing conditions are always damp. Most of those I tried to grow in my garden rotted. Last year was also a bad year for my health, the worst since steroids were first prescribed for me in eighth grade. I had life-threatening allergies and debilitating fatigue, accompanied by aches and pains.

After some new tests, my internist prescribed immunoglobulin injections to counteract a severe immune disorder. While I waited for the results, I wondered what to do with my tomatoes. "You're like me," I told them, "rotting from the inside out." As I began to pull the vines down, I found a few green tomatoes that weren't blighted. I took them indoors and spread them on my kitchen windowsill. Perhaps they could ripen before the rot got to them. All week I watched those precious few that had struggled to bud, blossom and ripen under less than adequate conditions. As they pinked up, turned red and softened right there on the windowsill, I, too, began to feel better than I had in twenty years.

"You *are* like me," I told my tomatoes. "We were both waiting to come to fruition in God's good time."

Thank You, God, for Your promise that fruit comes in its season Help me to trust Your promise.   — Brenda Wilbee

13 | F R I | *MY GIFT TODAY...* | *THE WASP*

He leads me beside still waters; he restores my soul....
                                          — Psalm 23:2–3 (RSV)

I don't know how the wasp got into my study this morning, and I certainly didn't suspect when I saw it that it was a gift from God.

I'd hurried down to my desk at 6:00 A.M., thinking of all I had to do before I caught a plane at noon. Half-finished projects and unanswered mail covered two card tables and a good part of the floor. As always, I'd taken on too much: getting up earlier and working later, trying to extricate myself.

And here was this witless insect frantically flinging itself at the walls and the ceiling. Ducking beneath its trajectory, I tugged the window up and with a magazine tried to fan it toward the opening. The senseless thing only hurled itself harder at the solid walls. There was its escape route, provided by someone who comprehended the situation. Someone who knew that no amount of energy could force a way through such obstacles. Why didn't it stop whizzing about and let me show it the way out?

Instead, it was I who stopped. Once again God had sent one of His creatures to show me myself. The wasp and I had the very same problem. Trapped, desperate, trying to solve things by going faster, trying harder. *I've opened a way out,* God seemed to say. *Slow down and let Me show you.*

I sat down at my desk and asked God one by one about the items piled there. Can that one wait? Should I turn to this job first? Does that project have my name on it at all?

The wasp had come to rest on top of the filing cabinet. I clamped my empty coffee mug upside down over it, slid a piece of paper beneath it, carried the improvised cage to the window and set the insect free. When I had to leave I still had a roomful of undone chores. But I'd get them done — those God intended for me — in His time, in His way, in His wondrous freedom.

Instead of running in all directions, Father, let me walk in the single path You have prepared for me this day.   — Elizabeth Sherrill

14 | S A T   *Know that the Lord has set apart the godly for himself....*
                                              —Psalm 4:3 (NIV)

My grandfather is good at "keeping at." Though eighty-seven, he still tends his family's cemetery plots, old graves that lie in an even older cemetery in Mt. Greenwood, Illinois. His parents were laid to rest there in the early 1930s. Brothers and sisters lie there also, their stones carved with dates from the 1950s and 1960s. I often volunteer to drive him on his rounds and cannot help being awed by his faithful commitment to his family and to honoring their memory.

I stand back and watch him as he tends the family memorials. He strides about, a wistful look on his craggy face, weeding and clipping as he goes. While he works, I notice he stands more erect, his pace quicker, his every action vital and purposeful. Bending agilely, he plucks a nettle from the grass crowding a small, weathered stone reading simply, "Martha Mutzbauer — Beloved Sister — 1903–1911." He doesn't forget Martha, who passed away when he was three — he promised his parents he wouldn't.

Driving home from the cemetery one day, "Pa" sat quietly, a contented, fulfilled look on his face. After reading in silence for a while, he seemed to search for the right words, then said to me earnestly, "Y'know, Jen, I'd like geraniums on my plot when my time comes. They sure do last the summer, don't they?"

His abruptness and the thought of his passing made me uncomfortable, and I teased, "Pa, if I get to be rich and famous, how do you know I'll even have time to visit, much less plant geraniums?"

He didn't miss a beat. He simply patted my knee and said, "You won't forget, Jen."

Lord, make me worthy of the faith others have in me, and strong enough to bear faith's burdens.   — Jenny Mutzbauer

15 | S U N   *Those things, which ye have both learned, and received, and heard, and seen in me, do: and the God of peace shall be with you.*   — Philippians 4:9

I've been going to Hillsboro Presbyterian Church since I was nine months old. I'm twenty-two now, and throughout the years the church has given me countless wonderful gifts. One of those gifts was Frank Clark.

Frank was an extraordinary man, a Harvard law graduate who worked his way to a vice presidency of a major corporation. When I talked with him, he was more interested in my achievements than anything he had done. And he was very honest about his faith. "I love the Lord, Brock," he would say.

When I was twelve, Frank gave me Eleanor H. Porter's *Just David*. "I was given this book when I was about your age," he told me, "and it had a major impact on my life." The story is about a young boy named David who never loses sight of the splendor of God's creation. He transforms rigid minds and hard hearts through his innocent approach and his violin playing. David is grateful to be a "player in the orchestra of life."

"This is God's day," the cheerless farmer who takes the orphaned boy into his home tells him one Sunday. "You should not fiddle nor laugh nor sing."

At first, David is puzzled, then his face breaks out in kind understanding. "Oh! That's all right then. Your God isn't the same one, sir, for mine loves all beautiful things every day in the year."

I grieved at Frank's death several months ago, but I smile to myself now as I think back to the hundreds of people from all over the country who gathered in his honor at his funeral. Frank's lasting influence makes perfect sense to me. He loved the Lord and was grateful for the chance to play a part in God's great orchestra of life.

Dear God, we honor those who show us good. Let us live by their example. —Brock Kidd

16 | M O N *You are all one in Christ Jesus.* —Galatians 3:28 (NAS)

When I was a child, living in the South, I could tell by the stories my father told that he had a low opinion of races other than his own Anglo-Saxon background. Because the children I played with at recess were Native Americans, I didn't agree with my dad.

When I was nine, our family moved to northern Illinois, and my sister and I were enrolled in our first urban school. There were no Native Americans, but there were Jewish students, African Americans, Hispanics, people like me from the South, and the sons and daughters of immigrants from almost every European country.

One day, during my freshman year at East Moline High, I was standing in the hall discussing the football team's chances with our archrival Moline and trying to eat an Eskimo Pie. Judy, one of the cheerleaders, reached up and pulled my hand toward her mouth. "Let me help you with that," she said and took a big bite. Everyone laughed, and I felt accepted.

Then Willie, our varsity squad's two hundred-pound tackle, grabbed my hand. "You still need help," he said and took a bite.

Suddenly, the prejudice I didn't know I had rose in me. All I could see was his huge black hand and face, and I panicked. I thrust what was left of my Eskimo Pie at him and said, "Here, take it all." The laughing stopped. I can still remember the look in his eyes as he turned away and the terrible pain in my heart as I saw that I was just like my father.

In the next few years, I began to look my prejudices in the face. But by the time I felt I could apologize to Willie, it was too late. Yet that one memory has had a profound influence on my life. I can now say, with the apostle Paul, "There is no such thing as Jew and Greek, slave and freeman, male and female; for you are all one person in Jesus Christ" (Galatians 3:28, NEB).

Lord, may Your Spirit continue to tear down walls that separate me from You and Your other children. —Kenneth Chafin

17 | T U E | *Act as free men, and do not use your freedom as a covering for evil....* —I Peter 2:16 (NAS)

Freedom. If there's one word that we like to think characterizes the United States, it's *freedom*. Our quest for freedom, our defense of freedom, our commitment to freedom have been our strength and identity. But freedom can be a weakness as well.

Twenty-five years ago, I took a political science course at Furman University in Greenville, South Carolina. I don't remember any of the lectures, the name of the professor or even much of the subject matter. But I do remember one thing, a quotation from scientist-philosopher René Dubos that I scribbled in my journal: "Civilizations commonly die from the excessive development of certain characteristics which had at first contributed to their success."

I was a freshman that year—a free man! No more parental decrees or guidance. I could go to bed when I wanted, attend class when I wanted, study only if I wanted. I was intoxicated with my newfound freedom. Little wonder that I remember almost nothing of my political science course. My freedom promptly led to academic probation and a trip to the dean's office, which I do remember with crystal clarity! For the rest of my college years, I made the dean's list, and eventually discovered that the discipline of study and scholarship led to the freedom of vocational choices. Through experience, I learned that freedom and discipline must always walk hand in hand.

As citizens of America, we can take our freedom for granted. Or we can accept the discipline of voting, taking part in civic affairs, working for our communities, even holding public office. Today, on Citizenship Day, and each day, we have the freedom to choose whether our freedom will be the source of our greatest strength or our greatest weakness.

Dear God, help me to be a citizen who exercises his freedom with responsibility. Amen. —Scott Walker

18 | W E D | *What you have whispered in the inner rooms shall be proclaimed upon the housetops.* —Luke 12:3 (NAS)

I work part-time as a photo stylist for several home decorating publications. My job takes me into a lot of different homes where I arrange flowers and food and help make a room look "picture perfect" for the camera's eye.

One morning, I was working alone in a guest bedroom and had just finished setting up a vase of roses, a pitcher of juice and some croissants on a wicker bed tray, when I began to think about the guests who would spend a night in that cozy room. I found myself praying for their comfort and well-being.

And so it was that I began my secret practice of whispering a prayer in every room at a photo shoot. At Thanksgiving time, as I helped the photographer move a heavy dining room table, I asked God to bless those who would gather there. Later, fluffing pillows in a toddler's bedroom, I prayed for a young life devoted to serving the Lord. Often, though, I wondered if my prayers did any good.

Then, one summer evening, I received a long-distance phone call from a homeowner. "You don't really know my daughter Amy," the lady said, "but I noticed you smiling at her picture the day you photographed our home. I wanted to tell you, her cancer's in remission."

That first of many such reports confirmed my decision to make every photo shoot (as well as every visit to a friend or loved one's home) an opportunity for prayer — prayer whispered in secret as I move quietly from room to room.

Lord, hear my prayers.　　　　　　　　　　　　— Roberta Messner

19 | T H U *Hatred stirs up strife, but love covers all offenses.*
　　　　　　　　　　　—Proverbs 10:12 (RSV)

At the traffic light on Drewville Road, a blue Plymouth ran into my car. I groaned at the impact and shakily got out. At first, it was a relief to find there wasn't much damage, but then the other driver got out. She put her hands on her hips and said in an exasperated voice, "Why did you run into me?"

My temper flared. "Me?" I shouted. "You ran into me! You're not supposed to turn left in front of oncoming traffic. I had the right of way!" We stood glaring at each other, two angry women facing off as passersby stopped to look.

"You'd better take a driving course!" I shouted to the woman, shaking my finger.

All at once there were tears in her eyes, and she broke down. "I'm so scared," she said. "Would you do me a favor?"

"What?" I asked, hesitating.

"Would you hug me?"

Suddenly, my heart softened. I felt my anger dissolving, and I put my arms around her. There, standing on the side of the road, with dozens of people watching, we hugged each other.

"I'm sorry I yelled," she said.

"I'm sorry I was angry," I replied.

We gave each other another squeeze before she got back into her Plymouth. As she pulled away, I waved good-bye, feeling a sweet sense of peace. For two of God's frightened children, that hug of love had changed everything.

Father God, You know how vulnerable I am. Don't let me be too proud to admit it. Or to seek Your protection.   —Susan Schefflein

20 | F R I *Greet one another with a…kiss….*
—II Corinthians 13:12 (GNB)

When I hear about "bad things" or read about them in the paper, I always manage to feel like a spectator, observing the tragedy from the sidelines. This past week, however, that all changed.

A boy I went to high school with died in a car accident only two days before he was to graduate. Two days later, in the state of Vermont, a girl I went to high school with was seriously injured in a freak car accident. And tonight I found out that a fourteen-year-old boy who went to camp with my boyfriend's little brother Geoff had committed suicide.

No longer feeling like a mere spectator, I raced into my parents' bedroom to tell them the terrible news as soon as I got home. My mother was getting ready for bed, and when I told her what had happened, she sighed and lay down in bed. "Oh, God," she said, "how awful. How simply awful."

"Imagine," I said, and swallowed hard, "only fourteen years old." Geoff was almost fourteen, and my twin sisters were fifteen. The thought of one of them taking his or her own life was unbearable.

"His poor family," my mother added sadly. "Please pray for that boy tonight, Jennifer."

"I will, Mom," I promised, and then bent down to kiss her forehead.

"To what do I owe the pleasure?" my mother mumbled drowsily.

"Since when do I need a reason to kiss my own mother?" I joked, but she had already drifted off, so I quietly left the room.

There are two extra mothers in this world tonight who won't be receiving

kisses from their children, I thought to myself as I walked to my room. And as I knelt beside my bed to pray for all the kisses lost by these children, I also thanked God for all the kisses I had yet to give.

Dear Lord, please help me to remember to take the time to bestow the kisses today that I want loved ones to remember tomorrow.

— Jennifer Thomas

21 | S A T | *Wisdom resteth in the heart of him that hath understanding....* — Proverbs 14:33

My friend Amy called with some bad news. "My job has been eliminated," she said.

Amy had been a librarian for fifteen years. "I don't understand," I said. "They'd have to eliminate the library to do that."

"They did," she replied, choking back tears. "They're closing our branch." She explained that the main library, like so many other public institutions, was cutting back its staff.

I could feel my friend's pain and immediately began to look for ways to ease it. "Do you have an up-to-date résumé?" I asked. She didn't. "Have you thought about where you might look for another job?" She hadn't.

"Phyllis, please stop trying to fix things!" Amy interrupted me. "Just *listen* to me!"

At first, I was hurt by her remarks. Then I realized that she was right. The kindest thing I could do for my friend was to be quiet and let her share her pain with me. "I'm sorry," I told her. "You talk and I'll listen."

For a long time I sat quietly while Amy spilled out her fears about her future: about competing with younger people for a new job; about getting along on less money; about leaving the world of books, which she dearly loved. Maybe I couldn't solve her problem, but she knew I was there for her. "I'll pray for you," I told her.

The good news is that Amy eventually found another job. She works in a store that specializes in locating out-of-print books, and her librarian's training is invaluable to the store owners. It turns out that she was able to fix her own problems. What she needed from me was the time, the attention and the love it takes to listen when someone hurts. I thank her for that lesson.

Beloved Jesus, make us sensitive to the times when it is better to put words aside and listen with our hearts. Amen. — Phyllis Hobe

22 | $\begin{smallmatrix}S\\U\\N\end{smallmatrix}$ *He that…believeth on him…is passed from death unto life.*   —John 5:24

April 6, 1990, marked the end of a long fight to save our family farm. We'd sold most of the land, and that day we auctioned off our equipment: tractors; the combine; the big white truck. Friends and neighbors surrounded and strengthened us, and we were thankful for many blessings. I had a good job. We kept our house and acreage— enough to allow Don to expand his hog operation into a full-time business. But our familiar way of life had ended, leaving behind empty, desolate feelings that surfaced at unexpected moments. I thought that they'd never go away.

Three years later they were still there when Don and I flew to Hawaii for my niece Amy's high school graduation and the first real vacation we'd had in years. "You have to see Volcanoes National Park," Amy said. So we took the Chain of Craters drive, which dead-ended where a 1994 lava flow blocked the highway. I was certain nothing would ever grow or live in the area again.

On the way, back we hiked mile-long Devastation Trail, which winds through the cinder outfall of the 1959 Kiluaea Iki eruption. I'd expected the trail to be a monument to its name. Instead, plants were abundant: ground cover like bougainvillea, with delicate purple flowers; small, bushy trees; hardy ferns and grasses. There were even lizards and birds! At the visitor's center, I learned that new life begins almost before the lava stops flowing. Plants spring up quickly in seemingly lifeless soil. Eventually, lush tropical growth replaces barren rock.

Don and I snapped pictures of each other, smiling and happy, framed by the ongoing process of earth's healing. As we looked at the pictures later, we rejoiced that our own healing, planned and perfectly timed by our loving Creator, was almost complete as well.

Gracious God of creation, thank You for renewing my spirit as You renew and replenish the earth.   —Penney Schwab

23 | $\begin{smallmatrix}M\\O\\N\end{smallmatrix}$ *Wonderful are thy works! Thou knowest me right well; my frame was not hidden from thee….*
                                       —Psalm 139:14–15 (RSV)

I am short. And it bothers me. My children laugh at me, now that they are all at least four inches taller than I. "Shortie, shortie, Mom," they tease affectionately.

Many years ago I went to boarding school in England. Every day for the nine years I spent there, my class marched in line into morning prayer, tallest first, down to shortest last. And I was always the last. All those years in school I'd hear in my head Jesus' words from the Sermon on the Mount: "Which of you by taking thought can add one cubit unto his stature?" (Matthew 6:27), and wished I could prove Him wrong somehow!

When I came to live in the United States, things got a little better. The many nations represented here include enough people who are naturally small that I stopped feeling self-conscious. All the same, I still wanted to wear long slim dresses and to be able to see across a crowded room to find a friendly face.

Some people worry about their weight. I worry about my height, even though I know it's foolish. Then one day I was walking to lunch with an old friend, and she admired an elegant cape in a department store window. "What a great color," she said. "It would really suit you."

"Oh, I couldn't wear that," I replied. "I'm too short."

"Really?" she said in surprise. "How tall are you? I've never thought of you as short."

What a moment! I realized that I had quite missed the point of those words in Matthew. Here on a crowded city sidewalk, by taking thought, my friend had added much more than a cubit to my stature. She had changed my self-perception.

God, I accept the body You've given me. Help me to treat it with respect.   — Brigitte Weeks

24 | T U E   *[Love] does not envy, it does not boast....*
                              —I Corinthians 13:4 (NIV)

I was disappointed when I discovered that I had a teacher's aide in the kindergarten class in which I'd been assigned to substitute. The five- and six-year-olds in the class loved "Miss Marsha" and didn't care much for "Miss Linda" (me!). One girl shrugged off my help in tying her shoe, saying, "You do it all wrong! I want Miss Marsha to help me!" Hurt, I envied the warm relationship they had with her.

But as the day wore on, I was glad Miss Marsha was there, for when two girls started squabbling, I didn't know how to handle it.

"Teacher," one cried to me, "we had a singing contest and I won first place. But now Sheila wants first place!" The two girls glared at each other, arms folded against their chests.

I was at a loss for words — mainly because I knew how she felt! I was used to being the best — and only — teacher. And now I was in "second place" to Miss Marsha. But I knew I couldn't say that, so I stood there, drawing a blank — until Miss Marsha came along and said, "Girls, why can't you have *two* first place winners?"

The girls' eyes lit up and both said, "Yeah!" and marched off arm in arm while I stared in disbelief.

Why had I been so small? I thought. Why did I feel that if the kids liked Miss Marsha that meant they didn't like me?

"That was a good mini-lesson for them…and for me!" I said to Miss Marsha. "Now, can you show me how to tie a shoe the 'right way'?"

Help me share the spotlight today, God, whether it is with a co-worker, a spouse or a friend.   —Linda Neukrug

25 | W E D | *"For in the resurrection there is no marriage; everyone is as the angels in heaven."* — Matthew 22:30 (TLB)

I've been single since 1985. In the following years, I've met and dated a number of different men, always looking for the "perfect" mate. But usually I only dated each one once or twice because they just weren't "perfect" enough. And they've left me wondering if the perfect mate really exists.

Then one day a friend suggested I put my family room to good use by letting that be the monthly meeting place for a women's group. After that, I made an effort to bring other people into my home, both male and female. I joined a few organizations, changed careers, helped start a Bible study group at church, worked hard at keeping the relationships with my married friends, and started visiting friends and relatives all over the country.

Oh, I still have those days when I wonder if God has someone perfect out there for me. But instead of feeling like part of me is missing, I make the effort to keep my life full by making sure it's filled with people. Today, I can honestly say that I'm enjoying the single life and, in fact, I can't ever remember being happier!

Lord, help me to be the perfect *friend to others and to stop worrying about finding the perfect* other *for me.*   —Patricia Lorenz

26 | T H U | *...Always giving thanks to God the Father for*
        everything....   — Ephesians 5:20 (NIV)

"We're almost out of water again," I say to my husband Harry. "Can
you make a trip to town today to fill our jugs?" The constant traveling down and up the mountain for water is a regular chore at our
house these days, our "house" being a thirty-foot travel trailer on our
property in Durango, Colorado. We're living here while we build a
new home.

Life here has demanded that we slim down our lives to the basics.
Frankly, we've been kind of surprised at how much stuff we can live
without. Water isn't one of them.

We're building the road now. Electricity, telephone, well and septic system are next on the agenda, then the house. It's all taking such
a long time, and I sometimes get frustrated with having to rough it.
My husband senses this in my tone of voice.

"Someday, Mary Jane, we'll look back on this and reminisce with
affection about it," remarks Harry. "We'll say, 'Remember those solar-
heated showers out under the juniper tree in the late afternoon sun,
enjoying both the warmth and the aroma? And all those months of
candlelight evenings, even if they were out of necessity? And the beautiful starry sky overhead when we made those bedtime trips to the la-
trine?'

"When we're in our house," he continues, "we'll have to take a moment now and then to smell the juniper, or to step outside at night
to see the stars."

"Yes, you're right," I reply. "And when we have running water
again, let's remember to say a 'thank-You' prayer every time we turn
on the tap."

*Lord Jesus, in the rough times and in the good times, help me to be
more conscious of the everyday abundance in my life.*
                                              — Mary Jane Clark

27 | F R I | *For everything God created is good, and nothing is to be
        rejected if it is received with thanksgiving.*
                                            — I Timothy 4:4 (NIV)

"Forewarned is forearmed," my husband said after watching a TV program on crimes in schools. He handed me a tiny black disk that fit in the palm of a hand. "If a student tries to attack you, press this little button." A horrible sound pierced my eardrums, then suddenly ceased.

The first day I carried it in my pocket, the small alarm felt as heavy as a battering ram. Instead of my usual confident stride, I walked slowly, hesitantly throughout the day. Everything and everyone on campus looked eerie, suspicious, sinister.

Then, coming through a secluded grove of trees on my way to my car, I spied a shadowy, menacing figure sprinting toward me. My eyes traced with alarm the stranger's hulking frame, the baseball cap turned backward, the gold earring sparkling in one ear, the hooded eyes.

I groped for the alarm. Yet as I found the button, the stranger's eyes opened wide, a grin spread from ear to ear, and a hand waved wildly in greeting. It was Pete, a favorite student. As he came into a patch of sunlight, the world suddenly shifted into focus and I saw him clearly, untainted by my unwarranted fears. Just Pete, a friendly young man in a friendly place where good things abounded.

I still carry the black disk. But I don't let it limit my perspective or make me see friends as enemies. More importantly, I go armed with the courage that faith bestows.

Lord, help me to look beyond my fears to Your good world.
— Linda Ching Sledge

28 | S A T | *I have learned, in whatsoever state I am, therewith to be content.* — Philippians 4:11

Today's Saturday — cleaning day. *Ugh!* It's a glorious autumn morning, temperature sixty-eight degrees, sun filtering through red and yellow leaves. A perfect day for a walk with a friend or a picnic together in the park. Instead, here I am stuck inside, keeping company with dust rags, brooms and the vacuum cleaner! Feeling a wisp of loneliness edging near, I decide that now's a good time to apply a recipe for satisfaction I learned from author Sue Bender: "Satisfaction came from giving up wishing I was doing something else."

As I straighten the living room, I stop thinking of the outdoors and try to enter fully into what I'm doing. Picking up the baby toys from Saralisa's visit last evening, I smile. How I love that little sugar-and-spice granddaughter of mine! As I dust Grandmother Morgan's fold-down oak desk and polish its glass doors, I am carried back to the days when that strong-spirited woman, born in 1865, homesteaded here in Nebraska. Brushing the throw pillow that was hand-sewn by women in Bangladesh, I realize that their lives touch mine every day when I lean on its soft, woven surface. And as I vacuum, I have a flight of fancy trying to picture the artist who chose the colors and planned the pattern of the braided rug in front of the fireplace. Did her hands weave it all together, too?

Now, looking over my nice, clean living room, I see it with new eyes. What an enriching morning it's been! And how satisfying.

When I wish I were doing something else, Lord, remind me again of the jewels You have buried for me to find, in this place, at this moment.—
Marilyn Morgan Helleberg

29 | S U N   *"How long will you hesitate…?"*
—I Kings 18:21 (NAS)

One day my husband Gene, who is pastor of our church, said, "Marion, I really think we should join the choir. It needs more members."

"That's fine for you!" I replied. "You can sing and read music. You know I'm practically tone deaf and can't read a note of music. I'd be a misfit."

Gene won, and our choir grew from twelve members to fourteen. People welcomed both of us warmly, even Ken, the director. It was discovered, somehow, that I "sing" alto. I left the first practice holding on to my big, black choir book, and it felt sort of good to carry it around — something like a freshman in college carrying new text-books. En route home, Gene and I sang the songs that we'd practiced. I was smiling as we sang.

That first Sunday in the choir, I discovered that I really liked looking out into the faces of the people, and I liked seeing the emotion in Ken's face as he directed us. I felt bonded with the other singers as well as the organist and pianist and Ken. I discovered that there's a lot more to being in the choir than just singing. We pray together, encourage one another, laugh together….

Sometimes when I lose the place in a song, thirteen-year-old April, who stands beside me (and reads music), quickly points it out to me.

Another newcomer told me, "You weren't singing alto exactly, but you were on key a lot of the time."

Sometimes I wake up early and seem to hear our little choir singing. It's a delightful way to start the day. I'm so glad I didn't miss out on joining the choir and making a joyful noise.

Sometimes, Lord, I avoid the very blessing that You have in store for me. Help me not hesitate to attempt new things. Amen.
— Marion Bond West

30 | M O N *Bear ye one another's burdens, and so fulfill the law of Christ.* —Galatians 6:2

I've always been one who believes that favors should be returned. If a couple invites us to dinner, we have them over for dinner. If a gift arrives in the mail, I feel beholden until I can give a gift in return. Then one month last year I found myself beholden to so many people, I could never pay them back.

It was a month when I had to be hospitalized for an operation, four-year-old Timothy broke his leg in three places and seven-year-old Willy came down with the chicken pox. The presents for the boys came so fast we couldn't keep up. People baby-sat, did our laundry, chauffeured and cooked for us. Our freezer and refrigerator were filled to overflowing with soups, quiches and casseroles. In desperation, I asked my sister Gioia (one of our many benefactors), "How can we ever pay people back?"

"You can't," she simply said. "That's what true giving is about— not expecting a gift in return."

A second answer to my question came a day later when I heard about a neighbor whose husband was going into the hospital, and she was at her wit's end. I knew precisely what we could do for her: make a casserole, invite her kids over, offer to do laundry....

"I found something to do for the kindnesses shown us," I later told my sister.

"What's that?" she asked.

"Pass them on."

This day, in some special way, I will pass on a kindness, Lord.
— Rick Hamlin

GIFTS OF LIGHT

1 _____

2 _____

3 _____

4 _____

5 _____

6 _____

7 _____

8 _____

9 _____

10 _____

11 _____

12 _____

13 _____

14 _____

15 _____

16 _____

17 _____

18 _____

19 _____

20 _____

21 _____

22 _____

23 _____

24 _____

25 _____

26 _____

27 _____

28 _____

29 _____

30 _____

OCTOBER

In the furthest corners of the earth the glorious acts of God shall startle everyone. The dawn and sunset shout for joy!... He prepares the earth for his people and sends them rich harvests of grain.

—PSALM 65:8–9 (TLB)

S	M	T	W	T	F	S
		1	2	3	4	5
6	7	8	9	10	11	12
13	14	15	16	17	18	19
20	21	22	23	24	25	26
27	28	29	30	31		

1 │ T
  │ U
  │ E
"I thank thee, Father...that thou hast hidden these things from the wise and understanding and revealed them to babes."
— Matthew 11:25 (RSV)

One morning at breakfast, when I was still a young mother, our little boy Mallory clambered down from the table and ran to the painting on the wall, shouting, "Look, look! The picture's come alive!"

All heads lifted, and sure enough, shafts of golden sunlight seemed to be pouring from the beautiful clouds and hills in the painting itself! Amazed, we gazed at the phenomenon. "Why, it couldn't be more effective if the artist had put it there," said my husband Lynn.

"An artist did," Mallory said. "God."

He was so casual about it that the rest of us laughed, and we began to discuss the chain of events that had led to this unexpected marvel. I'd found the painting in a swap shop when we were looking for a lamp. I meant to hang it in the living room, but Lynn discovered the light was so much better in the dining room, we might like it even more there. I agreed, and while I was at it, I decided it was time to stop saving that room for dinner or company and serve all our meals there.

"Just the old law of serendipity," Lynn reasoned. "Finding something better than what you were looking for. If you hadn't been looking for the lamp, we'd never have found the picture."

"And if we hadn't been having breakfast in the dining room, we'd never have seen that dazzling sight this morning. Serendipity," I repeated.

"No," Mallory insisted, "God!"

"He's right!" declared his oldest brother. "Who put the sunlight *there*?"

"Thanks, kids. Of course, it's God!" Their dad and I looked at each other, embarrassed but pleased. It's a strange but precious feeling to discover that your children's simple faith makes more sense than your own.

That night, after the children were asleep, we thanked God that no matter how often we had had to move, we had managed to raise them in church and Sunday school. We vowed anew to keep that commitment—which never failed us. It made us even stronger as a family and helped our sons and daughters become the fine men and women they are today.

Dear Lord, bless the wonderful churches that instill faith in our children. Lead all young families to the church just waiting for them.
— Marjorie Holmes

2 | W E D | *A desire fulfilled is sweet to the soul....*
— Proverbs 13:19 (RSV)

When my son Phil was in the ninth grade, he was asked to select a significant theme from Mark Twain's classic *The Adventures of Tom Sawyer*. I've never forgotten what he observed about Tom's character, and essentially his own. He wrote, "A sense of adventure is important to every young boy's childhood."

Phil was one of those insightful kids who realized how fleeting and precious it is to be a child, and he tried his best to wring every bit of carefree fun and adventure out of the experience. He did all kinds of memorable things: digging huge holes in our backyard (that stopped when his shovel collided with the drain field for our septic system!); unscrewing the decorative hardware from my living room tables ("To build a cuckoo clock," he said); going to the mall with me, dressed in his Superman getup (how the shoppers smiled at the little boy in the blue leotards and red cape).

As he grew older, Phil's adventures changed. One day I arrived home to find him and his friend attempting to make baked apples on our front step, using his dad's blowtorch (it didn't work!). Eventually, it was his snow machine that created the highest tracks on the mountainside and his motorcycle that "caught the best air" flying off the sandhill jumps.

Yes, my son had the adventurous kind of childhood he was hoping for. But there's something he doesn't know — his mother did a whole lot of praying! It didn't come naturally for me to step back and allow him his thrills and spills. "Cautious Carol" is my handle. Yet, in loving Phil, God opened my eyes to his unique needs and gave me that ability to set aside certain elements of my own personality so that Phil's personality could fully develop.

And, you know, after nineteen years of sharing life with Phil, "Cautious Carol" is becoming slightly more adventurous!

Dear Father, You made us in Your image and yet You encourage our individuality. Use our personalities for good in the lives of others as they seek to "catch the best air."
— Carol Knapp

3 | T H U   *Thou shalt have no other gods before me.*   — Exodus 20:3

I have a small tray that attaches to the arm of my chair. I keep my Bible there as well as other books and magazines. Sometimes the pile gets so high that everything topples over onto the floor. Then I clean it up and start over.

The first evening I came home from my month-long stay at the hospital, I looked down at the tray and saw a list and a catalog. My husband had left everything on the tray just as I had left it. Picking up the list, I was stunned at all the things I'd meant to order from the catalog for decorating my house. But now that list just looked frivolous. I was not the same woman who had left my house in an ambulance. Nor would I ever again be the same woman. Those weeks in the intensive care unit, the heart surgery with its resulting complications and the four code blues that had been called on me had transformed me into a totally different person. I reached out and threw both the list and the catalog into the trash can.

My husband looked at me curiously. "Why are you throwing your list away?" he asked. "I was careful to save it for you."

"Because I have everything I need, and I thank God for that," I replied. And now with the money saved on capricious purchases, I am able, once in awhile, to send donations to some of my favorite charities.

Dear Lord, let me never confuse frivolous wants with real needs again. Amen.
                                                    — Dorothy Nicholas

4 | F R I   *How great are your works, O Lord ...!*
                                                    — Psalm 92:5 (NIV)

One early, ordinary fall morning, I sleepily dragged myself to the deck to shake the kitchen rug. *Yuk!* A cloud of dog hairs and dirt dissolved into my backyard. I turned to go inside, but something out there caught the corner of my eye. On the edge of our pond was a dignified guest, a great heron, standing stock-still on one skinny leg, long sharp beak in profile, as if waiting for its portrait to be finished. Leaning on the railing, I watched it, thrilled at this out-of-the-ordinary, exotic creature visiting my common turf.

Finally, it turned its long beak my way, a spray of head feathers nodding, and gave me a haughty look that said, "Toodle-loo." Spreading enormous wings, it soared over the treetops and on to whatever place it goes for the winter. "Wait!" I wanted to shout. "Stay and be my guest. Live here, so I can thrill to your sight every morning."

I could almost hear it call across the sharp, clean breeze, "How long before I, too, become ordinary?" As I looked around at the wild ducks paddling sparkling wakes in a clear, oval pond, the cloudless sapphire sky spread like a tent pegged with rich crimson trees, the green carpeted field fringed in morning shadows, the calico cat expertly stalking the fence line, I knew the great heron had been sent to tell me, "Wake up and see your astonishing backyard!"

Lord God, please wash my jaded eyes with wonder more often so that I can see the everyday as You do.   — Shari Smyth

5 | S A T | *Love does not demand its own way. It is not irritable or touchy. It … will hardly even notice when others do it wrong.*
—I Corinthians 13:5 (TLB)

After a restless night, I was up early waiting for the paper, going over the all-too-familiar argument I'd had with my husband John the night before. Once again I had found myself shutting cupboard doors after him.

"It not only looks terrible," I had growled, "but one small shake from an earthquake would smash our dishes onto the floor!"

Instead of the apology I expected, he had muttered, "This is absurd! I put your garden tools away time and again after nearly tripping over them. Why complain to me? Just close the doors!"

As I brought in the paper, I heard a *swish* — an eerie, unidentifiable breath, like some phantom wind blowing past the front door. Turning, I saw it. Our beloved oak beside the driveway had fallen over! From the rings in its trunk, John estimated the tree to be more than two hundred years old. It had survived the most brutal assaults — earthquakes, torrential rains, Santa Ana winds.

"Look here," John pointed at the base of the trunk. "Borer bugs. That's what did it!" The tree had been toppled by the persistent gnawing of small bugs! I wept.

In bed that night, wide awake, I thought of our marriage. Like the oak, it had survived many brutal assaults: the near fatal accident of our son; my husband's heart seizure; financial problems. But now our love was threatened by small, insignificant things — "borer bugs"!

"I'm sorry," I whispered as I reached an arm out to him. "I'll shut your cupboard doors. I'm just thankful you're here to leave them open!"

"My fault," he responded. "I'll try to keep them shut, and I'll gladly put away your garden tools."

The next morning he called, "Lovey, come look!" There, just a few feet from the fallen tree was another small oak, growing straight and strong. No borer bugs will get this one, we resolved. And no borer bugs will get us anymore, either!

Help us, dear Lord, to keep the small borers out of our relationship by extending our tolerances and giving each other the love gifts of "I'm sorry" and "It's okay."
                                                            — Fay Angus

6 | S U N *This is my body which is given for you: this do in remembrance of me.... This cup is the new testament in my blood, which is shed for you.*   —Luke 22:19–20

For a while, a few years ago, it seemed that I didn't turn on my radio without hearing the popular song "From a Distance." In addition to an appealing melody, the lyrics were memorably touching. "God is watching us, from a distance," Bette Midler assured. Though I sensed there was something missing, some spiritual gap in the message, I didn't really look behind the words until our minister called them to my attention one day in a sermon.

The song, he pointed out, focuses on God's "awayness," forgetting His omnipresence through the Holy Spirit, Whom Christ promised to send as our Comforter, Helper and Guardian when He returned to His Father. It is good to remember that God is always with us on all days, but particularly today when we observe World Communion Sunday.

What a great word, *communion*, which comes from the Latin meaning "mutual participation." Though it appears only four times in the Bible, in Paul's first and second letters to the Corinthians, communion between believers and God is what the Last Supper is all about and why the Christian community will gather in all corners of the world today. Our celebration of Christ's life and death is testimony to our faith in His promises, one of which is that "where two or three are gathered together in my name, there am I in the midst of them" (Matthew 18:20).

If you don't feel Christ's nearness in your life when you eat His bread and drink His wine, then you can be sure of one thing: He has not moved away, you have. He may be watching us from a distance, as the song says, but He is also as close as our next breath.

> *We praise You, Lord, in our communion,*
> *Prologue to a grand reunion.*

— Fred Bauer

7 | M O N   *"Where is God my Maker, Who gives songs in the night."*
—Job 35:10 (NKJV)

Crickets' chirps, owls' hoots, a cat's meows. Sounds in the night. They can keep me awake. Or I can transform them.

A train whistle: "Thank You, Lord, for commerce that makes this nation's economy strong. Bless those who drive the trains and trucks and planes."

A bottle breaking: "Father, help those who struggle with bad habits. Undo their chains, and set them free for health and happiness."

A siren: "Bless those in health care who never sleep but watch over our needs day and night. Be close to those who are suffering."

A dog barking: "Thank You for those companions who love and accept us just as we are, with all our faults."

The party next door: "For friendship and laughter, I give thanks. They remind me of the coming celebration in heaven when all of us will be happy."

A dripping faucet: "Remind me, God, that little things are not so small. Help me fix the little leaks in my character before they become torrents of trouble."

A car radio: "How I love Your gift of music that sweetens our days with melody and puts a spring in our step."

Children squealing: "Take care of all the little people who often have no one to love them or fight for them when they are in need."

Wind in the trees: "The hope of rain. Without hope, I would die. Keep the breezes of hope ever blowing in my heart and bring refreshing showers of blessing."

A rooster crowing: "It's morning! Another chance at life!"

"I laid me down and slept; I awaked; for the Lord sustained me"
(Psalm 3:5).
—Daniel Schantz

8 | T U E | *Now be ye not stiffnecked, as your fathers were, but yield yourselves unto the Lord....* — II Chronicles 30:8

Most of us like to have our own way. I know that I bridle when some-one tells me what I must or must not do in my personal life. That stubbornness nearly caused a tragedy years ago when I began to have a problem with alcohol. Fortunately, over a period of time, God helped me break my addiction.

The tool God used is similar to one employed by a friend of mine in training horses. One summer day when Rick Thomas had just fin-ished his junior year in high school, a man appeared at his house pulling a horse trailer behind a pickup truck. "Son, I hear you're pretty good at breaking horses of bad habits," the man said. "Will you take on this mare?"

Rick took the challenge. It was his fundamental principle that you never hurt a horse, you just showed it who was in control. He got an experienced wrangler to help him put a training harness on the mare. They snubbed her to a tree, got her onto her side and tied one leg under her belly in the hope of making her less able to strike. Then they let her loose. With incredible prowess the horse jumped up and — on three legs — chased Rick around the grove, rearing up and lashing out at him so viciously that he had to dodge behind orange trees to keep from getting killed.

For days the horse fought the boy with hoof and tooth, but Rick never wavered. Patiently, steadily, day after day, Rick kept at his task until finally the horse yielded.

"When the man came to pick up his mare," Rick told me, "he couldn't believe the change in her."

That's the way God worked with me. For several years I stubbornly insisted that I could handle alcohol. During that long time, God let me struggle and thrash around. He never hurt me. But in the end, I gave up. There was no doubt Who was in control.

Lord, when You have finished Your work with me, I hope people can say of me, too, "I can't believe how much that stubborn man has changed." — John Sherrill

9 | W E D | *Owe no one anything, except to love one another....* — Romans 13:8 (RSV)

Recently, my daughter Charlotte fell in love. It had to happen, I realized, when she went away to college. It was just surprising that it hadn't happened sooner. I love her with the special intensity that a mother of rambunctious sons loves her only daughter, and think she is the nicest, most beautiful young woman I know.

When a young physicist from upstate came along, I knew from the first that this was different. I heard it in her voice, but I tried not to pry. Almost before I had time to worry about what his family was like, it was over. She was crushed, but I truly think I felt worse than she did.

"I don't have any friends," she told me sadly on the phone. "There's no one to talk to." I wanted so much to do something, but felt helpless. Then I remembered an advertisement I'd seen in the newspaper. It was for "BearGrams." One could dial an 800 number and send a teddy bear. I found the number and called.

"Vermont Teddy Bear Company," a bright voice answered. There were all shapes and sizes, clown bears, graduate bears and brown bears, but it sounded very expensive to me. With three children in college, it would be an unwarranted extravagance. But then she was lonely, unhappy and far away. A bear might just help.

Jesus tells us that "it is easier for a camel to go through a needle's eye, than for a rich man to enter into the kingdom of God" (Luke 18:25). Was that an invitation to extravagance or an indictment of material things? Could I justify this frivolity?

"Are you there, ma'am?" said the bright voice.

"Yes, I'm here," I answered, and made my decision.

What, I wonder, would you have done?

Thank You, God, for every chance to consider the feelings of others.
— Brigitte Weeks

10 | T H U | *Here are my directions: Pray much for others; plead for God's mercy upon them; give thanks for all he is going to do for them.* — I Timothy 2:1 (TLB)

For four years I have met every Thursday morning with a group of men to discuss our spiritual growth. One of the things we have promised to do is to pray regularly for one another. I never knew how important that was until recently.

I was in the hospital for what I was told would be routine surgery. When I came out of the operating room, swathed in bandages, groggy from anesthesia, feeling anything but well, I tried to pray and words wouldn't come. My mind felt dull, my spirit disconnected and despondent. Soon, though, I felt a curious buoying of my spirits. It was as though I were borne on the crest of a wave and riding with it smoothly into shore. Somehow it didn't matter that I couldn't think about God. The feeling of being carried lasted for days, until I could pray again.

Later, when I told my buddies about it, one of them said, "Think of all the people who were praying for you. Your friends, your family, your church, your office...us! You might have been struggling, but everyone else kept you close to God."

I do believe he was right. In my anxiety, I had lost touch with the Almighty. But through the watchful words of many, I was never far from Him.

*Dear Lord, today I will remember in prayer:*_____.

(List names)

— Rick Hamlin

11 | F R I | *"You will surely wear out...for the task is too heavy for you; you cannot do it alone."*   —Exodus 18:18 (NAS)

I studied one of the cards on the volunteer's desk at the American Red Cross that fall Friday afternoon. "I wanted to give you a special gift so I gave a part of myself," it said. "I was a blood donor today."

I'd once donated blood for a five-year-old boy with leukemia. But today was different. I was scheduled for major surgery in a week, and I was there to give the last of three pints of blood for myself. An "autologous donation"—just like me, it had an air of independence to it.

"How have you been feeling this week?" the nurse asked as she pricked my fingertip to test my hemoglobin. "Your blood looks a little weak today. I hope your count is high enough."

"Fine...just a little tired, that's all," I answered, shrugging off the fatigue and dizziness I'd been fighting. "Probably just the stress of everything."

She shook her head as she read the results. "Your count is too low, Roberta. I'm afraid you can't give any more blood before your surgery. Know anyone else with A-negative who might donate for you? We'd need them here Monday morning."

How I'd swelled with self-sufficiency and pride just five minutes before. Now I was going to have to ask for blood. *Who would do such a favor?* I wondered as I thumbed through my address book. Like a supporting cast in a play, friends and family began to help, and that afternoon my sister-in-law Ellen located a donor, Charlie Campbell, who said he'd take off work Monday morning to give me a gift I couldn't give myself.

This time I didn't do it alone. Come to think of it, I never have.

Father, teach me the joy of receiving Your gifts so freely given through others.   — Roberta Messner

12 | S A T | *Charm can be deceptive and beauty doesn't last, but a woman who fears and reverences God shall be greatly praised.*   — Proverbs 31:30 (TLB)

It was early fall, and my morning prayer routine was starting to slip by the wayside. Sort of the way my personal appearance had slipped since I quit my job at the radio station to stay home and work.

Just before my forty-ninth birthday, my sister Catherine arrived for a weekend. She plopped a gift bag filled with eight little presents on my lap. "Happy birthday! Here's to a new you!" she said, her eyes twinkling.

I opened box after box. Lipstick, eyeliner, blush, eye shadows, little brushes to apply them all and a case to keep them in.

While I was thinking to myself that I liked my "plain Jane" look, she whisked me into the bathroom and applied touches of highlighter, shadow and liner to my eyes. When Catherine finished my makeover, I couldn't believe my eyes. They looked bigger, brighter. Nice. I liked it all … the blush, the lipstick, the whole look.

"It takes a little time every morning, but if you do it every day it'll become a habit," she advised.

After Catherine's visit, I thought about my other "habit" that I'd let slip. Daily prayer. I thought, *What if I combined my prayer time with my makeup time?*

The next day, as I added a touch of eye shadow, I prayed, "Lord, please let these eyes of mine see the needs of others and respond accordingly."

With the blush brush in hand I said, "Lord, my cheeks are pretty full. Help me to watch the fat grams today and exercise. Keep these cheeks smiling, Lord. Help me to see the good in others and to pass out smiles by the truckload."

Finally, the lipstick. "Lord, help me to use my mouth and the words that come out of it to Your glory. Help me to speak only with kindness."

My makeup routine is now a habit. So are my morning "makeup" prayers.

Thanks, Lord, for all the daily reminders to come to You in prayer. Thanks, also, for a sister who wants me to be the best I can be!
                                              — Patricia Lorenz

13 | SUN

Live in harmony with one another....
                                              — Romans 12:16 (NIV)

My husband Gary and I sat side by side in church, but we couldn't have been farther apart. The tiff we had had before coming to church seemed to have erected a wall between us. I glanced at my bulletin to see what special music was planned. It seemed we were scheduled for a *duel*. I smiled at the typist's error. She had, of course, meant *duet*.

I looked across at Gary. *Duel* or *duet* — two people could be either, but what a difference in the outcome of that chosen relationship! I nudged his arm and pointed to the error. He smiled and, suddenly, that tiff didn't seem nearly so important.

I reached for his hand as the duet began.

Dear Creator, may the melody of Your love and patience be the tune we hum in our relationships with each other. — Mary Lou Carney

14 | MON

But my God shall supply all your need according to his riches in glory by Christ Jesus. — Philippians 4:19

Our lives changed dramatically when my husband Don and I made the painful decision to quit crop farming. Don had been a farmer most of his life, and I prayed earnestly that he would be able to remain in farming in some way. Of course, I had in mind the type of farming we'd always done, so I was surprised when he announced different plans. "When I was a kid, my dad and I raised pigs," he told me. "Good ones. We won prizes all over the state. It will take time and lots of work, but I can raise good pigs again — right here on the farm."

Pigs? I *hated* pigs! They required constant care; they escaped from the sturdiest pens and ate everything in the garden except zucchini;

worst of all, they smelled like pigs! I wouldn't look at them, talk about them, help feed the babies or even wash them.

One day, after I'd launched into another litany about the horrors of pigs, my friend told me a story about a woman who hung a plaque reading "Prayer Changes Things" over the kitchen sink as a reminder to pray daily. A few days later, it was gone. Finally, her husband admitted he'd taken it down. "Don't you believe in prayer?" she asked him. "Of course," he told her, "but I hate change!"

"Is it pigs you hate?" my friend asked gently. "Or is it change?"

Of course, it was change. I had a neat, tidy picture of how I wanted God to answer my prayers. Pigs weren't part of it. To be honest, I'll never share Don's enthusiasm for the pigs. But I'm making strides in dealing with them — and with change! This fall I even went to a pig show and cheered louder than anyone when Don's lean "blue-butt" was named grand champion.

Lord, help me to recognize and gratefully praise You for the changes that come through answered prayer. — Penney Schwab

15 | T U E | MY GIFT TODAY... THE LEAF

O Lord, how manifold are thy works!... — Psalm 104:24

My gift this morning circled slowly down and landed on the kitchen windowsill as I was making coffee: a gold and crimson maple leaf. But it wasn't the leaf's color that caught my eye. It was the graceful, spiraling descent.

I'd never noticed the varied ways leaves fall until last year when my husband John and I were walking in the woods one October day. "Don't you like the way each leaf," he said, "makes its own special pattern as it falls?"

I stopped there on the path, staring first at John, then at an oak leaf gliding by. I hadn't been aware of individual patterns at all. "Flutter" was about all I'd seen leaves do. John, though, is an artist, and artists are people who help the rest of us to see.

I watched a leaf tumble end over end, and another twirl like a spinning top. Over there I saw one drop almost vertically, here one floated by in a slow motion arc. Like an all-star ballet, each leaf performed its solo number as it bowed itself out. From that day on I've watched leaves with new appreciation.

I watched today, all day, from the time my gift dropped on the windowsill, aware of the infinite variety, not only of falling leaves, but of rocks and squirrels and shifting cloud shadows. And people, no two alike: neighbors and mailmen and store clerks and joggers. And artists, who open our eyes to the riches of God's world.

Give me an artist's eye, Father, and a lover's heart to revel in all You have made.
— Elizabeth Sherrill

16 | WED

All the believers continued together in close fellowship and shared their belongings with one another.
—Acts 2:44 (GNB)

Some years ago, one of the young men of our neighborhood became a source of anxiety to his family and friends. Freddy dropped out of school, grew his hair long, dressed in an unkempt manner and was running a mild war with his parents. I may have been the only person on our block who experienced no concern about his future. Here is the reason for my confidence:

When my son Ben was seven years old, he borrowed Freddy's bicycle. Freddy was eleven and just the week before had been given this brand-new ten-speed. This was an unlikely bike for him to have, for his parents were not wealthy enough to purchase things like that casually. He worshiped that bike and knew full well that if anything happened to it he should not expect another one until he was prepared to buy it himself. Nevertheless, he lent it to my Benjamin.

That is why Ben was crying as he lay beside the spilled bike in our backyard. He had caught a crack with the front tire, and now he had to tell Freddy he had bent and scratched the bike. I decided to soften the blow by finding Freddy and breaking the news.

He was around the corner. "Freddy," I said, "Ben crashed on your bike."

"Is he hurt?" Freddy asked. And that is all he asked.

From that moment to this, I have had no fears about what kind of a man Freddy will become.

Lord, teach me to value people before things.
— John Cowan

P.S. Freddy has taken a different path from that of his parents and siblings. He did not go to college. For a couple of years he washed dishes for pay. But now he is in technical school learning about the electronics he loves.

17 | T H U
Whenever you pray tell God every detail of your needs in thankful prayer. — Philippians 4:6 (Phillips)

I felt a bit apprehensive as I drove down the tree-lined driveway toward the Benedictine abbey a few miles from our home one recent morning. I'd never spent a day alone at a spiritual retreat center, but lately I'd been feeling overwhelmed by the adjustments of going back to work after staying home to raise a family. My days always seemed a jumble of too many responsibilities and too little time. So I made a reservation to spend this quiet day at the abbey, hoping to regain some strength and find some better ways of coping with the pressures.

When I rang the doorbell of the modest brick building, a nun with a gentle smile greeted me. "Come right this way," she said in an almost-whisper before leading me down a long hallway. She opened the door into a small room with a bed and a desk. "Our most important task here is to praise God and sanctify each part of the day through our services in the chapel," she said. "Our next one is at 11:45, and you are welcome to join us." With that, she disappeared back down the hall.

The idea of sanctifying the day — or setting it apart for God's purposes — intrigued me, so at 11:45 I slipped quietly into the back of the chapel and listened as the nuns chanted several beautiful psalms and hymns. They then ended with a prayer, asking God to bless the tasks begun that day and to give them strength to complete them. The words seemed spoken just for me, and when I got back to my room, I jotted them down as best as I could remember and tucked the prayer into my Bible. Later, as I drove home, I knew God had given me what I had come to find: a reminder that pausing to talk to Him in the middle of a jumbled day is the best way to find strength to cope with mounting pressures.

In case you need the same reminder, here is my new noon-time prayer:

Almighty God, in the middle of the day, I come to rest and ask You to bless the work I have begun. Make good its defects and let me finish in a way that pleases You. Amen. — Carol Kuykendall

18 | F R I
The trying of your faith worketh patience. But let patience have her perfect work.... — James 1:3–4

When I was in medical school, I had a most unusual teacher. At the time I met him, he was a lowly hospital resident, but before Castro took over Cuba, he had been the most famous professor of cardiology on the island. Dr. Torres and his family fled here for refuge, and he had to start his training all over in order to be licensed to practice in America.

Although he was much older than the other residents, Dr. Torres seemed to have more energy than the rest of us combined. One night when I was on duty, I watched another intern fuss and throw a fit after fifteen minutes of trying and still failing to get an IV into a little infant on our ward. Dr. Torres came along and took Stuart's place. Silently, the older man worked for an hour before the tiny needle slipped into a willing vein.

"Dr. Torres," Stuart confessed, "I'm so embarrassed. After a few minutes, I was cursing. But you, you stood there patiently for an hour and never said a word."

The tired older man kindly put his arm around the tired younger man. "Stuart," he said, "let me tell you something. After Castro, this was nothing!"

That vignette happened more than thirty years ago, but I remember it as if it were this morning. Each time I come to the end of my patience, I reach back in my memory, not only for Dr. Torres' lesson but for all the hardships in my own life that required a new level of patience. With God's help and godly examples, I can find the strength to do the seemingly impossible at least once a week and afterward say, "This was nothing!"

In Your plan for me, God, I see all the impossible things that have been made possible by patience, which could only come from You. Thank You!
— Diane Komp

19 | S A T *Blessed are the pure in heart: for they shall see God.*
— Matthew 5:8

One morning in autumn, my mother called me to her sewing room. I was a little boy full of energy and rough ways. I liked to chase my sisters with mud balls at that time.

"Christopher, I just finished knitting you this sweater. Let's try it on." The sweater was red and gray, a sleeveless vest with buttons in the front. As my mother slipped it on, I looked over her shoulder and made a funny face in the mirror behind her. "Now," my mother said, "look at yourself."

With my big ears, I looked like Dopey with a baggy sweater. It looked awful. But my mother had made it, so I wore it.

Later in the afternoon, when I was in the yard jumping into the pile of leaves my father collected, I noticed something. Each button on the sweater had two eyes, a nose and a smile. I was so delighted that I ran into the kitchen to show Mother the wonderful buttons. She gave me a big hug.

Of course, I now understand why a mother would embrace a child who noticed and delighted in something she did. Children know to take delight in the smallest things, but it is something I, as an adult, often forget. But perhaps, today, you and I can open our eyes and take a second look, to discover and delight in something special someone has done for us … something like buttons with smiles.

Lord of generosity, let me delight in the light of Your love.
— Christopher de Vinck

POINT OF LIGHT

THINGS THAT COUNT

Not what seems fair, but what is true;
Not what we dream, but the good we do.
These are the things that shine like gems,
Like stars in fortune's diadems.
—Author Unknown

---

20 | S U N | *Ye did communicate with my affliction.*
—Philippians 4:14

The phrase *pay attention* has always puzzled me. Where does this idea of payment come from? Shouldn't payment, if any, come from the receiver of attention, not the giver?

In any case, the art of giving (or paying) complete attention is one of the most important skills we can acquire. It's not easy, because it involves screening ourselves and our troubles out of the picture and focusing on someone else. But the payment brings great dividends.

I remember the story I heard once of a patient in a mental hospital in Nebraska. He was suffering from depression so profound that he never smiled, never spoke, never responded in any way to attempts at treatment. This had been the case for years; his condition was considered hopeless.

But there was a young chaplain who, for some reason, took a special interest in this man, visited him every day, read to him, talked to him, tried to reach through to him, never gave up. This went on for months. Then one day as they both sat facing a window, just to fill the silence the chaplain was describing the scene outside, the trees blowing in the wind, the pigeons, the squirrels. And suddenly, incredibly, a hesitant voice spoke beside him: "I...had a...pet squirrel once."

That was the breakthrough. From then on the patient began to get well. Why? Because someone paid attention. And paid it and paid it. And by so doing brought salvation to a lost and suffering soul.

Father, help us pay attention to others as You pay attention to us.
                                        —Arthur Gordon

21 | M O N *[God] comforts us in all our troubles, so that we can comfort those in any trouble with the comfort we ourselves have received from God.*   —II Corinthians 1:4 (NIV)

"Hello, this is Pastor John calling," the voice on the other end said. "I wonder if you'd be willing to call a young woman whose husband died very suddenly yesterday. I know you haven't met her, but I told her about you and she said she'd like to hear from you."

I went to see Barb this afternoon, and as I listened to her story, I was flooded by memories of my own sadness and pain of a decade ago: the phone call from the hospital telling me of Jim's death in a car accident; the bewilderment and loneliness and fear; the agony of telling my three young children that they'd never see their daddy again.

Yesterday, Barb's husband, in good health and in his early thirties, had dropped dead of a heart attack. No warning, no opportunity to say that final good-bye and "I love you." I can see in her face that she is still struggling to believe it, and I know from experience that the next weeks and months will demand lots of hard grieving work if she wants to find healing. To complicate matters further, their first babies—twins—are due in about six months.

We talked and cried together, and as I left she said, "Thanks for coming. Just meeting someone who has survived this gives me hope and courage to go on."

I'm glad Pastor John called. He knew what I now know: We can use our own pain to ease the pain of others.

Encourage me, loving Father, to use the painful, difficult experiences of my life to bring help and hope to others.   —Mary Jane Clark

22 | T U E   *Now there are diversities of gifts, but the same Spirit.*
                        —I Corinthians 12:4

Fifteen years ago, my wife Barbara and I bought a little farm in Texas. It was the dead of winter when the trees were bare and the pastures brown. We loved the tiny yellow house, the faded red barn and spring-fed creek, and we could picture how lush the pastures would soon be. But springtime only brought waist-high weeds. The county agent suggested that we plow everything under, then hire someone to plant Coastal Bermuda, a popular grass in the area.

Our neighbor George Wehrung had a better idea. "Go with the grasses that God put there," he advised. "Emil Fenner, whose farm you bought, kept the weeds cut so that the native grasses could get the sunshine and rain and nutrients they needed." That summer Barbara and I mowed a few acres each time we came to the farm, and as it rained, the grasses began to appear. In the fall, we counted more than twenty different kinds, including the prized bluestem, which had sustained the buffalo grazing there a century before.

Last summer, a mild stroke forced me to cancel my speaking and teaching responsibilities for the year. I discovered that the principle my neighbor had suggested for our pasture also worked for my life. Previously, I would rise early for overly full days and nights of preaching and pastoring, or heading for the airport for a week of speaking. Now, I sit quietly each morning, reading for an hour in my handmade rocking chair. With the heavy activities cut back, my soul is being fed. And I have both the time and emotional energy to begin developing gifts that my faster pace of living had stifled—even writing poetry!

I wonder what other gifts are waiting to be developed.

Thank You, God, for quieter times and the awareness of new opportunities to grow.   —Kenneth Chafin

23 | W E D *Who gathers crops in summer is...wise....*
—Proverbs 10:5 (NIV)

Is this really worth it? I wonder on a sweltering August afternoon, standing in the middle of a briar patch. *No one should pick wild blackberries in short sleeves. And I can buy jam already made!* Nor can you pick blackberries with gloves on. Each shiny blackberry has to be gathered one by one, while you try to avoid the twisting, clinging briars that scratch your hands and arms.

Back home after several hours, I pour a portion of my gleanings into a kettle. The deep purple jam bubbles on the range while jelly containers wait to be filled. I crush some fruit and thicken its juice for syrup. My stained hands still sting from scratches while I roll out dough, but the resultant pies, oozing juice through browned crusts, make me ask, *What if I'd missed the opportunity to create this wonderful scent?*

Each time I pick, peel, and can fruits and vegetables, I have moments of wondering if the labor is worth it. But now our pantry shelves are lined with color — not only purple blackberries, but golden peaches, yellow corn, red tomatoes, green beans and more. My husband and I already envision dull winter days brightened by breakfast toast spread with blackberry jelly, followed by dishes of spicy applesauce or mellow pears processed in pineapple juice. That's when I know the work was worth it.

Dear heavenly Father, thank You for the ability You've given us to work, and for the results when we do. —Isabel Wolseley

24 | T H U *They shall beat their swords into plowshares, and their spears into pruning-hooks: nation shall not lift up a sword against nation, neither shall they learn war any more.*
—Micah 4:3

One benefit of living near New York City is the opportunity to visit many of the interesting sites in the Big Apple. I never thought much of the United Nations until I went there to attend a conference in one of its many meeting rooms a few years ago. One of the men at the meeting suggested that he and I take the official tour afterward. At one point, we listened to the tour guide tell of the United Nations' goal of working for "world peace and security and the betterment of humanity." Somehow, the words rang hollow in the face of all the armed conflicts around the world.

After the tour, we were about to hail a cab when, looking across the plaza, we saw a huge statue of a man beating a sword into a plow. Curious, we walked over and found that it was created by a Russian sculptor, Yevgeny Vuchetich. "It was a gift to the United Nations from Communist Russia," my friend noticed. "And that was before the fall of the Berlin Wall."

"Imagine that," I said, "a country that officially denied the existence of God gave a statue to illustrate the Bible verse that defines the mission of the United Nations. So you see, there was always hope after all."

And with God's blessing, there always is.

Thank You, Lord, for letting the world conceive of a place where people can work to prepare for the future You have planned.
                                                    — Eric Fellman

25 | F R I   *But thou, when thou prayest, enter into thy closet*
                                                    — Matthew 6:6

My prayer life needed help. I'd been searching for a way to help me pray more consistently. The one I discovered is so simple, I almost hesitate to share it.

While I was cleaning out my walk-in closet one day, an eight-by-ten photograph of my twin sons fell from a top shelf. Jon and Jeremy were four in the picture, wearing navy sailor suits with short pants and white, starched collars and new, red-buckle shoes. I smiled at the picture I had thought was lost and started to replace it on the shelf, when an idea came to me. I taped the picture to the wall, eye-level, in a spot where no clothes hung. Then I bowed my head and prayed for each son. Later, I added pictures of my other children and grandchildren. My husband's picture is there, too — I know some special dreams and visions he has. I've included a picture of a friend who needs a big miracle, as well as pictures of other friends, and things to remind me of some of my dreams. It's become my prayer wall.

My intercession over my collage of prayer requests is sometimes lengthy. Then I sit or kneel amid my shoes. Other times I'm grabbing something in a hurry, and a glance at my prayer wall reminds me to pray on the go. But whether my prayer time is long or brief, I sense that in my closet I'm in a snug, secure cocoon of prayer, with no out-side interferences.

Lord, help me to create prayer reminders in my heart and in my home. Amen.   — Marion Bond West

Editor's Note: A month from now, on November 25, Guideposts will hold our third annual Family Day of Prayer. We invite you to become part of our prayer family by sending your prayer requests, along with a picture if you'd like, to Guideposts Prayer Fellowship, 39 Seminary Hill Road, Carmel, New York 10512. We will pray for you on November 25.

26 | S A T *Every branch that beareth fruit, he purgeth it, that it may bring forth more fruit.* —John 15:2

"Cut back the grapes," I once ordered my teenage son, and went on about my work, vaguely aware of the young figure chopping away. When I looked up later, I was aghast. He'd cut the vines clear to the ground!

"You've ruined them!" I wailed. "We'll never have grapes again." It looked hopeless. We had to build a big fire just to get rid of what he'd cut down. Yet the next year the vines grew back stronger than ever, the grapes so abundant they bowed the trellises — more than enough to give away.

And I think that applies to my life, too — those terrible cuttings and trials by fire. I look back sometimes, shocked but grateful as I remember the pain and problems I had to suffer. I wept and protested at the time; I only wanted to be spared. Yet now I realize how essential they were to my growth. How much pride and self-pity had to go, how much hostility and unforgiveness. Habits that only made the tribulations worse and disturbed my faith in God.

Why didn't God answer my prayers? Why did He let bad things happen? But I finally understood. Experience taught me: When we suffer, He wants us to be strong and to learn from what we must endure. To grow in sympathy and understanding, so that we can help others in their times of crisis and despair. Only then can we, too, bear abundant fruit.

Dear Lord, please help all those who are hurting. Comfort them as You and Your children have comforted me.   — Marjorie Holmes

27 | S
U
N | *For thou wilt light my candle: the Lord my God will*
enlighten my darkness.   — Psalm 18:28

My husband Bob and I sat in our car in front of the small rural church where he, a certified lay speaker, was to speak that Sunday morning. It was five minutes before the service was scheduled to start, but we were the only ones present, and the church was locked.

From a nearby house, an elderly woman and a middle-aged man walked toward the church. She nodded a "good morning" as she passed us and unlocked the door. Once we were inside, she said, "My name is Ellie, and this is my son Tom. We don't have many folks come to services anymore, since we don't have a regular preacher. But Tom and me, we keep up the Lord's house."

Ellie handed out hymnals and named three songs we would sing a cappella. After the hymns, Bob went up to the pulpit and announced we'd have prayer. While he prayed, I heard a car stop outside, and as soon as he said, "Amen," two well-dressed women slipped in the back door and sat down behind Ellie. One put an arm around Ellie's shoulder, hugged her slightly and touched her lips to the withered cheek. The other one smiled sweetly, and the warmth the three shared was obvious.

When the service was over and we all had gathered at the back of the church to talk, I looked around the small sanctuary. The pews, the altar rail and the bare floor were all clean and polished. A large vase of fresh garden flowers stood on a table beside the lectern. I thought of the time that Ellie and Tom had devoted to caring for this church. I thought of the hours Bob had spent preparing his message for the service, and the many miles the two women, no longer residents in the area, had driven to worship here. And then I said this prayer:

Father, bless these faithful servants of Yours and all those like them,
everywhere. Amen.   — Drue Duke

28 | M
O
N | *Let him have all your worries and cares, for he is always*
thinking about you and watching everything that
concerns you.   —I Peter 5:7 (TLB)

Life is one huge celebration on Alvaro Street in Los Angeles. The cheerful beat of mariachi music is enticing; huge clay urns are filled with bright paper flowers; papier-mâché piñatas shaped like donkeys, bulls and birds climb up vendors' poles; the food — tostadas, taquitos, tacos, tamales — is superb. Alvaro Street is a perfect place for a fun-filled stroll and for finding an unusual gift.

Browsing through one of the many shops of Mexican folk art, I picked up a small, hand-painted wooden box tagged "Worry Dolls." "What on earth…?" I asked the clerk.

"Ah," she laughed, opening it up to show several tiny, colorfully dressed stick dolls crowded inside. "These are for the children. Before they go to sleep at night, if they have a worry or a fear, they can take out a doll and tell it their trouble. The doll takes the worry, so the child can sleep. In the morning, the worry is gone!"

"Does it work with grown-ups, too?" I grinned.

"Why not!" she said.

So I purchased the dolls, and when I got home I gave each a name: Fear, Anxiety, Regret, Trouble, Health and Money. Now, when a worrisome thought comes, I take out the appropriate doll and stare it in the face. And I pray:

Lord, thank You that You are concerned about all my cares. With these symbolic dolls, I release my worries to You. Clothe me with the mantle of Your peace.   — Fay Angus

29 | T U E   *I will lift up mine eyes unto the hills….* — Psalm 121:1

"What a lousy day," I muttered as I climbed up the rough hillside. Nothing had gone right. I hadn't finished my homework, my best friend said she was too busy for me to come over, and I'd just had a stupid argument with my brother. It had been one of those days when things felt all mixed up and terrible, but I just couldn't explain exactly why. I had been feeling removed from God lately. It seemed as if I were lost and forgotten in the midst of everything.

I reached the top of the hill and looked around for a place where I could sit and feel sorry for myself. I spotted an oil well and climbed its ladder and settled myself on a precarious ledge. Now I was really alone. And I was lonely.

A soft wind blew and I heard it rustling in the trees, when a single maple leaf swirled through the air and became entangled in my hair. I reached up for it and held it in my hand. It was bright red with deep veins tracing through it. I think it was the first time that I'd ever thought of the intricate craftsmanship of this seemingly insignificant object, which God had created. There were millions of leaves — trillions of them — but not one like this one.

I got up, ran down the hill, and when I came home, I pressed the leaf between the pages of my Bible. It is there to remind me of the day I forgot about feeling lonely and neglected. How can anybody feel that way when God takes such obvious care with a single red leaf?

How precious my life is, dear Lord, with You in it.   — Hollie Davis

30 | W E D | *Though I walk through the valley of the shadow of death, I will fear no evil: for thou art with me....*
—Psalm 23:4

It was 5:00 P.M. when the call came about my former mother-in-law. Edna had only hours to live. "There's no need for you to come," the nurse said. "She's in a coma now, and the doctor said she'll not regain consciousness. There's nothing you can do." It wasn't a shock. Edna was ninety-nine and had been in the hospital many weeks. I decided not to go. What could I say or do anyway?

Then I began pacing. I couldn't get Edna out of my mind, even though I'd prayed for her smooth passage into the afterlife. Over the past weeks, I'd sensed that she was ready to die but that she couldn't quite let go. Now I began to feel a sense of urgency. Finally, I drove to the hospital.

She was alone in the room, skin a ghostly white, eyes half-open, glassy, unseeing. I reached under the covers and held her hand, looked into her eyes, and began to recite the Twenty-third Psalm. While I spoke the words, "Yea, though I walk through the valley of the shadow of death, I will fear no evil, for Thou art with me," Edna's eyes came alive and she looked directly at me. Then she sighed, closed her eyes, and as I finished the Psalm, all the hard lines in her face softened. I told her I loved her, kissed her good-bye and left, heavy with the sense of loss all final good-byes bring.

My phone was ringing when I got home. It was the nurse who had returned to the room just as I left. Edna had died peacefully at 6:04 P.M.

I'll never again stay away from visiting a sick or dying person because "there's nothing I can say or do." The Twenty-third Psalm will do more than my human words or deeds could ever do.

Spirit of God, thank You for Your trusted Word that leads the way from darkness into the Light. — Marilyn Morgan Helleberg

31 | T H U | *And now these three remain: faith, hope and love. But the greatest of these is love.* — I Corinthians 13:13 (NIV)

"Mom, the doctor is going to take the first ultrasound of my baby this afternoon!" Meghan's voice bubbled with enthusiasm over the phone. "Would you like to come and see your new grandchild?"

Would I ever!

A short while later I watched in awe as the small, curled-up shadow of Meghan's child appeared on the screen of the monitor. "There's the head," the doctor said, "and the torso. And look, you can see the heartbeat."

"Hello," I greeted the little one softly and thankfully. There had been certain medical problems that could have prevented Meghan from conceiving a child. More than thirty years ago, I had not been able to conceive a child. But through the miracle of adoption, our beautiful, loving daughter had come into Larry's and my life. Now, through the miracle of modern medical technology, a much-wanted child was about to come into Meghan and Pete's life.

Meghan touched her body in a caress for the child inside and said, echoing my thoughts, "Oh, Mom, what a miracle!"

What a miracle indeed!

Father, I praise You for Your many wonders, including the wonder of new life, and of older lives shared in faith and love.
— Madge Harrah

GIFTS OF LIGHT

1 _____

2 _____

3 _____

4 _____

5 _____

6 _____

7 _____

8 _____

9 _____

10 _____

11 _____

12 _____

13 _____

14 _____

15 _____

16 _____

17 _____

18 _____

19 _____

20 _____

21 _____

22 _____

23 _____

24 _____

25 _____

26 _____

27 _____

28 _____

29 _____

30 _____

31 _____

How precious is your constant love, O God!...You feed...[humanity] with blessings from your own table and let them drink from your rivers of delight. For you are the Fountain of life; our light is from your Light.

—PSALM 36:7–9 (TLB)

NOVEMBER

S	M	T	W	T	F	S
					1	2
3	4	5	6	7	8	9
10	11	12	13	14	15	16
17	18	19	20	21	22	23
24	25	26	27	28	29	30

1 | F R I   *The Lord ... preserveth the souls of his saints....*
                                            —Psalm 97:10

One of the things I like best about my small Midwestern hometown is its cemetery—complete with quaint wrought-iron fence and winding gravel driveway. Near that driveway is a small cement bench with these words engraved on its side: *Come Sit With Us.*

When I was a child, I thought it a strange invitation. But as I grew up—and people I cared about died—I often did just that. I would sit on the cool stone bench and look around at the headstones of those I had known: Roger, who died in an accident just after our tenth birthday. Mrs. Lytle, who always got the flower for being the oldest mother on Mother's Day. Ronnie Smith, who everybody said was the best trumpet player our school ever had. They buried his trumpet with him. And then there was Brother Ward. Every Wednesday night, when the pastor asked for testimonies, Brother Ward rose to his feet. Dressed in blue work pants and a flannel shirt, he gripped the pew in front of him and never said a word. He simply stood there, his broad shoulders shaking as tears rolled down his rough cheeks, and raised his hand toward heaven.

I don't often get back home these days. Whenever I do, I still visit that cemetery. My father and grandmother are there now, too. But I've found that I don't have to be actually on that bench to heed the invitation to "come sit with us." I simply need to stop my bustle and find a quiet spot of my own. And remember.

Dear God, today on All Saints' Day, I thank You for Your saints and the path they have left for us. Amen.   — Mary Lou Carney

2 | S A T   *He which soweth bountifully shall reap also bountifully.*
                                            —II Corinthians 9:6

We all call her Ronny. An ordained minister, her real name is Veronica. Recently, on her seventy-fifth birthday, friends sponsored an "almost surprise celebration" that established a scholarship in her name. The church was overflowing, and friends spilled out onto the street. What had she done to attract such a gathering?

When she was ordained in 1970, Ronny was one of two black woman ministers in her denomination. Now she is an interim pastor, bringing healing to a divided parish. She drives over a hundred miles each week to bring comfort and encouragement to others.

Ronny's concern and kindness have touched our lives also. When our son Oscar, Jr., was five, she rushed us to the hospital for his surgery because we had no car. When job demands threatened my health, she was there with strong advice about seeking other employment. When my wife Ruby shattered her knee, Ronny took care of personal errands for us and then stayed to comfort me as I wept.

Few are aware that this cheerful, energetic, enthusiastic person has a hearing impairment and no sense of smell. Her heart condition, acquired in childhood, is so severe she cannot raise her arms above her head. Yet her letters and telephone calls all end with, "Be of good cheer!"

"I wonder if God tires of hearing from me?" she said recently. "I'm forever thanking Him."

We who know Ronny feel that we are guests at her spiritual table, which overflows with warm friendship, sound advice and spiritual sensitivity. But more than that, she has shown us the secret of happiness: living for others with a grateful heart.

Providing Savior, examples of Your saints are all around for us to see and to emulate. Thank You.   — Oscar Greene

3 | S U N   *Therefore, rid yourselves of all malice....*
                              —I Peter 2:1 (NIV)

Just before my husband and I left for vacation, I learned of a betrayal by a friend that filled me with bitterness. I knew exactly how I would hurt her back. I carried my plan with me, thinking of it even as we lugged the suitcases into the hotel in Harper's Ferry, West Virginia, a small town carrying a burden of dark history dating to the Civil War.

The next morning, I got up early, leaving Whitney to breakfast and read the paper alone. I walked downhill to the foot of Harper's Ferry, where the Potomac and Shenandoah rivers merge together like old friends, and saw ugly stone stumps rising like tombs out of the water. Nearby, a uniformed guide was explaining to a group that they were once part of a railroad bridge. During the Civil War, it was blown up and rebuilt nine times by the North and the South. Both coveted the strategically located town where blood flowed, as first one side, then the other, conquered it. Loyalties were divided, families split.

"Now up there" (my gaze shifted as the guide swept his arm to a rocky summit far above on which a church stood alone, its cross piercing the sky), "is St. Peter's Roman Catholic Church. During the war it served as a hospital for both sides." When the war broke, the priest put aside his own loyalties and flew the British flag over the church, rendering it to a power that neither the North nor the South wanted to touch. Thus, St. Peter's survived the shelling and became a source of healing, both physical and spiritual.

I climbed the sixty-eight stone steps, worn smooth by time and tears, to the top of the summit, where the church stood larger than life, stronger than evil. I stepped inside the church's musty Gothic interior, eyes adjusting to the darkness, and moved up the bare wood aisle to kneel at the cross. Rendering myself to its healing power, I, too, found the church a hospital.

Back outside, I looked far down to where the river lapped at useless stone stumps and felt the start of a bridge in me. A bridge of forgiveness.

Heavenly Father, help us to pray the prayer of Your Son, when He conquered evil for the world: "Not as I will, but as thou wilt" (Matthew 26:39).   — Shari Smyth

---

4 | M O N *"Come to me, all who labor and are heavy laden, and I will give you rest....For my yoke is easy, and my burden is light."*   — Matthew 11:28, 30 (RSV)

Last winter, I decapitated a driveway light. *Great,* I thought, climbing out of my Jeep to survey the damage, *one more problem to tend to!*

"Humph," said my father, coming to take a look. He turned the broken fixture in his hand, examining the exposed wiring. I didn't like the sound of his grunt. But then he grinned and said, "Here's your chance to do what you really want. You aren't particularly attached to this fixture, are you?"

It was rather ordinary, come to think of it.

"How about making a fixture out of an old stump instead?" he suggested. "We could make it a hut for one of the elves you collect and hook a light up to that."

I started to catch on. My father doesn't ever *fix* things, he *creates* things. He's an artist. As I pictured his suggestion, the burden of fixing my broken light vanished. I felt, instead, new excitement and the thrill of creativity taking hold. This was going to be fun, not work!

In just moments, my father had transformed a frustrating burden into something joyful and new! I wondered suddenly, *Maybe this is what Jesus meant when He said, "My yoke is easy, and my burden is light."* Perhaps His yoke, at times, is one of creative response to our troubles, making our tasks less bother and more fun.

My driveway is still one light short, but it won't be when I find the perfect stump to do what I want!

Dear God, thank You for the gift of creativity, which lightens our load and brings energy and hope for new potential.

— Brenda Wilbee

5 | T U E *Now I beseech you, brethren... that there be no divisions among you....*   —I Corinthians 1:10

I used to think I was a pretty good citizen because I voted in every election. Then, about a year ago, I attended my first local public meeting because some developers requested a zoning variance that would allow them to build a lot of houses in my neighborhood.

The meeting room was packed. When the zoning board members filed in and sat at the long table in front of the room, they seemed a bit startled. The chairman grinned and said, "It's real nice to see all you people here. We're usually pretty lonely."

I felt ashamed. If I hadn't been looking out for my own interests, I wouldn't have been there. I'd thought it was enough just to elect people to represent me. It didn't occur to me to give them a hand in the difficult task of governing. But in the past year, I've learned through personal experience just how difficult it is, because in a democratic society we have to try to agree on what is right or best for everyone.

I still vote in every election. And when I pull the levers, I imagine all of those men and women sitting in an empty room, trying to do what we elected them for — decide what's best for the rest of us. In this presidential election year, I feel an additional responsibility: to give each candidate my attention; to be willing to listen to other points of view; to make my vote an informed and intelligent one. And I will continue to attend our local governmental meetings. It's a privilege to be part of the governing instead of just the governed.

Lord Jesus, may this Election Day be a time of personal commitment as well as personal choice. Amen.

— Phyllis Hobe

6 | W E D   *Let there be thanksgiving.*   —Ephesians 5:4 (RSV)

A few weeks before Thanksgiving, I was surprised to receive a letter from an old friend of my mother's. "I came across this clipping in my files," the note said, "and wanted you to know how much it meant to your mother." Tucked inside was a folded, yellowing copy of a Mother's Day column I had written for our local newspaper.

The urge to do it had come from Hospice, the group that helps families cope with death and dying. "Take care of all unfinished business with the people you love," is their advice. "Say what you need to say. Don't save your words for a tribute at a funeral."

I had written:

> That's good advice for any relationship....To me it means that I must tell my mother right now how many things she's done well in her life and how much I appreciate some of the qualities, characteristics and indelible memories she's given me.

The column went on to highlight some of those memories and to touch upon those parts of me that will always aim to be like her. At the bottom of the clipping, my mother had penned this note to her friend in her shaky handwriting: "This is the best message a mother could hear." She died of emphysema a couple of months later at age sixty-five.

As I put the letter down, I began thinking about other messages I could write — to my husband, our children, a couple of surrogate mothers who have encouraged me, our minister who nurtures me through his sermons. Later that afternoon, when I went to the grocery store, I bought a bunch of Thanksgiving cards, ready once more to tell others what they've meant to me. Now. Because those messages matter.

Father, remind me to take the time to pass on the messages that matter. Now.   — Carol Kuykendall

7 | T H U   *And lo, I am with you always....*   —Matthew 28:20

Last year, I sat in a doctor's office, holding my wife's hand, and heard the surgeon say, "Joy, the lump on your thyroid has grown very fast in the last year. This presents a high possibility that it is cancerous. We have to do surgery to find out and remove your thyroid, if necessary."

In the days that followed, I was frozen by fear. In the previous eight months I had helped three good friends bury their wives. Two had succumbed to cancer and one to a tragic fall. How could I pray for healing when prayers for them had gone unanswered? Why should God be any kinder to me than He had been to them? The result was that I couldn't pray at all.

In my fear, I pushed away friends and family. On the day of the surgery I found myself all alone in the waiting room. By now, I didn't even *want* to pray because I feared the answer that might be given. Finally, the loneliness became so great that I whispered, "God, I'm afraid of You. I have no right to ask for everything to be all right, but I feel so helpless, and I know I can't live without Joy."

In the quietness that followed, the verse "My strength is made perfect in weakness" (II Corinthians 12:9) flooded my mind. Somehow, I said back, "You'd better be pretty strong today, God, because I'm shot." I still couldn't pray, but I felt God's presence.

Much later the doctor came out and said, "Relax, Mr. Fellman, it's benign." As I burst into tears, I thanked God for the answer to the prayer I had never made. But then as I thought about it, God had known all along what my real prayer was.

Lord, thank You for being with me in my darkest moments and for hearing the prayers I cannot put into words.   —Eric Fellman

8 | F R I | *And the Lord's servant must not be quarrelsome but kindly to everyone, an apt teacher, patient.*
—II Timothy 2:24 (NRSV)

In college I majored in chemistry, but I dreaded the final course that crowns that path of academic endeavor—physical chemistry! The older students added fire to our fear as they enveloped the course description in mystery. They never explained why it was so difficult. It simply was so. The catalog description was more neutral, but hardly a source of comfort.

There were only four of us in the class, the lone survivors of the chemistry major, and we dreaded the first exam. Professor Fred Shannon, a bit of an Irish imp, bounced into the classroom that day and handed out the booklets. We held our breath and opened them. "Welcome to the wonderful world of Thermo!" we read. Professor Shannon had woven all of his questions on the laws of thermodynamics into the mythical adventures of a character named Thermo.

He had found a way to get us over our fear of the subject. We smiled, relaxed and plodded through the exam in peace.

I'm a teacher now myself. Although not as witty and patient as Fred Shannon, I learned from him that consideration for my students is just as important as focusing on my subject. Fear is a poor teacher, whereas humor and understanding put everyone — not just students — at ease.

In every situation, O God, may all my words be delivered with grace and kindness.   — Diane Komp

9 | S A T *Incline your ear, and come unto me: hear, and your soul shall live....*   — Isaiah 55:3

My wife is a singer. A couple of years ago she was preparing for a concert at Radio City Music Hall when she lost her voice. Her throat doctor diagnosed swollen vocal cords due to over-rehearsing and prescribed total vocal rest. "Don't speak a word," he said. "Not a sound until the morning of the show."

Julee, I can tell you, is not the silent type, and those few difficult days were an odyssey. Everywhere she went Julee carried a pad and pencil. Our apartment was festooned with those little yellow stick-on notes. And when it came to our having a simple difference of opinion, I would have my say, then wait for Julee to write out her response. That lull in the action invariably gave my hackles time to go down a bit. Julee's words, tempered in the very writing and devoid of vocal inflection and volume, seemed so much less threatening. I had to focus on what she wrote if I were to understand her. The funny thing was the less Julee said, the harder I had to listen. We learned a lot about communication — the importance of a passing touch, a lingering look, the communing comfort of shared silence.

Julee's voice returned stronger than ever, and the concert was a success. While she chatted with friends in her dressing room afterward, I slipped across the street and got her a small box of fudge, chocolate having been at the top of the disheartening list of foods forbidden by the voice doctor. As I put the box in her hand, she was about to say something. Then she grabbed her pad and scribbled, "Thank you!"

Thank You, God, for showing me how to listen. In Your words I find all wisdom.   — Edward Grinnan

10 | S U N   *Lord, I believe; help thou mine unbelief.*   — Mark 9:24

Lord, I believe; help thou mine unbelief. After my husband's father John David Kidd died in 1992, we found references to these words time after time in his papers and books.

How strange. Here I was with an indelible memory of a peaceful man who sat every evening of his life in a worn chair, haloed by an old floor lamp, reading his Bible. He seemed so steadfast. He had turned that Bible's pages so often that the gold was worn from their edges. He had studied the book from cover to cover until the entire volume was soft and pliable. And yet penciled here and there, the same words kept coming up: "Lord, I believe. Help my unbelief."

It's been more than four years since Dad Kidd died. In those years, it would be impossible to count the number of times those words have come to comfort me. *How can I ever have Keri's tuition saved by August?* "Lord, I believe. Help my unbelief," I whisper. *I don't think I can handle all of the things I have to do ... the house, the job, the church work.* "Lord, I believe. Help my unbelief," I whisper again.

The way I see it, there's something so hopeful in knowing that a man as faithful as Dad Kidd struggled, as I struggle, to maintain what seemed to be an imperishable brand of faith. He, too, needed a touchstone to strengthen his believing. So I hold his reminder, penciled in the margins of his life on earth, that God is close, even when I doubt His nearness. Like Dad Kidd, I want to believe that I have an unshakable partnership with God. I want to believe that God is with me in all that I do. I want to believe that God will carry me over the rough spots and set me down in cool, sweet places of rest and happiness. I want to believe that I will live with God forever....

Lord, I believe. Help my unbelief.   — Pam Kidd

11 | M O N   *Endure hardship with us like a good soldier of Christ Jesus.*   — II Timothy 2:3 (NIV)

Veterans Day is an important day in our American culture. We celebrate and honor those who have served our country in our armed forces. We recognize that many of them had to endure hardship, and because of their sacrifice we have the privilege of enjoying a better quality of life.

Today we are learning how to celebrate and honor *all* of those who have served in our armed forces. But though they have fought in every war from the Revolution to the Gulf War, African Americans have tended to be forgotten or overlooked. Near Mendenhall, Mississippi, there is a small town that decided to put up a prominent marker containing the names of all deceased veterans from the surrounding community. Yet not one single African American veteran was mentioned, though I know of several, nor were any African Americans invited to the celebration. *Were we not important enough to be recognized?* I wondered, as I watched the TV news broadcast of the event.

One day, I believe, all the veterans' names will be listed there, just as they are on the Wall — the Vietnam memorial in Washington, D.C. In the meantime, I take comfort in the fact that "God does not show favoritism" (Romans 2:11, NIV). So I celebrate Veterans Day, thankful that we have the freedom to worship God openly because of the sacrifice of American veterans of every race.

Dear Lord, I thank You for the sacrifices of all the men and women who endured hardship as good soldiers in service for this country.
— Dolphus Weary

12 | T U E | *Remember the wonderful works that he has done....*
— I Chronicles 16:12 (RSV)

After reading about the world's fourth-best bird-watcher, Peter Kaestner of Lansing, Michigan, who has seen almost seven thousand bird species, my husband Alex and I were inspired to start a list of our own sightings over the years.

As we reminisced, delighting again in scarlet rosellas right on our balcony in Australia and pretty pine grosbeaks that visited our feeder here in Michigan one winter, I thought of other sightings I wished I'd recorded over the years: glimpses of God's presence. I told Alex about God's miraculous protection when camping with my college friend Joann in the Porcupine Mountains. Two drunken men started unzipping our tent — we prayed very hard, and they suddenly fled.

Then Alex mentioned our rescue in a blizzard in Wisconsin. "Remember that state trooper who followed us on the shoulder and guided us to an exit?"

I found another notebook, and we began recording our sightings:

God's bringing Alex and me together, and helping us through our long, dark tunnel of infertility, wondrously answering our prayers for children; His leading us to a loving church family; shining a light of guidance on when and where to go for Alex's sabbatical; providing a renter for our house two weeks before we left; hearing Him in the laughter of our children....

We want to keep recording our "sightings" for grandchildren to read someday, but also for those dark times when we feel God has flown, so that we may recall glimpses of His golden wings.

Lord, help us recall special sightings of the past, and grant us eyes to see Your wondrous presence today. — Mary Brown

13 | W E D | *...To give... beauty for ashes, the oil of joy for mourning, the garment of praise for the spirit of heaviness....*
— Isaiah 61:3

"A medium supreme?" I asked my daughter Rebecca as we settled into a booth at her favorite pizza place a few years ago.

"I hate supreme!" she snapped. "Make my half pepperoni."

We can't even agree on pizza, I thought wearily. Since Rebecca had entered the "terrible teens" two years earlier, our relationship had become a disaster. Our discussions usually turned into shouting matches. In between, there were long stretches of stony silence, punctuated by icy glares (Rebecca) and tightly compressed lips (me).

As we waited for our food, a burst of laughter from a nearby table caused me to turn and look. Another mother and daughter were engaged in animated conversation, obviously enjoying each other's company. I looked at Rebecca, then back at them. Tears welled in my eyes. *How I wish we were like that!* I thought as I hastily dabbed my face with a checkered napkin. I wished for, longed for, prayed for that kind of relationship with Rebecca, but the barriers between us seemed insurmountable.

Last week, we were back in the same restaurant. We ordered the same half and half combo, reversed: supreme for Rebecca and pepperoni for me, laughing at the way we'd influenced each other's tastes. While we waited for the food, I caught the eye of another woman, sitting in silence with her sullen teenage daughter. The mother was looking at me with the same longing I'd felt when my daughter was fourteen.

I wanted to wrap them both in my arms and comfort them. I didn't. So I'm taking this opportunity to speak, loud and clear, to mothers of difficult teenage daughters and to daughters of difficult middle-aged mothers. "Be patient. Be prayerful. God willing, in time you'll be more than mother and daughter—you'll be friends."

Lord, pour Your blessings on mothers and daughters who are struggling toward love and understanding. —Penney Schwab

14 | T H U *...That ye may be able after my decease to have these things always in remembrance.* —II Peter 1:15

He was an old, black, hound-type dog with brown patches above his eyes and a heart like no other dog who ever lived. Kiloh had been my daughter's pal and loyal friend for more than fifteen years. Karen had nursed him through a broken leg, pulled porcupine quills out of his nose and sandburs out of his paws, provided the best of veterinary care, bathed and petted and loved him through heart trouble and arthritis.

Near the end, Kiloh started having trouble walking, and one day he just couldn't get up. Nothing could be done to help him, so Karen called the vet, who came to her house and put Kiloh to sleep. "It's so hard to let him go," said my daughter.

"Is there anything you'd like to send with him?" asked Dr. Neil. Beside Kiloh on his bed, Karen placed his favorite chew bone and her own slippers that he loved to rest his head on.

As the truck drove away with Kiloh inside, Karen and I held each other and cried. "I'll miss my old buddy so much," she said. "But sending those things with him helped me to let go."

I want to remember to perform some act of love, however small, at my own letting-go times. Even in the daily good-byes that are part of life, I can send a cookie with little Saralisa, my granddaughter, or an interesting clipping with my son John, or tell Karen how pretty she looks. And to those who have moved away, like my friend Jan, I can send a card or a note. It's the little things that bridge the parting gap and keep love alive in the heart.

Today, Lord, inspire me to perform the little acts that give form and continuity to love. —Marilyn Morgan Helleberg

---

POINT OF LIGHT

MY HOUSE HAS WINDOWS

My house has windows that are wide and high;
I never keep the curtains drawn
Lest I should miss some glory of the sky,
Some splendor of the breaking dawn.

My soul has windows where God's sun streams in;
They never, never shuttered are,
Lest their closed blinds hide in my soul some sin
And keep some lovely thing afar.

—Anna Blake Mazquida

---

15 | FRI | MY GIFT TODAY... THE PHONE LISTING

He is able to deal gently with those who are ignorant and are going astray....   —Hebrews 5:2 (NIV)

My gift today is a listing in the telephone book, the name of a restaurant that doesn't exist.

There *is* a small Italian restaurant in our local shopping center. So when our house guest Andrew van der Bijl told us this morning that he liked Italian food, I went to the phone to find out if the place would be open tonight.

But what was it called? I drive right by it several times a week. It began with *S*, I knew, a long name with a *c* and a *p*....My husband couldn't remember either, but he thought it was something-*arelli*. "Scapparelli," we decided. I looked in the phone book and there it was: *Scapparelli's Restaurant*.

There was no telephone number, though. Just a second line beneath the first. "See *Spaccarelli's Restaurant*."

I called Spaccarelli's and, yes, it was open tonight. "How did you come to list the misspelled name?" I asked.

"You'd be amazed, lady, how many people get it wrong."

But I wasn't amazed, not about getting it wrong. What amazed me was that they'd taken my error into account, met me at the place where I was off course and steered me in the right direction.

How often, today's gift reminds me, God does just that. When I'm confused and lost and looking in the wrong place for answers, there He is.

When I've fretted and lost sleep over a decision, I'll hear Him say, *Have you prayed about it?*

When I've talked myself hoarse trying to correct a misunderstanding, there He is again: *Will you trust Me to reveal the truth?*

Following each false start, His gentle correction: "This is the way, walk ye in it" (Isaiah 30:21).

I'm so glad, Father, that You are the answer, even when I get the question wrong.

— Elizabeth Sherrill

---

16 | S A T | *Jesus wept.... so the Jews were saying, "Behold how He loved him!"*   —John 11:35–36 (NAS)

During a break at a meeting I was addressing, one of my students from years past approached me with a request for help. He took a small photo from his wallet and handed it to me. It was of an attractive young woman with a little boy sitting in her lap.

"That's my daughter and my only grandchild," he offered. "Though she tried hard to make her marriage work, it's over and the two of them are back home." Then with tears, he explained that, though they had been close, he could no longer communicate with his daughter. In his pained expression I saw that he doubted whether I could understand what he was experiencing.

As I looked from his face to the picture, I was seeing myself as a teenage boy lying face down on my parents' bed, weeping my heart out for a whole afternoon. I had just learned that my parents were getting a divorce. There was no one to help me with my pain.

I did understand. Out of that memory came my answer to my former student. "What would you do for your daughter if, instead of this, your son-in-law had been killed in a car accident? The failure of a marriage is like a death in the family—but without the usual support system. People don't usually come with hugs and tears and food, or send cards, or even telephone when there's a divorce. But the pain is just as great—perhaps even greater."

"Thanks," he said as he put the picture back in his wallet. "I think I know exactly what my daughter needs from me." As I watched him head for the parking lot, I was grateful that God had created out of my suffering a larger compassion for people affected by the pain of a failed marriage.

Look around yourself, in that circle of family and friends, for people who are trying to deal with some sort of bereavement. Your presence and caring can have God's healing in it.

Dear Lord, make me more sensitive to all those kinds of pain in life to which You want to bring healing and comfort through me.
— Kenneth Chafin

17 | S U N | *Where two or three are gathered together in my name, there am I in the midst of them.* — Matthew 18:20

Home from college for the weekend, I was telling an old friend about something that had been troubling me. "It bothers me that so many of my classmates are unbelievers," I complained. "It even makes me question my own faith in God."

That Sunday evening I was back in my dorm room, going through a pile of piano music books, when I came across my old battered hymnal. I began leafing through the worn pages and before long I was humming the familiar tunes. My roommate, who was reading on her bed, laid down her book and began to sing the words to the hymn I was humming. I looked at her surprised, for she had been raised in a different church, and I had not thought she would know "my hymns." I smiled. Within minutes, we were working our way through the hymnal, locating hymn after hymn that we both knew, refreshing each other's memory. Before long, other girls in the hall were wandering in, their curiosity aroused by our voices. Some sat listening, some joined in, but everyone was drawn into the room.

It dawned on me that many of the "unbelievers" I had thought were all around me had never known I believed in God. It was not that they did not believe; it was that they didn't know I did. Now, when I feel my faith wavering, I share it with someone else. Try it. Surprising things can happen…like an impromptu singing session.

Dear Lord, help me to share my belief in You and to seek out others who believe, so that we may strengthen our faith together.
— Hollie Davis

18 | MON

And He shall wipe away every tear from their eyes; and there shall no longer be any death; there shall no longer be any mourning, or crying, or pain.... — Revelation 21:4 (NAS)

Because my parents were missionaries in the Philippines, I had many opportunities to sail on ocean liners. In fact, by the time I was twelve years old, I had sailed completely around the world. Recently, my mother found in a scrapbook a copy of the passenger list from the last voyage we made in 1965, from Manila to San Francisco via Japan. As I gazed over the list, I found the name of Diane McLane. A flood of fond memories broke loose.

We were both fourteen years old. Diane was blonde and beautiful, and I was freckled and shy. We struck up a great friendship. The truth is, I was bitten pretty hard by puppy love. But ports are reached and voyages ended. I remember standing on a street corner in Yokohama, where the McLanes were to stay, telling Diane good-bye. Something ripped inside. My father placed his hand knowingly on my shoulder, and we walked away. I've never seen or heard from her since.

In these past thirty years, I have only thought of her fleetingly. But when I read her name on that yellowed passenger list and remembered the painful farewell, I was seized by the conviction that good-byes are not forever. We will not be separated forever by time or distance or death.

I don't know where Diane McLane is today. And I haven't seen my father for thirty years. But in God's good time, we'll sail together again.

Dear God, help me to believe in Your promise of eternity and life together with You. Amen. — Scott Walker

19 | TUE

Be not afraid... for the Lord thy God is with thee whithersoever thou goest. — Joshua 1:9

I have no sense of direction, and getting lost on a highway scares me. So when everyone was excited about the new superhighway section of Route 316 to Atlanta, I wasn't. "But it will help you get to my place so much more quickly, Mom," my daughter Jennifer said.

"The trip will be so much simpler on the main highway," my husband Gene said.

Finally, I decided to try it. I drove to Jennifer's the old, comfortable, long way — the way with eighteen turns that were sweetly familiar, the way that took one and a half hours. When it was time to leave, Jen drew me a map. As she smiled and waved from her front steps, she called out, "Don't turn onto I-85! That goes to Greenville!"

Already afraid, I waved and backed out of her driveway. At an unfamiliar intersection, I waited for the light to change. *Wasn't this where I turned?* Hopefully, I made a left. Within moments I read the dreaded bright green sign: "I-85. Greenville, S.C. 90 miles." Absolute terror shot through me. *I'll have to drive to Greenville and call Gene. Maybe no one will ever find me! What shall I do?*

I made myself pray out loud. "Lord, I'm lost. Turning around scares me as much as being lost, but I'm refusing this terrible fear— by faith. Please help me turn around."

I'm with you, I sensed God speaking to me. *I'll help you. You'll be fine.* With His help, I figured out how to get off at the next exit, cross the bridge and get back on, going in the opposite direction. And when I got off I-85, I found Route 316, and got home just fine.

How exciting, Father, that when I do the thing I'm most afraid of, fear lets go of me. Amen.   — Marion Bond West

20 | W E D   *Continue steadfastly in prayer....*
                    —Colossians 4:2 (RSV)

I do not sleep well nowadays. I've heard that happens often to people as they get older. I've been getting up and going out to the living room to sit in my large, comfortable recliner to pray. In the quietness of the night, it's very easy; God seems very near.

After awhile I realized that I was totally losing track of time during these prayer sessions. I'd suddenly feel my eyes beginning to droop with sleep, and upon checking the clock I'd find I'd been up for perhaps three or four hours. I'd go to bed then and fall almost immediately into a sound and dreamless sleep.

One night I found myself saying, "Lord, let me count for something in this world. I'm housebound now and my active life is over, but isn't there something I can still do to help others?" But, alas, I could not stay awake long enough to wait for an answer.

Next morning I awoke with the very distinct feeling that I should call an elderly lady I knew who was in very poor health. She was elated and so eager to talk. As I hung up the telephone, I suddenly knew that this was the answer to my prayer the night before. After breakfast, I called another shut-in, and another, and another.

My husband commented, "You do have 'telephonitis' today."

"No," I replied, "it's just that God has shown me an opportunity to make a difference in the lives of others, even after I'd started thinking my days of activity were over."

"Then go for it," he replied.

From that day onward I've continued calling at least six people every day, sometimes an even dozen. It's when I lose count of my calls that I know I can still count for some good in this world.

Dear Lord, I want to work for You. Reveal Your plan to me. Amen.
— Dorothy Nicholas

21 | T H U "*...Things too wonderful for me to know.*"
— Job 42:3 (NIV)

My husband's grandmother turned 102 last year. Her memories of growing up in England are rich and vivid. For example, she still remembers being let out of school when Queen Victoria died! But, of course, she doesn't remember a childhood with automobiles, airplanes, telephones or television, because they either didn't exist then or hadn't reached her village.

"Maybe you should try living in your grandmother's time," my friend Janine commented as I complained about how slowly traffic was moving as we carpooled one day.

"What do you mean?" I asked.

"If you lived early in this century, for example, you'd be dreaming that one day you'd be fortunate enough to ride in a car just once in your lifetime!"

"Oh, I see," I said. "And here I am — not even a hundred years later — complaining because there's too much traffic, or the line at the tollbooth is too slow."

"Yes, and if you were part of the crowds around Orville and Wilbur Wright," she went on, "you'd be trembling with pleasure at the idea of taking a hundred-foot flight!"

"You're right," I laughed. "And on my last flight what did I do, but complain about the bad food and that I'd seen the movie already."

"Look to the future," Janine said. "Maybe someday you'll be

chosen to go on a rocket to the moon. Do you want to enjoy the wonder of the ride, or will you be complaining about being weightless?"

God, let me see and enjoy the wonder of Your inventions today, not their inconveniences. —Linda Neukrug

22 | F R I | *Then the Lord opened the eyes of Balaam, and he saw the angel of the Lord standing in the road....*
—Numbers 22:31 (NRSV)

"Steph," I wrote, "you are an angel in my path!"

"It's a lovely thing," she answered, "to think of oneself as an angel in someone else's life, though to me, an angel seems a being of light, something outside human boundaries. For sure, I don't feel like an angel of any kind right now."

My friend Stephanie and I have a lot in common, but our views on religion have been far apart throughout the years of our friendship. She was a devout Episcopalian as a teenager, but as a young adult became quite cynical about the church and all the hypocrites she saw sheltered in it. We became friends despite my Christian commitment.

But in recent years, a series of personal crises has driven Stephanie to look deeply for the meaning of her life. For at least ten years now she has been earnestly searching for truth. Her conversations and letters are a revelation to me. I marvel at her desire for spiritual enlightenment, and I am often reminded of Jesus' story of the man who sold all to buy the field where the treasure was hidden. Her periodic reports on her spiritual journey often surprise me.

"I focus on survival mostly," she wrote in the middle of multiple disasters. "I list over and over the cushions that have come with every blow to make the blow less awful than it might have been. I meditate and visualize God's hand under me—but I can't help remembering Job. Hanging in there didn't save him from the next blow."

I remembered some years before that I had told her that once when I was very ill I imagined myself in the hand of God. I could fall down. I could even hurt myself. But I could not fall off. And now I heard her wrestling with my childlike image with a maturity that put me to shame.

So when I said, "Steph, you are an angel in my path," I meant it literally. An angel is a messenger of God, and that is what Steph continues to be for me. Her probing questions make me think carefully before I give what may prove a too-facile answer. The integrity with which she searches makes me examine my own journey for living evidence of the faith that I proclaim.

Lord, let me heed the angels You put in my path.

— Katherine Paterson

23 | S A T *[Jesus] said…"If any one of you is without sin, let him be the first to throw a stone at her."* — John 8:7 (NIV)

For a few years now, my wife Rosie and I have been reaching out to a young lady (I'll call her Lucinda) who is addicted to crack-cocaine. You might think drugs wouldn't be a problem in a small Mississippi town like Mendenhall, but they are. With Lucinda, we've been on a roller-coaster ride. She's been in and out of one treatment place after another. Periodically, she seems to improve. But then she's back, sitting in our living room, telling us, "I need an additional thirty-five dollars to pay my car note. Everybody is against me. My family is against me. Nobody loves me…."

At one point we got Lucinda into a treatment center, but she was released earlier than expected and was soon back on the streets. Her family was upset at our "interference." They wanted to wash their hands of her and let her take the consequences of her habit. This hurt us deeply.

About 2:30 one morning recently, the phone jarred us awake. It was Lucinda. This time she was in jail. As I drove there, I was overwhelmed with the desire to give up on her. Because of her, a great deal of my time was being diverted from my wife and children. And none of our caring seemed to help. What was the use? That day, however, I did what I could to help her… one more time.

If she calls again, will I respond with a loving and caring spirit? If she gets a prison sentence, will I walk beside her, praying, encouraging and writing to her? Or will I say, "I've tried," and give up? No, God won't let me.

Lord, You've never given up on me. Help me to remember this when I'm frustrated and confused. Amen. — Dolphus Weary

P.S. Lucinda is now out of jail, has a job and is in a care program for recovering addicts. Rosie and I keep in touch and keep praying. Perhaps you will pray for her, too.

24 | S U N   *I Paul have written it with mine own hand....*
                                          —Philemon 19

"Attention, class! You must write something every day," Mrs. Schibley told us in high school English. "At least one page." She passed out blank notebooks. "Reading makes a full man, conversation makes a ready man, but writing makes an exact man," she said, loosely quoting English philosopher Francis Bacon.

I panicked. "But what if I can't think of anything to write?" I asked.

"Then you may copy a page out of a good book or magazine."

I did a lot of copying in the ninth grade! But I also discovered that copying a chapter out of the Bible in longhand helps me feel closer to God. On this National Bible Sunday, as I form the words on a yellow tablet, I feel like the original author, laboring over word choice and phrasing. Often I discover that passages I thought I knew well don't really say what I thought. Like the verse I Timothy 6:9 that says, "They that *will be* rich fall into temptation," and not "they that *are* rich," as I have always quoted it.

Since my motor skills are used in copying the text, I tend to remember it exactly, often at critical moments when I need God's thoughts to solve a problem or to comfort me. Instead of my having a vague idea about Scripture, it's locked clearly in my memory, and I can recite any one verse at a time. Length doesn't seem to matter. When rushed, I may copy a short Psalm or a pinch of Proverbs. It's the act of copying God's words that does the trick for me.

I invite you to try it for a week, and share in one of my more rewarding devotional practices.

Class dismissed!

Lord, make me an exact man.   —Daniel Schantz

25 | M O N   *It was good of you to share in my troubles.*
                                          —Philippians 4:14 (NIV)

The ten-word, Red Cross letter had somehow made it halfway around the world, from Massachusetts to Shanghai, in November 1944. It was one of the few letters our missionary family received during our two-and-a-half-year internment by the Japanese. Dated May 1944, it read something like this: "Uncles Willis, Milton, sixty cousins at reunion prayed for you." The sender's name, Mrs. Chester Allen, was strange to me.

"Every year since at least 1897," Daddy explained, "the descendants of my grandparents Jonathan and Betsy Howes have been meeting together somewhere in central Massachusetts for a reunion. Adele Allen is my cousin."

The fact that so many relatives I'd never heard of knew we were in an internment camp and cared enough to pray for us and write us amazed me. I felt blessed and protected by these cords that stretched across the ocean in the midst of war.

The wonder of being thought of and prayed for by people I didn't know has never left me. It is one reason I'm so glad to be part of Guideposts Prayer Fellowship every Monday morning at 9:45. There I can do the same for those who write us with their requests. And it's good to know that each person gets a letter (longer than a ten-word form) from Prayer Fellowship saying that we prayed for them, and offering reassurance, encouragement and God's blessings.

Today, on the Guideposts Family Day of Prayer, we remember in a special way all of our Guideposts Prayer Fellowship family. In our business office in Carmel, New York, we display their pictures on our Prayer Wall, and here in New York City, we pass them around the table as we share in their joys and troubles and pray for them. And we remember you, too, our *Daily Guideposts* family.

Thank You, God, for the privilege of being part of Your praying family.
— Mary Ruth Howes

26 | T U E *Examine yourselves to see whether you are in the faith....*
Not that people will see that ... but that you will do what
is right....   — II Corinthians 13:5, 7 (NIV)

Last winter, the decorating magazine where I work part-time as a photo stylist featured my own country-style kitchen. I worked for days so everything would look warm and homey. I stuffed everything I didn't want photographed in a closet or drawer and hauled all our small appliances to a faraway corner.

When Mike, the photographer, arrived, he set up his lights and a camera, the one with the wide-angle lens. As he gazed through the viewfinder, he said, "You might want to take a couple of those crocks off the counter, Roberta. It looks too cluttered to the camera's eye. If you'll move that bread box to the right about an inch, I think we'll have all the cords covered. Also, the papers bulging from that drawer and that coffee pot and can opener need to be moved." I thought I'd safely hidden them from view.

As I carted all the stuff to the family room, Mike surveyed the mess and joked, "As I always say, it's a good thing our readers don't know how people *really* live."

I felt as exposed as a roll of film. Suddenly, I saw not just my kitchen, but my real self. There was a cobweb of fear in the corner of my heart about my dad's health. I'd panicked instead of prayed when he'd confided his new back pain to me. And that resentment over a hurtful remark a friend had supposedly made, instead of talking to the Lord about it or confronting the issue directly, I let it smolder in the closet of my soul. I pretended it didn't bother me, but those secondhand words mocked my joy at unexpected moments.

I saw that Jesus' all-seeing, wide-angle lens doesn't just zoom in on the areas of my life I've carefully dusted and polished and displayed. I asked Him to rid my heart and mind of those spirit-snuffing emotions I thought I'd so carefully tucked away, and He did just that. Oh, the joy of a clutter-free heart!

Dear Lord, expose those areas of my life that I need to work on.
                                        — Roberta Messner

27 | W E D | *I will praise God's name in song and glorify him with thanksgiving.*   — Psalm 69:30 (NIV)

Thanksgiving was the focus of a big flap back in 1939. The traditional date for this holiday had always been the last Thursday in November. But that year the month had five Thursdays and the fifth one fell on the thirtieth, the final day. President Franklin D. Roosevelt moved Thanksgiving a week ahead to extend the retailers' Christmas season. Many disagreed with his decision, including a number of state governors who issued their own proclamations, recognizing the last Thursday date.

Everyone was confused. Pastors were unsure when to schedule special worship services; school administrators didn't know which day off to give students; families had to specify which of two Thanksgivings they were inviting you to. My dad put his foot down: "The last Thursday was good enough for Abraham Lincoln — it's good enough for us!"

The wrangle continued into 1940 and was the butt of many jokes.

A calendar company attached a red pencil and note to its product: "Mark your own holidays." Finally, in 1941, Thanksgiving was officially established as the fourth Thursday in November.

But since that brief flap, I've taken it upon myself to "mark my own holidays." Last year, when there were five Thursdays in November, I offered up special prayers of thanks on the last two Thursdays. After all, I thought, two days spent in celebration of God's boundless abundance was the very least I could do. And anytime throughout the year, when I feel the urge, I mark some more of my own holidays. There's reason for more than one occasion to celebrate God's graciousness.

Keep me ever thankful, Lord, for You and Your everlasting gifts.
— Isabel Wolseley

28 | T H U *On this mountain the Lord Almighty will prepare a feast of rich food for all peoples....* — Isaiah 25:6 (NIV)

The cornerstone of our Thanksgiving feast in Hawaii was potato dressing. The recipe had entered our family via my *tai kung* or great-grandfather, an immigrant from Canton, China, who had learned it from the New England missionary family for whom he had cooked at the turn of the century.

The family recipe went with me when I moved to New York. For years, the dressing graced our Thanksgiving table, enjoyed by my husband, myself and our growing family, which now included our small son Tim, my brother Jerry and his wife Donna.

When Jerry and Donna moved to Oregon (taking the recipe along), I grumbled to a girlfriend about the futility of making turkey and dressing for three.

"Could I join you?" my friend asked, and kept coming for six Thanksgivings. By the time she moved to Wisconsin with my recipe and her two babies, I had gained an appreciation for the dressing's miraculous ability to change strangers into participants in an ongoing Thanksgiving tradition that had, over the course of a century, traveled from continent to continent, culture to culture, and family to family.

This year, new friends will join our family at the table. The Bertrands will bring Haitian rice and a cousin or three; the Gaspariks a Southern-style pecan pie; Una will cook up Shanghai noodles; my brother's son Brian, visiting from college, will bring his two hungry roommates. And at the center of the feast will be my tai kung's potato dressing, still feeding and binding our family across the years and the miles in marvelous ways.

You Who fed the multitude, we come to Your table with thanks this day, one family strengthened and renewed by Your grace.
                                                        —Linda Ching Sledge

29 | F R I | *Everything God made is good, and we may eat it gladly if we are thankful for it, and if we ask God to bless it....*
                                        —I Timothy 4:4–5 (TLB)

One bright and sunny Thanksgiving, my daughter Charlotte came home from college. The house was full of young people, relatives and the smell of turkey. Grandma made green Jell-O salad while Dad cooked the rest of the meal. Feeling blessed, I contemplated my assembled family.

As usual, Charlotte looked pale, her skin was broken out, and the food she was snacking on would have made a nutritionist faint. I can't remember how many arguments we must have had over the years about salad or fruits or vegetables. My pleas for a healthy diet fell on deaf ears, and Doritos and Diet Coke ruled.

This year, she had brought home a new boyfriend, a young scientist, the first she had been serious about so far as I could tell. We all sat down around the big dining room table. Trying not to spoil a rare family occasion, I held my tongue as my daughter left her salad untouched and pushed aside everything but some mashed potato and a small piece of turkey.

A few minutes later when I got up to go into the kitchen, I noticed Charlotte and Joshua (the boyfriend) arguing earnestly in low voices: "...idiotic. Mammals can't live on starch. You've got to...."

"Oh, dear," I said to my husband as we served dinner, "I think they're having a fight."

I went anxiously back to the dining room and saw something I had never before witnessed. With a sour face, my daughter Charlotte was steadily eating the head of incontestably green broccoli, which she had earlier pushed to the side of her plate.

There it was—so simple. One piece of broccoli marked the end of childhood. A few stern words from the new man in her life accomplished what I had failed to do in twenty years. I took a deep breath, wished her well with all my heart and hoped that whoever did become the most important person in her adult life would love her as much as I did. Three words, unspoken in the bustle of that Thanksgiving Day, summed it up for me: "Godspeed, my daughter."

Lord, help me to step aside lovingly as my child builds a life of her own.   — Brigitte Weeks

30 | S A T | *The...prayer of a righteous man availeth much.*
                                                     — James 5:16

I have a friend named Michael who writes me letters from time to time. Instead of ending them with a conventional *Sincerely* or *Best regards*, the word above his signature is always *Praying*.

That single word always has a calming effect on me. I'm sure Michael ends his letters to everyone in that fashion, but I have the feeling that in each case he really is praying for the recipient. Without knowing what the cares or troubles of that person may be, he is praying nevertheless.

The other night at dinner with Michael, I asked him if this was so, and he admitted that it was. "I start and end each day with prayer," he said. "Then all day long I try to find little cracks of time between necessary activities and try to fill those cracks with prayer. Sometimes with requests for people I know. Sometimes for the patience and persistence and strength I need to get through the day myself. It's a constant thing. At least, as constant as I can make it."

I had brought something to share with Michael, a newspaper clipping that showed a photograph of Mother Teresa celebrating her eighty-fourth birthday by standing at the doorway of her Missionaries of Charity in Calcutta, passing out leaflets to passersby. On each leaflet was a message that I read aloud to Michael: "Prayer enlarges the heart until it is capable of containing God's gift of Himself." I handed the clipping to Michael. "I think that's true of you," I said.

Michael smiled his slow, self-deprecating smile. "I hope so," was all he said.

Lord, hear our prayers and let our cry come unto Thee.
                                                    — Arthur Gordon

GIFTS OF LIGHT

1 _____

2 _____

3 _____

4 _____

5 _____

6 _____

7 _____

8 _____

9 _____

10 _____

11 _____

12 _____

13 _____

14 _____

15 _____

16 _____

17 _____

18 _____

19 _____

20 _____

21 _____

22 _____

23 _____

24 _____

25 _____

26 _____

27 _____

28 _____

29 _____

30 _____

For once you were darkness, but now you are light in the Lord; walk as children of light.

— EPHESIANS 5:8 (RSV)

D
E
C
E
M
B
E
R

S	M	T	W	T	F	S
1	2	3	4	5	6	7
8	9	10	11	12	13	14
15	16	17	18	19	20	21
22	23	24	25	26	27	28
29	30	31				

JOURNEY TOWARD THE LIGHT

One might think it easy for Pam Kidd, mother of two and wife of a minister, to keep Christmas and the celebration of the birth of Christ in clear focus. But as she shares her Advent with us, we discover that it takes thought and fierce effort to slow down, to remember one can't do everything perfectly, and to hold on to the shared joy of gift giving. "The pure love of Jesus Christ," she reminds us, is the best gift of all.

—The Editors

1 | S U N | *The people which sat in darkness saw great light....*
—Matthew 4:16

Early on this first Sunday in Advent, I sit alone in the dark living room. Thinking about the weeks ahead, I go to the hall closet and pull out the box that holds our family's most beloved Christmas treasure, a wooden structure three feet high called a Christmas carousel. My father purchased this beautiful, hand-carved creation in Germany when my son Brock was just a baby and my daughter Keri wasn't yet born. My mother remembers that Dad thought it so precious he held it in his lap on the long flight back to America.

As I place the carousel in its traditional spot on the dining room table, it occurs to me that I might allow myself a small Advent celebration before the house erupts into its Sunday morning busyness. I light the candles on the bottom tier, and soon the rising heat turns the wooden blades at the top of the carousel. As the blades spin, carved shepherds and wise men and angels on the three tiers begin to turn, as though traveling toward the Holy Family on the highest tier. In the soft candlelight, the journey to Christmas seems so sim-

know full well how exhausting the season can be. *What can d, to find the real Christmas amid the frantic activity?* I pray. the stillness for an answer.

Focus on the light, God seems to say. Clear the path that leads to the real Christmas by saying no to the events that hold little meaning. Bring the family together for the cookie-baking, tree-trimming and visits to shut-ins you remember from your childhood. Above all, keep your eyes set on the light of the manger where the Christ Child waits.

Father, as we anticipate the coming of Your Son, fill every dark corner of our preparation with Your light. Lead us toward the real Christmas.   —— Pam Kidd

2 | M O N   *These things have I spoken unto you, that my joy might remain in you, and that your joy might be full.*
—John 15:11

One morning I received a phone call from my daughter's best friend, asking how to reach her. "I can hardly wait to tell Melanie. I've got some exciting news!"

"I'll have her call the minute she comes in," I said. "Oh, Diane, I'll bet you're getting married!"

"No, no. You'll never believe it. I just won a million dollars! In the sweepstakes! But please don't tell her until I can. I want to hear her scream!"

Thrilled, I promised, hugging the secret all day. And what fun it was to hear that joyful scream myself when Melanie got the news firsthand that night. We were both laughing and crying when she hung up, hugging each other. "She's so deserving, Mother. She works so hard and does so much for people. God surely wants her to have it."

Then, with Diane's permission, we began calling other friends to spread the glad tidings. We were both ecstatic with that unique privilege of being able to proclaim good news — even if it was somebody else's. It is so rare, so wonderful, when good news happens to people like us, we simply cannot contain our exultation. And it's even more exciting when you are the first to tell someone you love: "You job!" "You won the contest!" "You're on the team!"

But all our good news, large or small, could never a news that burst upon the world at the birth of Jesus, the Messiah. The very angels in heaven first revealed it to shepherds, who rushed to Bethlehem to behold the selves and spread the word. And the most marvelous news of all had to come after the tragedy of His crucifixion. *He is risen! Jesus has risen, as he said!* (Matthew 28:6).

Let's all take that good news with us and share it with someone else today.

Dear Lord, please come again soon, and let us spread the wonderful news. We need You now more than ever. —Marjorie Holmes

3 | T U E | *The Father that dwelleth in me, he doeth the works.*
—John 14:10

Some people believe that miracles only happened in Bible times, but they are mistaken. Miracles happen every day. I talked to a couple of miracles just the other day. They are David and Barbara Anderson, Christian musicians from Phoenix, who survived a 1993 plane crash in the Bering Sea.

On their way home from a trip to Russia where they had gone on a short mission assignment, their plane went down off the Alaskan coast. Amazingly, the Andersons and five others survived the ditching without serious injury. Amazingly, they escaped from the plane, which sank in seconds, hanging on to floating empty gas cans that had been loaded on their plane by chance. Amazingly, the pilot of another plane, running late, saw what he thought was a whale splash in the sea. When he heard of the crash, he remembered the splash, turned his plane around and "miraculously" located the surviving seven minuscule specks in the vast sea. Amazingly, two helicopters were available and, amazingly, rescue workers were able to pluck the Andersons and their troupe out of the icy sea before hypothermia could claim their lives.

"We can't find enough superlatives to describe the work of our ic rescuers!" Dave Anderson exclaimed. "Or thank God enough aring our group."

xperience gave new meaning to that old Cowper poem: "God a mysterious way/His wonders to perform/He plants His the sea/And rides upon the storm."

You, Lord, are the miracle of all,
Mindful of our needs before we call.

—Fred Bauer

4 | W E D *MY GIFT TODAY...* *THE TABLE*

"Thus far has the Lord helped us."   —I Samuel 7:12 (NIV)

The table is in my study now, where it holds a word processor, a stack of manuscripts and, usually, a coffee mug. It's the kind of furniture we all bought in the 1960s: wrought-iron legs, imitation-wood Formica top.

In the very center of the table is a circular, black burn-scar. I see that ring of blistered Formica each morning as I sit down to work, but today, because I actually stopped to look at it, it became my gift.

The scar sent my thoughts back over thirty years, to the last Sunday of Advent, 1964. This was our brand-new dining room table then, replacing the old wooden one with the mismatched legs. The Advent wreath the children had created from pine cones made a festive centerpiece.

We'd finished dinner that night, the four lighted candles in the wreath showing that Christmas was very near, when I remembered the "Christmas Spectacular" on TV. I ran to turn on the set. "Come on, everyone!" And it really was spectacular, with ice skaters and marching tin soldiers and dancing snowmen.

It was eight-year-old Liz who first smelled the smoke. We raced through the kitchen, pushed open the dining room door and stared at a solid wall of smoke. Shouting, bumping into one another, we managed to fill pails of water at the sink. When at last we could close the windows on the frigid December air, we surveyed the damage. The rug and the walls would have to be washed. The wreath was a pile of ashes, four puddles of purple wax all that remained of the candles. Our new table had a blistered black ring in the center.

And that was all. Just days earlier there would have been a wooden table beneath the burning pine cones; the flames would have reached the curtains, the ceiling....

Today, we have smoke detectors in every room, a fire extinguish in the kitchen and a proper respect for open flame. But we also a scarred table to remind me of God's care even in our careles

How often, Father, do You protect me without my knowir
me to trust Your unfailing care, today and in the year abou
                                        —Elizab

Editor's Note: As we wrap gifts this month, we think o

that knows no season. All year long we've been opening His gifts, simple, earthbound things, but bright with the glory of the Father of lights. As we look over our gift list of the past year, let us prepare to receive the greatest Gift of all: the coming of God's Son to dwell within us.

5 | T *Teach us to number our days aright, that we may gain a*
    | H *heart of wisdom.*   —Psalm 90:12 (NIV)
    | U

"Only nineteen more shopping days until Christmas!" the announcer reminded his radio audience. "Will you be ready?"

I mentally began going down my list of things to do, things to buy. I was wondering if I could, indeed, be ready when my glance fell on the small crèche atop our mantel. *Only nineteen days to prepare your heart for the Christ Child's coming,* a voice seemed to say. I thought again about my list, ashamed how few of the "to do" chores would really help do that.

So I made myself a cup of hot cider and sat down to make a new list, one that would help me truly prepare for the coming of Christmas.

- Spend a few minutes each day praying for missionaries who can't be home for Christmas.

- Send half a dozen cards to people who aren't expecting them— local nursing home residents or county jail inmates.

- Make an effort each day to do something for my earthly family that Jesus might have done for His: help with a difficult chore; rub an aching back; give a hug instead of a lecture.

- Write God a thank-You letter and read it aloud on Christmas Eve.

Yes, there was plenty to do, and some of it really worth doing.

ear Father, help me move past the hustle. I long to welcome Your
? with fresh reverence.   —Mary Lou Carney

We are the children of God.   —Romans 8:16

py child, but I longed for one thing that I never had—my
?. When my husband Gene and I recently bought a new
?ddaughter Jamie, nine, helped me select wallpaper for

one of our guest rooms. Excitedly, she picked out a pattern with a bouquet of blue and pink flowers held by a blue ribbon.

"This is what I'd want for my bedroom," she said.

"Me, too," I told Jamie joyfully.

Now there's a bedroom in our home that suggests a little girl lives with us. A quilt nearly matches the paper and covers an old, painted iron bed. Dolls, pillows and handmade stuffed kittens are piled on the bed. Old-fashioned storybooks are spread out on it, and an old trunk holds some ancient paper dolls, waiting to be dressed. There's even a deck of well-worn "Old Maid" cards. In a corner, small animals and dolls enjoy a tea party set up on miniature wicker furniture. The white wicker baby scales that I was weighed on as an infant hold some of my children's first shoes. Little girl clothing hangs about the room. There's a child's straw hat for dress-up occasions. A pair of china dolls sits primly, waiting to be picked up and loved. This, at last, is the room I wanted as a child.

But it's more than that. It's a room where I can go and feel the freshness of youth again. It's a special place for talking to God about our children and our ten grandchildren (Gene has four, and I have six). In my little girl room, I pray them into His care.

Thank You, Father, for loving all the little children of the world— no matter how old we are.   —Marion Bond West

7 | S A T   *When I became a man, I put away childish things.*
            —I Corinthians 13:11

I turned forty this year, and it wasn't the crisis it was supposed to be. All around me friends were having birthday parties with black balloons and gifts like hair restorer, denture cream and Ben-Gay. Me? I couldn't wait for the day. And I've decided to let you know my secret.

Ten years ago, I visited a church in Hong Kong where, after the service, they had a big party for the man who preached the sermon. They were celebrating his fortieth birthday. Following the party was another service of some sort, very solemn and proper. I learned that the preacher was being ordained. In their culture, a male is not fully a man until he turns forty and therefore cannot take the final rites of ordination until that birthday arrives.

Right there I decided to adopt the Chinese approach to aging, which made the day something to be anticipated, not dreaded. By the way, the Chinese have another big birthday when you turn seventy. Then you become venerated and sought after for your wisdom. I can't wait!

Lord, thank You for every birthday and the experience, grace and wisdom that each year brings.   —Eric Fellman

8 | S U N | ## *JOURNEY TOWARD THE LIGHT*
Thou...coverest thyself with light as with a garment....
—Psalm 104:1–2

By the second Sunday in Advent, decorating Kidd-style is in full swing. "Keep moving or Mom will decorate you," my husband David teases the kids, but I'm too consumed with seeking perfection to laugh.

"Put the heaviest ornaments on the bottom of the tree, Keri. Brock, can't you remember how we always arrange the greenery on the mantel? David, would you get the rest of the stuff from the attic? No, I don't have time to cook supper. Why don't you order a pizza?"

Dashing through the dining room with my arms full of garland, I pause to find Keri sitting there. "Mama," she asks, "do you remember this old Snoopy ornament?"

Remember? How could I forget? It was the year Keri was four. A month before the holidays, we had gone to an amusement park with the Niblack family. Their little son Ty had his heart set on a toy Snoopy dog from the ball-toss booth, but no one in our group could hit the mark. Ty went home tearful. Later, during Keri's visit to Santa at the mall, she asked for only one thing...a Snoopy for Ty. Santa not only granted Keri's request, but he left her the ornament she was holding now with a note commending her on her act of Christmas kindness.

I look at my daughter, now in college, sitting in my Christmas clutter. She's probably a bit weary of being ordered around by a mom who has lost her focus. "Keri, why don't you light the carousel? It would be nice to sit down and rest for a minute." I know that as the tiny figures continue their pilgrimage toward the Christ, I can reroute my own journey. And within the hour my family is sitting together, munching on pizza and reminiscing.

On this second Sunday in Advent, I have a choice. I can run myself ragged trying to create a picture-perfect Christmas, or I can relax and bask in the glow of good times pulled from our memories of Christmas past, memories that light the way to the real Christmas.

Lord, today, let the best of our past influence us, so that we may make memories that will forever fill our hearts with Christmas.

— Pam Kidd

9 | M O N   *Thanks be to God for his inexpressible gift!*
                                  — II Corinthians 9:15 (RSV)

"There is nothing that lasts nowadays."

That cynical statement blurted from my kitchen radio this morning as I was cooking breakfast. I reached over and snapped off the sound.

"I could make a long list of things for that guy," I said, "if I had the time to do it."

I reached into a drawer for a pot holder. The one my hand brought out was washed thin, formerly blue-and-yellow gingham. Looking at it, my mind swept back over ten years. I was a stranger in a strange town, moved into a house I hadn't even seen the week before. Boxes, stacked high, dared me to open them and try to arrange their contents into a home.

Then the doorbell rang. A young woman stood there. She wore blue jeans and a plaid shirt and held out a pair of blue-and-yellow pot holders to me. "Just to say 'Welcome to the neighborhood,' and to ask if you could use a pair of unbusy hands this morning."

And now, I hold those same pot holders gently. They are faded, yes, and a bit scorched. But they are treasured, given to me years ago at the start of a wonderful friendship that is still strong, still lasting.

I smile as I pick up the skillet to get on with my cooking. As soon as breakfast is over, I'll make a list. Not for that fellow on the radio, but for myself. And topping all other things that last will be the pot holders, representing one of life's lasting treasures — friendship.

Thank You, Father, for the many blessings that do last. Make us ever mindful of them. Amen.   — Drue Duke

10 | T U E   *Thou hast taken account of my wanderings; Put my tears in Thy bottle....In God I have put my trust....*
                                  — Psalm 56:8, 11 (NAS)

Emily was a pretty little seven-year-old girl when I first met her. Her parents had recently moved halfway across the country, and Emily was missing her hometown and the friends she'd made there. I saw her standing in the hallway of our church one day, looking very sad.

"Emily," I asked, "where did you move from?"

"From Missouri," she replied with a shy smile.

"Well, where in Missouri?" I persisted.

For a moment Emily stared at the floor. Then looking at me with twinkling eyes, she said, "I know exactly where. I found it on my map last night. I can always find it easy 'cause I stained a tear on it."

Now, eight years later, her words still ring in my head. They remind me that all things we hold dear in this life — friendship, family, places we love — are marked at one time or another by our tears. The map of our lives without their stains would be devoid of richness and meaning.

Last night I grew melancholy as I remembered my days in South Carolina. Perhaps I was homesick. Then I remembered Emily's words. Thank God I had stained a tear on that place, on those people...so I know where to find them.

Dear God, may I not be afraid of my tears. I thank You for the gift of tender feelings. Amen.   — Scott Walker

11 | W E D *For God loveth a cheerful giver.*   — II Corinthians 9:7

While driving through Albuquerque, New Mexico, recently, I saw a sign that read: *All that is not given is lost.* Intrigued by those words, I printed them on a piece of paper when I got home and taped them to my kitchen cabinet.

The following week my five-year-old granddaughter asked me to read to her when I was in the middle of making a pie. I started to say I was too busy when those words caught my eye, and I realized I was about to lose an opportunity to share the gift of books with my grandchild. "Okay, let's read," I said as I set the pie aside and reached for an illustrated story of *Noah and the Ark.*

A few days later an acquaintance called to tell me her troubles. Again, I started to make an excuse to hang up, but then I glanced toward that sign. Maybe this was the day that she truly needed the gift of a sympathetic ear and a little of my time. Maybe this was another opportunity that shouldn't be lost. "Okay, let's talk," I said.

When she had finished her recital of woes, I did something I hadn't done before. Instead of offering advice, I said, "Let's pray together about this." So we did.

After the prayer she exclaimed, "I feel so much better! I think I now know what I'm going to do!" And for the first time she outlined a practical, sensible plan for straightening out her problem.

Giving to others. Giving time, comfort, prayer, knowledge. Today might be a good day to "give away" the good news of Jesus' love.

Father, You have given me so much! Time to pass it on.

— Madge Harrah

12 | T H U   *In every thing by prayer and supplication with thanksgiving let your requests be made known unto God.*
— Philippians 4:6

Does your mind ever wander during prayer? Mine does all the time. But when it happens, I refer to a method my father used during evening grace.

Dad's dinnertime prayers were legendary. Long-winded, rambling colloquies, they included all the news of the day: petitions for peace in places of war; guidance for newly elected leaders; mercy for the victims of natural disasters; thanksgiving for sports victories; healing for the hospitalized. But in the midst of his words, there were always interruptions.

Undeterred, Dad incorporated them into his prayers. "Thank You, God, for our daughter's popularity," he responded to the phone that always rang for my older sister during her teen years. "God bless Rick's high spirits," he said when I got the giggles. "Thank You for our dog," he said about our mutt Andy barking in the backyard. "God bless this food and the hands that prepared it," he concluded when the buzzing kitchen timer called Mom to rescue the rolls from the oven.

So when I pray, I make the interruptions part of my prayer. And often I find that what has interrupted me is just the thing I should be praying for.

Let all my thoughts lead to You, O God.   — Rick Hamlin

13 | F R I   *The light shines in the darkness, and the darkness has not overcome it.*   — John 1:5 (RSV)

At 5:00 P.M. on this short December day, it was already dark. *As dark,*

I thought, *as the headlines this week*. Wars around the globe, violence in our cities … it was hard to prepare for Christmas in a world of gloomy news.

An hour later I'd feel quite different.

We'd gathered at St. Mark's Episcopal Church in Mt. Kisco, New York, for a traditional service of Evensong. After the closing prayers, however, instead of the choir recessing down the aisle, the lights in the sanctuary went out. In the near-total darkness, through the side door, came a procession of children holding candles. As the glowing column wound its way along the dark aisles, from the choir stalls came the strains of "Santa Lucia." For this was the Festival of St. Lucy, the third-century Christian martyr whose name means "light." Our new minister Ralph Peterson and his Swedish wife Birgitta were introducing this Scandinavian celebration to St. Mark's.

The original Lucy lived in a Roman Empire callous to human suffering. An aura of light, it was said, accompanied her as she ministered, in defiance of imperial edicts, to the homeless and the hungry. Lucy's fame spread throughout Europe, but it was in the long winters of Scandinavia that her feast day became the year's most joyful celebration. *Like this candlelit procession in the shadowy church*, I thought, *light shines brightest where darkness is deepest.*

Maybe when things are blackest is the very best time to prepare for Christmas. Acts of compassion in pagan Rome. Acts of reconciliation in our own splintered world. Harbingers of the One Who came as the Light of the world in the darkest time of the year.

Lord, help me to carry Your light today into a waiting world.

— Elizabeth Sherrill

14 | S A T | *Jesus said to him, "… He who has seen me has seen the Father…."* —John 14:9 (RSV)

What would a space creature make of us, if it visited earth after being told that human beings have been created in God's image? Writer Bob George imagines that scenario in his book *Classic Christianity*, and goes on to ask, "What would he [the space creature] discover about God if he followed you around for a day?"

Some days he might see some pretty good stuff, I thought, *but other days I wouldn't want him anywhere near me, because he'd certainly get a distorted view of God.* For example, I get so mad over a trivial incident involving my children that I almost swear at them. *Misconception:* God must be quick-tempered and doesn't like kids. Or, at the grocery checkout stand I'm the "galloping gossip." *Misconception:* God is disloyal and talks too much. Or, after saying I don't have time to volunteer at the school, I stay home and read a novel. *Misconception:* God appears to be deceptive.

It is an overwhelming task to represent the true nature of God without slipping up. Yet the question from *Classic Christianity* really challenges me, because God has given me the unique opportunity to stand for Who He is. I may not have any space creatures trailing me, but there are plenty of human beings who observe me every day. What I am wondering is, *Am I living the truth about God?*

Dear God, it would be my great joy today if, because of me, someone could see You as You truly are.   — Carol Knapp

15 | S U N *JOURNEY TOWARD THE LIGHT*
Whoever loves his brother lives in the light....
—I John 2:10 (NIV)

On this third Sunday in Advent, I'm feeling good about my Christmas journey. My husband David and I have limited the whirlwind of activities, set aside good family time with our children Brock and Keri, visited church shut-ins and hosted our ritual viewing of *It's A Wonderful Life.*

Now it's time to concentrate on shopping. Reviewing last year's list, panic sets in. *Too many presents, too little time, even less money!* Buying gifts for some of the people on my list seems like an exercise in futility. Take my Aunt Ann. Retired, living in an apartment, she has everything she needs and not an inch of room for anything extra. David's Aunt Kate is in a similar situation. And then there's Walter Williams, a retired widower, well-off. There's nothing we can give him that he can't buy for himself.

I know from experience that the all-around stress of gift-giving can create a roadblock between me and the light of the Christ Child. *Father,* I ask, *show me Your way to give.*

I make myself a cup of spice tea and go into the living room to re-group. I think of Aunt Ann filling her car with day-old baked goods and making deliveries to the poor in her south Georgia town. Aunt Kate is in her eighties now, but in other days what feasts she set before us! And when David and I were first married, Walter and his beautiful wife Carolyn were so good to us, taking us out to restaurants we couldn't afford.

Suddenly, a new kind of giving is ignited in my heart. I will provide Christmas for a needy child in honor of Aunt Ann and present her with a detailed description. Aunt Kate still entertains frequently; she would love a basket of homemade goodies to share with her friends. And Walter, well, money couldn't buy the experience of a dinner in the Kidd household!

To be a part of this thing called Christmas, I will choose symbols of the life-gifts the people on my list have given to me and my family. May you find joy in doing the same.

Father, let my gifts to others reflect Your timeless love.

— Pam Kidd

16 | M O N *"It is not those who are healthy who need a physician, but those who are sick."*   — Matthew 9:12 (NAS)

As a nurse, I've sometimes asked patients and their families what attributes they value most in medical workers.

"Someone who listens," a man with multiple sclerosis confided to me. "Speak my language, not all that medical talk," echoed a single mother who recently suffered a heart attack. "Don't forget to return my phone calls," the husband of a patient with cancer commented. "The best ability is dependability." A fellow nurse summed it up like this: "People don't care what you know until they know that you care."

I discovered all of this myself when I became a patient. Last year, a team of doctors removed a large tumor from my head, and my eyes were bandaged for days. I couldn't see anyone, but I felt their love by the prompt response to my call bell, the compassion of a touch, the kindness of a hearing heart. They were competent, to be sure, but it was their caring that drew me to them.

I'm making these characteristics the standard for my own work, now that I'm recovered. And I can't help but think of Jesus, the Great Physician, Who not only healed the body, but the mind and the spirit as well. I keep in mind that He is always with me, a Doctor Who still makes house calls.

Oh, Great Physician, grant me the ability to dispense tender loving care, as You always do for me.   — Roberta Messner

17 | T U E

I will lie down and sleep in peace.... —Psalm 4:8 (NIV)

I can picture myself on *Oprah Winfrey* now. She looks at me somewhat sympathetically at first, then almost sneers. "Let me get this straight. You're seventeen, and you still enjoy being tucked in and saying nighttime prayers with your mother?" Collective gasps begin to roil from the audience while younger members laugh. An eminent Austrian psychiatrist on the panel ventures, "I had a case very much like this in Vienna once. We cured her with shock therapy." Oprah pauses, reflects, then finally confesses that she had a similar problem as a young adult but cured herself with herbal teas and vitamin supplements.

What can I say? I'm an incurable "lay-me-down-to-sleeper" and "tuckaholic." Being comforted by and saying my prayers with Mom is a traditional luxury I know won't last forever, so we enjoy it while we can. Sleep, I find, comes easily when you know you're being watched over and loved.

When I go away to school next fall, I'll miss having Mom near, but I'm sure that around our usual bedtime she'll find some excuse to putter in my room, straighten my desk and absently plump my pillow. We'll be close in thought, and God will be there to "tuck me in" before I sleep.

Lord, let me find my place in the world with You always by my side.
                                                            —Jenny Mutzbauer

18 | W E D

He...was sent to bear witness of that Light. —John 1:8

I am sitting in my office at *Guideposts* magazine on a blinding winter morning the week before Christmas—not a week when much work gets done. The sunshine bouncing off the huge building across the street makes it hard to look out the window. All is brightness and light.

Down the hall somewhere I can hear voices, mostly members of the editorial support staff. They are engaged in the good-natured holiday brawl they call Kriss Kringle, where everyone gives a gift to the person whose name they have drawn. I feel a little neglected, but grumpy editors are not traditionally included in the ceremony. With a flicker of annoyance, I start to close my door, then leave it open.

I hear Nilda squeal, followed by roaring laughter. I wonder what she got? Dana snorts and says, "I'll get you for this!" I hear the hiss of a jug of pop being opened and more wrapping paper being clawed. Amy got something good, because she sounds authentically pleased. Then again, she's always polite, and this is her first Kriss Kringle. Hope scurries past my door, the bells on her Christmas bracelet jingling, Celeste trailing her with a hastily wrapped package. Stephen says, "You're too late!" and Celia tells him to be quiet. Alan guffaws. Everyone *oohhs* and *aahhs* as Surujnie opens her present from Colleen. Everyone howls when Stephen opens his.

I'm glad I didn't close my door. This is a nice place to work. Especially the week before Christmas. When not a lot of work gets done. And everything is Light.

Father, You prepare me for the coming of Your Son. Make me worthy.
— Edward Grinnan

POINT OF LIGHT

THE CHRISTMAS STAR

Stars rise and set, that star shines on:
Songs fail, but still that music beats
Through all the ages come and gone,
In lane and field and city streets.
And we who catch the Christmas gleam,
Watching with children on the hill,
We know, we know it is no dream—
He stands among us still!
—Nancy Byrd Turner

---

19 | T H U | *She opens her mouth in wisdom, and the teaching of kindness is on her tongue.*   —Proverbs 31:26 (NAS)

The Christmas trees were breathtaking. No two were alike: exquisite Victorian ribbon and golden lights; clever handmade animals; starfish; silk roses. Local organizations had decorated Christmas trees for a Parade of Trees, and passersby voted for their favorite one by putting a contribution in a box.

Then my eyes fell on the next to last tree. A big plastic school bus perched on top in place of a star; unsharpened pencils dangled from the branches; the tree was covered with huge, square, rumpled snowflakes, which from a distance gave the appearance of being simply sheets of paper. "Those are the ugliest snowflakes I've ever seen!" I blurted to my family.

In a small voice, my seven-year-old son Andy spoke up. "Our class made them."

Immediately, I wished my words back! I stumbled all over myself trying to remedy what I had done, but Andy simply led me to the tree and found his snowflake. Suddenly, I saw the snowflakes through different eyes. Little second-grade hands, still learning to use scissors; eager hearts, so happy to participate. I cast my vote for the "snowflake tree."

After the tree was taken down, Andy brought his snowflake home and gave it to me. I hung it in my office — a visible reminder to think before I speak and to look for hidden beauty.

Father, words are powerful and can be tools or weapons. Please help mine to be constructive, kind and wise.   — Joan Rae Mills

20 | F R I | *And the multitude of them … were of one heart and of one soul … they had all things common.*   — Acts 4:32

"Mom, what's an olive stuffer with seven letters?" said my daughter as she bent over a crossword puzzle on the train.

She had joined me for my evening ride home. Commuters are not very sociable. Usually, I get on the train and take refuge behind a newspaper, shut out the world with a Walkman, or take a nap — just like everyone else.

"I have no idea," I answered. "I'm no good at crosswords."

"What on earth can 'Borden's ruminant' be?" she persisted. "What's a ruminant?"

"A cow," said the older woman across the aisle with a happy smile. "It must be E-l-s-i-e. You know, the cow on the milk cartons."

"Great. Thanks," said Charlotte and printed it in.

She read out the next clue in her young clear voice. "Mice," chimed in the raincoated man in front, quickly as if to win a prize.

In no time, the clues were bouncing up and down the car. Charlotte was scribbling at top speed. The olive stuffer turned out to be "pimento." The newspapers came down, and the smiles came out. The atmosphere was almost collegial. I wanted to preserve the moment as a crystal liquid, so I could dispense it drop by drop. I'd use it to heal anguished parents wondering what is wrong with their young, or give hope to those who feel that the world is going downhill with every new generation. God gave us young people for a reason. He needs their work, the kind of work that, without realizing it, Charlotte was doing on the 5:44 train.

Dear God, may each of us become part of Your plan to draw us together. — Brigitte Weeks

21 | S A T *For unto us a child is born, unto us a son is given....*
—Isaiah 9:6

When I was a senior at the University of New Mexico in Albuquerque, there was a shortage of dormitory space. Clint and Beulah Morrow, an elderly couple whom I knew at church, offered to rent me a room and let me take my meals with them. They were wonderful people, and I soon felt very much at home.

But as the holidays drew near, I became restless. Christmas was a close family affair, and I wasn't family. Besides, the Morrows' children and grandchildren were coming from out of town, and would no doubt need my room. So without mentioning it, I reserved a room for the Christmas vacation period at the university.

I was packing up, getting ready to move out, when Mom Morrow came into my room. "What on earth are you doing, Ken?" she asked. "Where are you going?"

"I need to study," I told her, "and I'm sure you'll be needing my room for your family."

Mom Morrow sat down on my bed and cried. "Kenneth," she said, "you're a part of our family. You can't move out. It wouldn't be Christmas without you!" Taking me to the Christmas tree, she started pulling out wrapped gifts to show me. "See," she continued, "there are already presents under the tree for you."

It was my turn to cry. Clint and Beulah Morrow showed me that at Christmas, especially, we are part of one family — God's family — and that's a family of love.

Because You have made me a part of Your family, God, help me to reach out to others who also need to experience Your love.
— Kenneth Chafin

22 | S U N *JOURNEY TOWARD THE LIGHT*
Walk as children of light.   —Ephesians 5:8

On this fourth Sunday of Advent, the house is decorated, the presents wrapped. As my son Brock says, "It's time to kick back and enjoy Christmas."

But earlier today, instead of "kicking back," I willingly entered the mayhem of commercial Christmas. After church, I went to the most hectic of all holiday places, the mall. Everywhere there were lights and glitter, elves and big, colored balls. The music was loud. At Santa's village, kids stood in a long line. An older lady looked at me and smiled. A young mother laughed as a saleslady scooped up her child and set her right in the middle of a teddy bear display. Several people gathered around, delighted with this sight. They exchanged pleasantries as I went on.

"May I help you?" a young man asked when I reached a department store. I explained my need for a tie, and the clerk made suggestions until one was chosen. "Have a great Christmas!" he said. Later, in the gift-wrap line, the spirit was the same. Smiles, and laughter, and "Happy holidays!"

Every year, I purposely save a bit of my shopping until right before Christmas because I love the rush, the feel, the way people who usually don't even look to the right or to the left look straight at me and smile. The spirit of Christmas shows us what our world would look like if we followed Jesus' lead every day to love, love, love.

So before this Christmas passes, go to the mall or to some gathering place. Take a bag of smiles and give them to everyone you meet. The spirit of Christmas is waiting for you.

Father, today, I saw You in the faces of happy people. Thank You for this opportunity to see how love looks when we put others first.
                                                        —Pam Kidd

23 | M O N *"I bring you good news of great joy that will be for all the people."*   —Luke 2:10 (NIV)

It was Christmas Eve. This year our family had taken a trip to Stowe, Vermont, far from the cozy, familiar church service we'd always loved in our hometown of South Salem, New York. As it got later into the evening, my husband Whitney and I were torn. Another church wouldn't be the same, but we both felt the need to worship on this special night. Leaving our teenaged children in our rented cabin, we drove down to the foot of the mountain where a small, family-sized church glowed in the darkness. We parked against a snowdrift. Through the windows we could see people holding hymnals, mouths moving in song. We were late. "Should we go in?" I asked.

"Let's," Whitney said.

The church was packed, and we had to be separated. The usher, apologizing that they'd run out of programs, led me to a front pew where I squeezed into the corner, the stares of a hundred strangers shrinking me into my bulky coat. I gripped one gloved hand in the other, feeling as frozen and distant as the icicles hanging from the roof outside. I stared miserably at the tabled crèche, with its small circle of shepherds and wise men.

I felt a nudge. The woman next to me smiled and gave me her program, pointing to the place. A man across the aisle handed me a hymnal, opened to the next song. The person behind offered to take my coat and hang it up.

Simple, small gestures. But their warmth melted my distance. I looked back at the crèche with its tiny circle of celebrants and thought how for two thousand years people have been pulling in people, not with words, but with gestures of warmth and love.

Lord Jesus, help us to pass along that heavenly touch that You began in Bethlehem.   — Shari Smyth

24 | T U E *JOURNEY TOWARD THE LIGHT*
The true Light... cometh into the world.   — John 1:9

"In your whole life, what was the most memorable Christmas present you ever received?" a friend asked me once. It didn't take long to recall....

I am seven years old. It is Christmas Eve and present-opening time. My father hands me a big box. I shake it. Not very heavy. My mother and brother Davey sit with unopened presents on their laps. All eyes are on me. "Open it! Open it!" Davey urges. I pull off the ribbon and tear away the paper. The box is blue, sprinkled with little pink flowers. So carefully I lift the lid. So slowly I fold back the soft pink tissue paper. My breath catches. I never expected nor could I have imagined anything as beautiful as the bride doll lying in the box.

Now that I'm a grown-up, things that come in boxes no longer offer that same incredible childhood thrill. Still, Christmas Eve is "hold your breath time," as I move toward December 25 with my eyes focused on the Christ Child. Tonight, I make my way into a church sanctuary bathed in candlelight. I walk silently forward for communion. I find a quiet mystery here, a gift waiting to be unwrapped.

My name — your name — is written on the tag. Tear back the paper of Christmas Eve. Open the box. The best of all presents — something so beautiful we could never have imagined it — waits for you and me. It's the pure love of Jesus Christ. It is ours — the children of God — for the taking.

In the hush and wonder of this silent night, Father, I hold the gift You offer. I will claim the love of Jesus for my very own.   — Pam Kidd

25 | W E D *JOURNEY TOWARD THE LIGHT*

Arise, shine; for thy light is come, and the glory of the Lord is risen upon thee.   — Isaiah 60:1

Early on Christmas morning, long before the sun rises, I set a huge pot of wassail on the back burner of the stove. Soon the house is filled with the smell of oranges and cloves and cinnamon, and a flurry of activity. In an hour, twenty-two people will be arriving for our annual Christmas breakfast, which we have traditionally shared with single friends and those who are lonely or without family near. Son Brock is off across town to pick up Frances Faulkner. Daughter Keri is checking to see that there's a remembrance under the tree for each guest. My husband David is working with my stepfather Herb to set up tables and chairs. My mother Bebe and I are working as fast as we can in the kitchen.

Later, seated around our stretched-out table, the faces of the guests blend with those from other years: an old couple who spent their lives as missionaries in China; a family of refugees from Vietnam; a lonely widower; a young family far away from home; a sweet woman, mentally challenged. All sizes, shapes and colors of people have gathered round our Christmas table this year. In their midst, David smiles, Bebe and Herb chat happily. I see Keri reaching over to hug ninety-one-year-old Frances, and Brock refilling wassail cups.

Then I see that in the rush I have forgotten to light the candles of the Christmas carousel in the center of the table. When I do so, the shepherds and wise men take up their journey, and the candlelight flickers on the faces of the guests. I smile in recognition: The Light, which enlightens everyone, has come (John 1:9). Christmas is here!

Father God, may all of us sit in joy at Christ's Christmas table, then vow to live always in His light. —Pam Kidd

26 | T H U *Then I heard every creature in heaven and on earth and under the earth and on the sea, and all that is in them, singing: "To him who sits on the throne and to the Lamb be praise and honor and glory and power, for ever and ever!"*
—Revelation 5:13 (NIV)

It's been thirteen years since I received that phone call from Mom, but every December I relive the shock. Her trembling voice sobbed, "Oh, Mary, Dad is dead." Snowmobiling with his friend in the wilderness of northern Minnesota, they broke through the ice and never made it out.

We buried Dad on Christmas Eve. That evening we wrapped a few last gifts, wondering how to get through the next day, the next year, without Dad.

Christmas morning we filed into church, our large family filling a pew. As the organist played the introduction to the first hymn, I squeezed my eyes tight, choking back tears. But then, somehow, it seemed as if God wrapped a warm blanket around my shoulders and whispered, *It's okay. Don't try to sing. Just listen.*

"O come, all ye faithful, joyful and triumphant." *But I feel sorrowful and crushed.* The voices swelled and rose with "O come, let us adore him, Christ the Lord," and inwardly I heard, *Come to Me in your sorrow. Come, draw near.* "Sing choirs of angels, Sing in exultation. Sing all ye citizens of heaven above." *Your father is now a citizen of heaven. As you worship Me, you are with him.*

As that realization dawned on me, an incredible joy welled up and I could join the singing. Worshiping Christ, Dad and I were together again. All of us singing in our church were united with those who had gone before us, adoring our Lord.

I would still have months of grieving ahead. Each December, especially, I miss Dad. But that joyful Christmas morning remains in my memory. And I can rest in its truth. Dad is home in his own country...heaven...a cause for celebration.

Thank You, God, for giving me a picture to remember every

Christmas. As we come to adore You in a manger, we also gather with loved ones around Your throne, united once more in worshiping You.
— Mary Brown

27

F R I

For I know the thoughts that I think toward you, says the Lord, thoughts of peace and not of evil, to give you a future and a hope. — Jeremiah 29:11 (NKJV)

I'm grappling with the decision to move to the Canadian Rockies. God — and my instincts — seem to say, "Go!" The schools are good, the air is dry and much better for my health, and the job situation is fruitful. But I still have a lot of fears. So, recently, as a test, my children and I went to the Rockies for a vacation.

One day my daughter Heather and I dropped the boys off at the ski slopes and headed east for the prairies. We had lunch at an old cowboy restaurant outside Calgary, everyone in boots and Stetsons. On the way back, Heather drove. "Let's take the back roads," she suggested.

As we wound up through the foothills, she saw a sign: "Buffalo Paddock." Next thing I knew she had veered off the road, bumping and flying on narrow dirt tracks over the terrain until we came to a screeching halt. There they were! A whole herd of buffalo, milling about just below the cliff. Heather was quite pleased with herself. I was, too. Such a marvelous sense of adventure!

Remembering that afternoon, I can see my way a bit more clearly now. I've wanted God to guide me, but I've been ignoring the signs that point to adventure, afraid to leave the main road. But now, like Heather, I'm going to search for something wonderful, even if it means a rough and bumpy road. Because I'm trusting God to guide me.

Father, give me that sense of adventure that propels me toward my dreams. — Brenda Wilbee

28

S A T

Teach me good judgment and knowledge....
— Psalm 119:66

One Christmas, my daughter-in-law Marie gave me a book by humorist Erma Bombeck. Marie had inscribed it, "To dearest Dad. This is for you to enjoy. Not to study, compare or pick apart!"

The words hurt. What did Marie mean? I was aware that my work as an engineer, technical writer and bank director had demanded attention to details, accuracy and the need to question all information. But was I carrying this into my home life?

Finally, I asked Marie what she meant. "We never see you relaxing for enjoyment," she said. "You're always reading for information or study. When was the last time you took Momma to a movie?" (It was twenty years ago to see *Fiddler on the Roof*!) "When was the last time you took her on a vacation?" (The year was 1982, when we visited Oahu.) "Momma says getting you to visit friends is like collaring a gorilla!"

Marie was right. I hadn't spent a lot of time just being with my family. But that was just the way I was — always needing to be busy and productive. I didn't feel right relaxing. Could I change?

Unexpectedly, an answer came from our Bible study. Commenting on Jesus' words, "Let anyone with ears to hear listen!" (Mark 4:9, NRSV) the leader said, "Jesus selected for His disciples ordinary people who would listen to Him, accept His words and change. If you are too pleased with yourself, or you feel you are overflowing with knowledge, you don't have room to change and grow."

That statement gave me the incentive I needed to listen to Marie's words. I wanted to grow. So I have worked at changing my approach on the home front. I still read too much, but I take time to enjoy some television with Ruby, to visit friends with her and even to take weekend vacations! I think I am more fun to live with. Just ask Ruby.

Understanding Father, there are numerous roads in life, but only Your way brings peace and understanding. —Oscar Greene

---

29 | S U N | *If it were not so, I would have told you. I go to prepare a place for you.* —John 14:2

In the letters I received after my husband's death in December 1993, a great many friends — perhaps you were one of them—seem to have been especially touched that Norman died on Christmas Eve. Looking back I, too, am moved by the correlation of his leaving on the anniversary eve of our Christ's coming. And yet, this timing pales in significance when I think of the overpowering meaning of what came to pass so softly on that most silent of nights.

Norman and I had been married for sixty-three years on that Christmas Eve. I was aware that day that his life on this earth was coming to an end. His physical body had been wearing down, and for several days Dr. Morrison had been coming to the Hill Farm both morning and afternoon. This day he was making his third visit.

Outside, the sky was growing dark with approaching night. Inside, various members of our family were quietly coming in and out of the bedroom where Norman lay. About four-thirty Norman was finding it increasingly difficult to breathe. Everyone left the room except me. As his struggle intensified, I leaned close to him. "It's all right," I whispered in his ear, "you can let go now."

His breathing grew slower. And slower. Slower. There was no sign, yet that was a sign. The breathing had stopped. I called the family.

"What do we do now?" my daughter Margaret asked.

"Pray," I said. "We pray." And I turned to Dr. Morrison and asked him to lead us, which he did, simply and beautifully, speaking to God with gratitude for the life of Norman Vincent Peale.

And that was it. Except it wasn't. A death? Yes, but the beginning of a new life for Norman. "Because I live," Jesus said, "ye shall live also" (John 14:19). I took hold of those words and held them fast. I hold them close now.

And so must you.

Oh, yes, Father, I believe, I believe.   — Ruth Stafford Peale

30 | M O N *Therefore we will not fear, though the earth should change, though the mountains shake in the heart of the sea.*
—Psalm 46:2 (NRSV)

Never has there been a time in my life with so many changes. For one thing, the greenhouse where I used to grow orchids has come down to make room for a new garage. I hadn't exactly planned it, but the orchids died in one of the hard freezes we had last winter. And then the friend who introduced me to orchids died himself. So these days I earn my green equity outdoors.

Then there's Babu. This half-pint pup came into my life because my beloved Ashley passed on in January. Two months of Yorkie-free life was about all I could handle, so I'm back training a puppy. Babu tries to help me in the garden but gets into every stickle burr on the acre. He doesn't yet know how to care for his Yorkie coiffure.

The biggest change of all has been in my career. I went to half-time at Yale to have more time to share the things that God has been doing in my life. And more time to love a puppy. And more time to transform a weedy patch into a wildflower garden.

The oddest thing of all—for a year with so many changes—is that although I've grieved, I've not been afraid. It's as if each step were ordered and planned and linked to the next. I wonder what changes next year will bring?

God of changes Who never changes, hold my heart in Your hands so that I shall not fear.   —Diane Komp

$31 \left|\begin{smallmatrix}T\\U\\E\end{smallmatrix}\right.$ *...Forgetting those things which are behind, and reaching forth unto those things which are before.*
                                    —Philippians 3:13

My children and grandchildren, who spent the early evening with me, have left to celebrate the new year with their friends. The lovely silence of the house nestles around me like a warm blanket as I settle into my prayer chair for a ritual I've practiced for several years. I turn off the lamp on the end table so that I can fully enjoy the Christmas tree lights and the lovely angel with silken hair who adorns its top. Then I light a candle and think back over the year, month by month.

What comes to my mind is a mixture of things. I find that I still feel strong emotions as I recall those things that marred the year, such as arguments, tears and losses, hurricanes, wars of greed, and a relationship that ended. It's hard to let the pain go. But there are also happy memories I want to cling to: the moment of my granddaughter's birth; a favored friendship; a fresh spiritual insight; a satisfying work project; a trip to California.

But life is change, and I need to remind myself that endings lead to beginnings, and that even good things must be held lightly in order to grow. So one by one I offer them up, the sad ones and the glad ones, knowing that forever and in all ways, these released events of the past year are safe with God.

Now, as the clock nears midnight, I sit quietly in the stillness, feeling lighter and freer. The future, still a mystery, glistens with the promise of a Light beyond time, a Light that shines in the darkness, a Light that cradles overflowing hope.

Loving Lord Jesus, Light of the world, You are the moon that shines on the shadows behind; You are the sun that illumines the path ahead. Keep me walking in Your Light throughout the coming year.
                            —Marilyn Morgan Helleberg

GIFTS OF LIGHT

1. _____

2. _____

3. _____

4. _____

5. _____

6. _____

7. _____

8. _____

9. _____

10. _____

11. _____

12. _____

13. _____

14. _____

15. _____

16 _____

17 _____

18 _____

19 _____

20 _____

21 _____

22 _____

23 _____

24 _____

25 _____

26 _____

27 _____

28 _____

29 _____

30 _____

31 _____

FELLOWSHIP CORNER

WHO'S WHO IN DAILY GUIDEPOSTS

This is the time for us to catch up with the lives of those who share so generously through their contributions to Daily Guideposts. *As our writers share their search for lights in the darkness, their successes and failures, by the end of 1996 we have come to know each other and become friends. Here is what those very important people have been doing this past year.*

 "This was indeed a year of light and shadows!" remarks FAY ANGUS of Sierra Madre, California. "One filled with brilliant joy as my husband John attended his fifty-year high school reunion in Vancouver, Canada, where he was able to shrug off many childhood hurts and misconceptions that had weighed him down for much of his life (see page 177). Then the shadow of grief as we mourned the death of two dear friends whom we miss most dreadfully. I was going to write *loss,* but then remembered a little boy at his grandpa's memorial service. As people hugged his grandma with condolences over the *loss* of her husband, the youngster suddenly pulled on her sleeve, 'Grandma, we ain't lost Grandpa. Jesus done found him!' "

 A couple of "do-it-yourselfers," ALMA BARKMAN and her husband Leo built the bungalow in which they live. It is located in a suburb of Winnipeg, Manitoba, right in the center of Canada. "Our three sons and a daughter have grown up and moved away, so when we get lonesome and want a change of scenery, we have an excellent excuse to travel all the way west to British Columbia and as far east as Toronto. We have three grandsons, Ben, 13, Dan, 11, and Sky, 3, and a granddaughter, Desirae, 1. In order to enjoy Manitoba's climate, we've learned to live in rhythm with each distinct season. As I cope with winter's bitter cold and darkness, I can trust God for summer sunshine, knowing that in His good time, He will bring about the difference."

FRED BAUER of Princeton, New Jersey, says the past twelve months were filled with lots of traveling for him and his wife Shirley: to Alaska to see son Chris; to Georgia to visit son Daniel; to Florida to see Shirley's mother; to California to watch the Rose Bowl; to Ohio for Christmas at Mother's; to Pennsylvania for son Steve's wedding; to Indiana for a vacation with daughter Laraine and her family. "When have I found lights in the darkness? Symbolically, all of my life. Literally, one example, the cold, rainy night that my first car broke down on a desolate country road. Sixteen and scared, I can still see my father's flashlight approaching out of the gloom. Though my father's gone now, he still lights my life with his love — just as my heavenly Father does."

For **MARY BROWN** of Lansing, Michigan, last year was full of "firsts." Daughter Elizabeth started first grade, and she and Mary began ice skating lessons. "We're skating backward and mastering one-foot glides!" The family went camping last summer, a real first for 2-year-old Mark and husband Alex, who is now hooked on the outdoors — as long as he has an air mattress and a hot shower. "Living outside, we experienced the joy of light... basking in the sun at Lake Michigan, watching golden sunsets, chasing fireflies, singing together around the campfire under sparkling stars. At home, we've tried to savor God's light in a different way. By beginning and ending the day reading Psalms, we find this wraps our days in God's light."

MARY LOU CARNEY, editor of *Guideposts for Kids*, and her husband Gary continue to live in Chesterton, Indiana, but "the house is getting bigger!" Last year, they moved daughter Amy Jo into her first apartment when she accepted a position as marketing specialist for AT&T in Dayton, Ohio. With Brett away at Ball State University, his room, too, is empty most of the time. "When I was little, I loved to run through the fields at dusk, watching fireflies scatter into the approaching darkness. The darker it got, the brighter the fireflies seemed. That's what God calls us to be. Not revolutionaries, perhaps. But definitely bright spots. Our acts of love and kindness must leave the world a bit more brightly lit."

KENNETH CHAFIN of Louisville, Kentucky, says that at his and wife Barbara's farm there is a light out by the barn that only comes on when it gets dark. "My past year must have looked full of darkness to others. My body rejected a silicone joint in my left index finger, causing months of pain and leading to more surgery. Then I suffered a mild stroke and had to cancel all my teaching and speaking plans. It was a dark moment. Then a light came on in the form of a suggestion: 'This would be a wonderful time to decide not to return to the fast lane but to focus more on your own growth and on writing.' I've had a wonderfully productive year, discovering that the creative springs of my life were clogged more by hurry than anything else."

MARY JANE CLARK and her husband Harry finally settled into their new home in Durango, Colorado, this past April after a year-long project that included building a road, drilling a well and putting in utility lines. They found a new church home, too, and Mary Jane dusted off her high school flute and joined the contemporary service's music group. "One of our primary reasons for moving here was the abundance of sunshine. Harry and I have learned that sunlight is important to both our emotional and physical health, so we designed our house with lots of windows. In the same way we want to open ourselves even more to the Light of life, allowing Christ to bring health and growth to the spiritual dimensions of our lives."

JOHN COWAN of St. Paul, Minnesota, and his wife Edith Meissner spent much of last year getting used to living in an empty nest. His two recent books, *Small Decencies: Reflections and Meditations on Being Human at Work* and *The Common Table: Reflections and Meditations on Community and Spirituality in the Workplace* (HarperBusiness), have included stories about his two sons Benjamin and David. So this year has included prayerful reflection about the next phase as a father to two adult sons. "It has been a most difficult year in many ways, but my experience has been that all important lights in my life have come at the end of tunnels." John works as a consultant and serves as the parish priest to an Episcopal congregation in the historic river town of Frontenac.

HOLLIE DAVIS, 21, is a junior at West Virginia Wesleyan College in Buckhannon, West Virginia, majoring in English and history. She plans to attend graduate school and pursue a career in law or counseling. Hollie spends her free time reading, writing or at home with her family. She also works as a proofreader in Wesleyan's Learning Center. Her father Gerald, her stepmother Arleta and her brother Kelly, 18, live in Glenville, West Virginia. "My brother has been having a lot of problems with my parents recently, and going home has become really difficult. I guess the knowledge that God has some plan that involves whatever is in my best interest has been the light in all this confusion or darkness."

After years of writing his *Daily Guideposts* devotionals in the basement, CHRISTOPHER DE VINCK and his wife Roe of Pompton Plains, New Jersey, converted their sun porch into a writing room. "I have left the darkness and entered the light," says Chris. "Our children, David, 16, Karen, 13, and Michael, 11, continue to be children of light, playing the trumpet, reading, bathing the new dog. My wife and I continue to work at our marriage, at our home and work responsibilities with glad hearts. It is, as the saying goes, 'better to light one candle than to curse the darkness.'" *(Photo credit: Alex Gotfryd)*

This has been a year of "enlightenment" for the family of Sheffield, Alabama's DRUE DUKE. "Our grandson Bob graduated from the University of Alabama and enrolled for a master's degree. Granddaughter Christy completed junior college and moved on, with an academic scholarship, to

Athens College. Emily, our daughter, has two more quarters to complete and she will receive her degree. And I am still enjoying teaching writing in the adult education division of our local community college. Parkinson's disease slowed down my husband Bob, but he still enjoys reading and his workshop. We bought a new camper and look forward to some travel throughout the next year, and to continue visiting elementary schools where I read aloud to children."

ERIC FELLMAN, the president and CEO of the Peale Center for Christian Living in Pawling, New York, faced some darkness last year when a suspected cancerous tumor was found on his wife Joy's thyroid. Son Nathan was dating a girl whose mother had died of cancer a year earlier. One evening, his emotions bubbled over and he blurted out, "Dad, don't ever lie to us about Mom!" The resulting discussion opened a path to tears and deeper trusting that lasted well beyond the passing of the crisis with the words, "It was benign." Joy has fully recovered to pursue her nursing career part-time while the boys, Jonathan, 14, Nathan, 16, and Jason, 18, progress through school. Dad stood by in pleasant bewilderment, even during the frantic search for colleges for Jason.

"This past year has been one of living with people who come from other countries," says ROBIN WHITE GOODE of South Monsey, New York. "For several months a couple from Venezuela lived with my husband Harley and my children David, 6, and Jamie, 4, and me. Now, we have a Swedish au pair whom the children just love. I read recently that the Amish simply accept the 'darkness'—the bad things that happen. They feel comfortable with not knowing, not understanding. They receive the deep comfort of God, assured that everything is in His hands. 'I can trust God, or not trust Him,' I once heard a missionary say. 'I choose to trust Him.' For me, trust is what enables me to see lights in the darkness."

Savannah, Georgia's ARTHUR GORDON and his wife Pam say that the past year had many bright moments and a few darker ones. The good times included two trips, one to see Pam's sister Diana in England and their beloved Nannie, now 96, but still sharp as a tack and telling everyone how to behave. The second trip was to spend Christmas in California with Alexandra, the most recent grandchild. A less happy moment came when Arthur leaped from a seawall, fishing rod in hand, landed too hard and damaged his back rather badly. "I guess something in me thought I was 28 instead of 82," Arthur says ruefully. "Very painful for a while, but better now. (P.S. The fish got away!)"

OSCAR GREENE of West Medford, Massachusetts, and his wife Ruby enrolled in a Monday evening Bible study and were amazed at the amount of work and participation required. During March, Ruby retired from the church choir after forty years, and after fracturing her left wrist twice in five months. For the first time since 1966, they did not visit their beloved state of Maine. Instead, they painted their home and completed needed repairs. Oscar's "lights in the darkness" came when he was asked to deliver the eulogies at the funerals of two dear friends. "I now realize this was a precious honor, being asked by the families to share when they were broken and vulnerable."

Though he has been an editor with *Guideposts* magazine since 1987, this is EDWARD GRINNAN's first appearance in *Daily Guideposts*. "For a good while now my friend Van Varner has been after me to try my hand at devotional writing. I always found some excuse to put him off. What did I have to tell about? But this year I was determined to give it a try. I was amazed to discover myself being able to put parts of my life into spiritual focus by writing about them. That's given me tremendous satisfaction and has been a new light for me." Ed lives in a Manhattan apartment with his wife Julee and their two energetic dogs Marty and Sally. "I spend a lot of time attached to the end of a leash. They tend to eat the furniture if they don't get enough exercise."

"Last year, we went through a month (and more!) of family crisis," says RICK HAMLIN of New York City, "with 4-year-old Timothy in the hospital for almost a month, 7-year-old William sick at home and me in the hospital all at the same time. The morning after my surgery, I looked three blocks north to Timothy's hospital, and I prayed for God to look after us, especially Carol who was under the greatest strain from trying to hold everything together. As the sun lit the skyscrapers, I could see where the lights in our darkness had been: from the friends and family members who had sustained us with their baby-sitting, carpooling, laundry service, grocery shopping and prayers. From this juncture of good health and well-being, that light seems far more memorable than any darkness."

MADGE HARRAH of Albuquerque, New Mexico, spent part of her time this past year conducting writing workshops for elementary and middle school students throughout the state and adjoining ones. "I like working with young people because they are enthusiastic and filled with hope. If I can make a difference in even one child's life, light a spark in their creativity, then it's all worthwhile." Madge's tenth book, *Comet Luck* (Avon), a children's historical novel based on a true story, is being used by teachers in their whole language programs. She and her husband Larry, now retired, have two children, Eric and Meghan, and five grandchildren.

MARILYN MORGAN HELLEBERG of Kearney, Nebraska, says her best spiritual practice this year is being a loving grandma to her seven grandchildren, including the two newest arrivals, Saralisa, 2, and Joseph, 1. "When I was a child, I was afraid of the dark, so Mother left the closet light on for me. But on visits, Grandmother Morgan said I could not waste electricity at her house. So my Aunt Alta told me to look at the candle as I said my prayers. Afterward, as she leaned close and blew it out, she whispered, 'See? The light's still there — inside of you!' Sure enough, I could still see it, and I went to sleep unafraid. But it wasn't till many years later that I saw that the Light of Christ is the same way."

PHYLLIS HOBE of East Greenville, Pennsylvania, says, "Living in the country, I take a lot of things for granted — that there will always be grass in the fields, leaves on the trees, birds and wildlife I can see from my window, long walks with my dog along country roads. Then I saw a sign that read: 'This is God's earth — please take care of it.' It dawned on me that many of our God-given blessings will not last forever if we don't protect them. So I'm learning how to recycle, how to avoid substances that harm the environment and how to share my space with some of God's other creatures. It took a little doing and some studying, but it's getting easier by the day. And it's comforting to know that even one person can pitch in and care."

MARJORIE HOLMES of Manassas, Virginia, says, "My daily 'light in the darkness' is walking at sunrise every morning beside the lake where I live, thanking God for the beauty all around me and feeling close to Jesus. I come in for breakfast revived and refreshed. Other lights? My grandsons Alexi and Adam, 10, and 12, come here to fish and swim, and my daughter Melanie, their mother, is teaching them to drive the boat and water ski. How lucky I am to be here! They live only an hour away. And my older daughter Mickie and her husband Stan are right next door." Marjorie's two sons are farther away. Mallory, who's studying photography, is in California, and Mark, an accountant, lives in South Carolina. But all four children were home for Christmas! *(Photo credit: Fred Kligman)*

"Since entering my sixties, I have had to think of myself as a senior citizen," says MARY RUTH HOWES of Jersey City, New Jersey. "I find it completely surprising that I have reached this exalted age! My father died two years ago, at the age of 94, and I miss his sense of humor, his interest in everything and his commitment to prayer. The effects of his life remind me of the magical afterglow I saw last fall during a week in Mexico.

I was keeping a friend company at a clinic there, and several evenings after supper we'd walk to the beach and watch the sunset. The sky would go quite dark, and we'd head back in. But five minutes later, the western horizon would turn a glowing orange and then a gold that would last for another five minutes."

"In a sense, 1996 is the beginning of my light in the darkness," comments BROCK KIDD of Brentwood, Tennessee. "After graduation from the University of Tennessee in Knoxville, I was told that the job in investment that I thought I had locked was gone. I was furious that my dream job had been taken away from me. For two very dark months, I was filled with doubts and anger. But through the support of my family and friends, I was able to hand it over to God. And, as always, the light returned. I was offered the exact same job at a different bank. Now I look forward to 1996, for opportunities to grow, to reach for success in a new career, always striving for the light."

"Lights have been turned on" in the Brentwood, Tennessee, household of PAM KIDD. Keri, 18, a premed student at Birmingham Southern College, interviewed John Seigenthaler, a journalist who played an important role in the Freedom Rides of the 1960s. Brock earned his broker's license in record time. David's church, Hillsboro Presbyterian, was featured in the book *Acting On Your Faith: Congregations Making a Difference* (Insight). And Pam wrote and appeared in a film for the Discovery Channel called *Angel Stories*. "Being alive is a constant journey through shadow and light. Experience teaches us that a new morning is always on the horizon, so I guess our faith-job is to hold on to that reality when the night is at its darkest."

Such a year for high*lights* in the Big Lake, Alaska, household of CAROL KNAPP and her husband Terry! "Tamara turned 21 on the Arctic Ocean, during a multicultural studies program through Whitworth College. We were so glad to get Phil graduated from high school, we rang a cowbell!

Kelly, now a high school senior, received a national science award. Brenda, a junior, spent a summer in Okinawa, Japan, staying with our former exchange student. The year my daughter Kelly was in sixth grade, her friend died in a car accident. She and I sat one night before our lighted Christmas tree, trying to make sense of it. And the consolation we found was in the lights. They reminded us that Jesus came into the world as Light, so that death and darkness, though real, are not all-consuming."

DIANE KOMP's dog has finally come to peace with being displaced from her lap by a computer. As long as Babu can stretch out behind Diane's neck on the couch and rest one paw on her shoulder, cheek to cheek, work can progress. Progress this year included a new book about mothers, *Hope Springs from Mended Places* (Zondervan). Diane, who lives in Guilford, Connecticut, and is a pediatric oncologist at Yale University School of Medicine, saw lights banish the darkness many times this year as she visited with hospice groups around the country. "I wish the health care reformers would look at this model for bringing professionals, patients and the community together to solve our other health care problems. In the hospice movement, the spiritual always has a prominent place."

Within a twelve-month period, CAROL KUYKENDALL's children will have graduated: Derek last spring from the University of Puget Sound; this spring, Lindsay from Westmont College; Kendall from high school. "My husband Lynn and I are perched on the edge of the empty nest, the subject of my latest book *Give Them Wings* (Focus on the Family). We've been through some dark times this year with a fairly serious health problem with one of our children. In the midst of that painful darkness, I am learning again that Jesus always walks alongside me, shining just enough of His light on the path ahead so that I can merely take one small step at a time. I don't have to worry about the unknowns much further ahead than that."

PATRICIA LORENZ of Oak Creek, Wisconsin, says the best way to bring lights into darkness is to fill her home with people. "Now that Jeanne, Julia and Michael are all graduated from college and living on their own, it's just Andrew, 16, and me in a house big enough for a large family. In March 1994, I opened up our three extra bedrooms as a Milwaukee-area 'crash pad' for airline pilots who are based in Milwaukee but choose to live elsewhere. On those nights when there's a pilot or two staying, our lives are filled with new friends, good conversations and lots of laughter. The Light of Christ is burning in each one of them, and I've discovered the more light you have in your home, the brighter and happier it is."

ROBERTA MESSNER, who lives in Sweet Run, West Virginia, with her husband Mark and their dog Cleo, is looking forward to a year of continued physical recovery in 1996. This past year, she underwent several major surgeries to remove painful nerve- and vision-threatening tumors caused by neurofibromatosis (also known as the "Elephant Man's disease"). "It was a year of learning to trust God in the darkness, and of coming to terms with the fact that God's insight is even more precious than physical eyesight." Roberta continues to work as a nurse and a part-time stylist for home decorating magazines.

KEITH MILLER and his wife Andrea, both writers, speakers and consultants, live in Austin, Texas. Keith's three married daughters live in different parts of the state and each has two children — a boy and a girl — between the ages of 2 and 12. "I am particularly glad to be participating in *Daily Guideposts, 1996*, because of the theme 'Lights in the Darkness.' This is what the Lord and the Gospel have meant to me from the time of my own conversion in 1956 — light, hope, and learning to receive and give love in the midst of the struggles to live for Christ in a world that often seems filled with the darkness of negativity and fear. I am especially grateful that I was asked to relive and write about Holy Week [see pages 86 to 96]. What a great experience!"

JOAN RAE MILLS lives with her husband Johnny and their children Kelly, 12, and Andrew, 8, on a 500-acre dairy farm in Greenwood, Delaware. Living only thirty miles from the Atlantic Ocean and the Chesapeake Bay, they delight in playing in the waves, watching for blue herons, visiting the boardwalk in winter and sitting down to a pile of steamed crabs for supper. Joan is a teacher of GED classes, Sunday school and a Bible study. "Recently, my husband gave me a lovely signed print of a cardinal entitled 'Winter Light I' by W. Goebel. Against the cold, dark background of grayed evergreens is this flash of brilliant scarlet, made even more beautiful and noticeable by the contrast. So like God's grace — how His light comforts me in those winters of my life."

JENNY MUTZBAUER lives with her parents William and Ilse, sister Brigitte, three cats and a dog in Alsip, Illinois. A freshman at St. Xavier University in Chicago, Jenny is pursuing a degree in communications with strong concentration in liberal arts. "Lights can be found in the darkness if we only begin to define the world in terms of God's light and goodness," Jenny believes. "Perhaps we all spend too much time peering inquisitively into the darkness and being lost in the negative. When I was a little girl, I simply avoided closets where I knew darkness lurked and would hurry past to find Mom in her bright kitchen."

"This has been a year of stability for me," says LINDA NEUKRUG of Walnut Creek, California. "I am still substitute teaching and practicing my sign language studies a little each day. My husband Paul's grandmother is still going strong at age 102. My 'light in darkness' this year was a simple thing. After days of darkness in my mailbox (no mail) — and I love getting mail — I got an uplifting letter from a woman named Linda in Chili, Wisconsin. She wanted to get a pen pal named Linda in every one of the fifty states. So I became her 'California Linda Pen Pal.' My goal for 1996? The same as for 1995. I'd still like to learn to sew on my machine. That way, I could use it for its intended purpose rather than as an end table."

DOROTHY NICHOLAS has a daughter, Donna, three grandsons and four great-grandchildren, a girl and three boys. She lived for the twenty-five years of her first marriage in Barboursville, West Virginia, then just five years ago moved back there where she lives with her husband of twenty-nine years, Fred, in a house they named Journey's End. Dorothy has some very serious health problems, but she has been able to come to terms with them through the light found in God's love. "I have just put everything in His hands and live one day at a time." Dorothy hopes that when her time comes to leave this earth she'll depart from her own bed right at Journey's End.

KATHERINE PATERSON began the year at a speaking engagement at South Pacific College in Fiji, a bright and beautiful island nation, where some light is beginning to break through the political darkness of the past six years. She and her husband John, a Presbyterian minister, live in Barre, Vermont. They have four grown children: Lin, who is married to Stephen; John, Jr., whose wife is Samantha; David, who is wed to Ariana; and Mary. They also have two granddaughters, Katherine, 5, and Margaret, 2. Katherine is a writer of books for children and young people, including *Bridge to Terabithia*, *The Great Gilly Hopkins*, *Jacob Have I Loved* (all from HarperCollins), *Lyddie* and, most recently, *Flip-Flop Girl* (both from Lodestar). *(Photo credit: Jill Paton Walsh)*

"My excitement reaches a high level when I think of more than one million people reading *Daily Guideposts* every morning," says **RUTH STAFFORD PEALE** of Pawling, New York. "Through this we all have a spiritual experience together. The theme for 1996 reminds me that light and darkness invade our lives constantly. In darkness, I find that prayer helps keep a balance. When light shines upon me, I give thanks and try especially to tell others of God's loving care. My life continues to be filled with daily activity at Guideposts. Our eight grandchildren are all graduated from college and in careers. I now have three great-grandchildren, and family reunions are high on our list of once-a-year activity to keep in touch."

For their thirty-first anniversary, DANIEL SCHANTZ and his wife Sharon of Moberly, Missouri, took a summer trip to Michigan to visit nostalgic roots of college days: Lansing, where they both attended Great Lakes Christian College and were married; Holland, where they honeymooned; South Haven, where Dan first ministered to a church. With the passing of years, he has come to see the blessing of "blindness to the future." "I have found lights in a dark world by learning to trust the Good Shepherd. After all, it's not the job of the sheep to know the way, but to follow the One Who does." Dan still has many questions, but "I know now when to stop asking and to start trusting God Who dwells in unapproachable light."

SUSAN SCHEFFLEIN of Putnam Valley, New York, says, "This has been a busy year for my husband Ernie and me. With his concerts and teaching schedule and my increased activity on local boards, it seems there's not much time to be together. So at least once a month we spend a Sunday afternoon at the Metropolitan Museum in New York City. How well Rembrandt, Vermeer and the other Old Masters knew the power of light and dark to convey the dimensions of the soul and our struggle to grow toward the light. My work at Guideposts puts me in daily contact with people who are experiencing that struggle, and how wonderful it is to be able to pray and provide inspirational materials during those times. Faith can put a candle in the darkest night."

PENNEY SCHWAB and her husband Don are delighted to have all three children, Patrick, Michael and Rebecca, and grandsons Ryan, 6, and David, 3, living in Kansas and close enough to Copeland for frequent visits. Her job as executive director of United Methodist Mexican-American Ministries is moving in new directions, focusing on community solutions to problems of health care access, employment and education. "Each of us alone is as fragile as a candle flame," she says, "but together we can bring God's light and hope to many people." Getting to know Rebecca's birth mother was another example of God's light and grace making a loving difference in the lives of both families.

Once more, travel has been the theme of the year for ELIZABETH SHERRILL of Chappaqua, New York. "New Zealand was the longest through space. Longest through time was the trip John and I took tracing the medieval pilgrim route from Paris to Santiago de Compostela in Spain. For two months we tried to stop where they stopped, see what they saw, feel what they felt. In many of the hotels, corridor lights are on a sixty-second timer. In an unfamiliar hallway, looking for a room number, you're suddenly plunged into total darkness, groping along the wall. As I stumbled against unseen obstacles, I felt some of the threat the word *night* held for Jesus' original hearers — and some of the potency in His promise to be our Light." *(Photograph © 1990 Helen Marcus)*

JOHN SHERRILL of Chappaqua, New York, learned quite literally what it is to have light come into a shadowy world. For months he'd noticed that the vision in his right eye was becoming blurred. Examination revealed a cataract, and an operation to remove it followed. Today, John's sight is once again clear, colors once again alive. "The world of beauty had not changed, but the way I saw it changed. In the coming year, I hope the same will be true of relationships. Most of my family and friends are as full of beauty as they ever were. But occasionally a misunderstanding can cloud that reality. In 1996, I choose to work at removing any hurt or regret — inner cataracts — that keeps me from appreciating friendships that mean so much to me."

"The incense turns to ashes, the candle dissolves in tears." This sorrowful line from a 1,000-year-old Chinese poem characterized pivotal moments last year for LINDA CHING SLEDGE and her family of Pleasantville, New York. They mourned the passing of Gary's father and faced the darkening of Gary's vision when the retina in his right eye tore. Yet there were also bursts of incandescent light: Timothy's graduation from the University of Pennsylvania and his job as a Wall Street broker; Geoffrey's happy transition to high school; the completion of Linda's second novel; Gary's healing at the hands of a skilled ophthalmologist, who pushed back the darkness with beams of green laser light!

"Give me a faith that pierces the darkness!" was the Sledge family prayer for the year.

"Our four children are pretty much grown and establishing their own lives," SHARI SMYTH of South Salem, New York, says, "though they're always in my husband Whitney's and my heart. My Sunday school students are lights to me. One week, 5-year-old Daniel played with some toy sheep, stopping them for a drink and then moving them toward a tunnel. 'Oh, no,' he exclaimed, 'one is stuck!' I watched as he reached a finger into the tunnel, patted the sheep and said, 'Don't worry. The Good Shepherd knows where you are. He'll get you out.' How often have I felt like that sheep, stuck and afraid in a place of darkness. But the powerful, sustaining truth is Jesus knows exactly where I am and, in His time, He will lead me out. He always has. He always will."

JENNIFER THOMAS of Pleasantville, New York, has fifteen new "lights" in her life now that she works as a nursery school teacher. "I never imagined that working with 3- and 4-year-olds could be so physically demanding, yet rewarding at the same time." Jennifer, who graduated from Pace University last year, gives the children she works with credit for shaping her future. "After I graduated, I was still unsure about what I wanted to do with my life, but I put my faith in God that all would work out. Indeed, working with 'my kiddies' has removed all uncertainty." In the spring, she began on the road toward getting her master's degree in Elementary Education and started putting ideas together for a young adult novel.

"So what about my life?" says VAN VARNER. "Mostly, it's a slowdown in my career at Guideposts where, after forty years, I am coming in to the office three days a week. It's called half-time. Meanwhile, I continue to live happily in New York City. I think New Yorkers are really friendly, helpful people, yet too often are lacking in society's lubricant — simple civility. But this quality is not lacking in the token clerk at the subway station I enter every day. Her name is Mary Wiley, and an entire neighborhood of our tough city responds to the bright benedictions she gives our days: a smile; a 'Mornin''; 'How are ya?'; 'Thanks, you too.' Talk about lights in the darkness — Mary knows how to turn them on, and are they appreciated!"

"This has been a year of a Southern family exploring a Western world," says SCOTT WALKER of Waco, Texas. "This past summer my wife Beth and our children Drew, 13, Luke, 10, and Jodi, 7, visited Colorado where my paternal grandfather was one of the first ranchers in the area. Visiting the old deserted home place was a 'lights in the darkness' experience for us as we discovered an important part of our family's history and heritage. It helped us appreciate the courage and industry of the generations that have preceded us. It caused us to understand that their faith in God gave them the security to launch out into the unknown of a new land, spend a winter in a sod house and place the first plow point into prairie sod."

DOLPHUS WEARY of Mendenhall, Mississippi, experienced a year of mountaintops and valleys. The great mountaintop experience took place when he and his wife Rosie went to Hawaii to minister with Hawaiian Island Ministries. The valleys were Rosie battling with carpal tunnel syndrome, which is causing her pain in both arms, and having son Reggie expelled from high school because of misconduct on campus. But Reggie graduated in the summer and is now entering his sophomore year at Tougaloo College in Jackson. Danita, 21, is a senior premed major at Rhodes College in Memphis, and Ryan, 8, is a third-grader. "There were many tunnels throughout the year. But my entire family agrees that God is faithful and provides lights for us in the midst of the darkness."

BRIGITTE WEEKS commutes from her home in Port Washington, New York, to the Guideposts office in New York City where she is editor-in-chief of the Book Division. She joined Guideposts in July 1994, having previously worked at the Book-of-the-Month Club and The Washington Post. "Working in the worshipful and committed atmosphere of Guideposts has brought calm and light into my daily life after many years in the tense and competitive atmosphere of corporate America," she says. Brigitte and her husband Edward Herscher, who is a high school English teacher, have three grown children, Hilary, Charlotte and Daniel.

This year was a time of some exciting firsts for MARION BOND WEST of Watkinsville, Georgia. She got her first pair of contacts, joined her first choir and got her first golden retriever puppy. "Often at three in the morning when Lovey would whimper, I would venture out into the night with her. My husband Gene's powerful flashlight sliced right through the darkness, and I felt secure. As I watched it pierce the darkness faithfully, I began to remember dark times in my life. But *always, always* in His time, God illuminated the overwhelming darkness with His Light. I've decided the dark, painful times equipped me to really rejoice and fully appreciate the bright, joyful times. I've finally come to thank Him for both the darkness and the light."

BRENDA WILBEE of Bellingham, Washington, is an artist and author. This year's "highlight" was a personal, unsolicited note from the president, thanking her for something she'd written. When she wrote back, thanking him, her son Blake said, "Mom, you are not best friends with Bill Clinton!" Three weeks later, another note arrived from the White House. Blake's response? "Mom, you *are* best friends with Bill Clinton!" So between chats with the president, Brenda keeps busy with her writing, handcrafting Christmas and Easter eggs out of eggshells, and trying to keep up with her two teenage boys Blake, 15, and Phillip, 17, and her daughter Heather, 20.

"During this past year, my oldest grandchild married," says ISABEL WOLSELEY of Syracuse, New York. "My mother, 97, decided Kristen should have the pearls my father gave her for their own wedding exactly seventy-five years before!" One dark/light happening in Isabel's life last year was when she broke her left hand. "My right hand — the 'important' one —

was of little use alone. During those helpless, dark days, I finally developed a new appreciation for all that my supporting left hand had done over the years. Left hands are a bit like people who remain in the background, supporting those whose photos often make the papers because of their accomplishments. All of us 'left handers' are part of the 'body,' the Scriptures say. Thus we're needed!"

THE READER'S GUIDE

A handy, three-part index
to all the selections
in Daily Guideposts, 1996

SCRIPTURE REFERENCE INDEX

Acts
1:8, 129
2:3, 137
2:44, 272
4:32, 331
9:36, 182
20:35, 53
22:28, 174
26:18, 232

Chronicles I
16:12, 296
17:27, 14
22:5, 212
Chronicles II
30:8, 266
Colossians
1:9, 62
1:10, 111
2:2-3, 134
3:12, 140
3:13, 233
3:16, 41
3:19, 83
3:21, 161
4:2, 303
4:5, 191

Corinthians I
1:10, 291
4:10, 152
9:25, 9
10:31, 196
12:4, 277
13:4, 250
13:5, 263
13:11, 321
13:13, 284
14:1, 15
Corinthians II
1:4, 276
3:18, 183
4:6, 63
6:18, 43
9:6, 288
9:7, 324
9:15, 323
12:9, 91, 293
12:10, 154
13:5, 7, 308
13:7, 77
13:12, 247

Daniel
1:15, 113

Deuteronomy
12:7, 223
23:14, 79
30:14, 135
31:6, 109
33:27, 210

Ecclesiastes
2:4-5, 11, 209
3:1, 36
3:3, 207
3:4, 27
5:19, 219
7:10, 79
9:4, 157
9:7, 224
9:10, 29
9:11, 180
Ephesians
1:16, 217
2:14, 8
4:13, 136
4:31, 109
4:32, 54
5:4, 292
5:8, 315, 333
5:16, 30

FIRST FEW WORDS INDEX

AUTHORS, TITLES AND SUBJECTS INDEX

A NOTE FROM THE EDITORS

This devotional was created by the book division of the company that publishes *Guideposts*, a monthly magazine filled with true stories of people's adventures in faith.

Guideposts magazine is not sold on the newsstand. It's available by subscription only. And subscribing is easy. All you have to do is write to Guideposts, 39 Seminary Hill Road, Carmel, New York 10512. A year's subscription costs only $11.97 in the United States, $13.97 in Canada, and $15.97 overseas. Our Large Print edition, for those with special reading needs, is only $11.97 in the United States, and $13.97 in Canada.

When you subscribe, each month you can count on receiving exciting new evidence of God's presence, His guidance and His limitless love for all of us.